Exploring

1 & 2 THESSALONIANS

THE JOHN PHILLIPS COMMENTARY SERIES

Exploring 1 & 2 Thessalonians
Exploring 1 Corinthians
Exploring 2 Corinthians
Exploring Acts
Exploring the Book of Daniel
Exploring Colossians & Philemon
Exploring Ecclesiastes
Exploring Ephesians & Philippians
Exploring the Epistle of James
Exploring the Epistle of Jude
Exploring the Epistles of John
Exploring the Epistles of Peter
Exploring the Future
Exploring Galatians
Exploring Genesis
Exploring the Gospel of John
Exploring the Gospel of Luke
Exploring the Gospel of Mark
Exploring the Gospel of Matthew
Exploring Hebrews
Exploring the Love Song of Solomon
Exploring the Minor Prophets
Exploring the New Testament Book by Book
Exploring the Old Testament Book by Book
Exploring the Pastoral Epistles
Exploring People of the New Testament
Exploring People of the Old Testament, vol. 1
Exploring People of the Old Testament, vol. 2
Exploring People of the Old Testament, vol. 3
Exploring Proverbs, vol. 1
Exploring Proverbs, vol. 2
Exploring Psalms, vol. 1
Exploring Psalms, vol. 2
Exploring Revelation
Exploring Romans
Exploring the Scriptures

THE JOHN PHILLIPS COMMENTARY SERIES

Exploring
1 & 2 THESSALONIANS

An Expository Commentary

JOHN PHILLIPS

KREGEL
MINISTRY

Exploring 1 & 2 Thessalonians: An Expository Commentary

Published in 2005 by Kregel Publications, a division of Kregel, Inc., 2450 Oak Industrial Dr. NE, Grand Rapids, MI 49505.

Scripture quotations are from the King James Version of the Holy Bible.

Library of Congress Cataloging-in-Publication Data
Phillips, John.
Exploring 1 & 2 Thessalonians: an expository commentary / by John Phillips.
p. cm.
Includes bibliographical references.
1. Bible—N.T. Thessalonians—Commentaries I. Title. II. Title: Exploring First & Second Thessalonians. III. Title: Exploring 1 and 2 Thessalonians.
BS2725.53.P48 2005 227'.81077—dc22 2005003129

ISBN 978-0-8254-3398-6

Printed in Colombia

23 24 25 26 27 28 29 / 11 10 9 8

Contents

Preface

A Jew! A Roman! A Greek! That was Paul. He was reared a Jew, was trained to be a rabbi, and was a disciple of the renowned Gamaliel. Some scholars think that he had once been a member of the Sanhedrin. Doubtless he had been one of its most promising sons.

He was also a freeborn citizen of Rome, a rare thing in those days, something that was worth his weight in gold. It kept him in touch with the world of the caesars and the far-flung empire of Rome. He traveled its roads and sought the protection of its laws.

He grew up in a busy Hellenic world, was at home with the Greek language, and was an observer of Greek culture. Those who taught him secular subjects in his school days doubtless caught his imagination with stories of such giants as Caesar and Alexander. Perhaps he was as insistent in saying "I must see Athens" as he was in saying "I must see Rome." All about him were eloquent reminders of the greatness that was Greece and of the empire that was Rome. Paul was not nearly so repelled by the Gentile world as were his Jewish friends. Doubtless when Paul saw in a vision "a man from Macedonia" calling to him for help, he would be reminded at once of that other and earlier man from Macedonia, Alexander the Great.

Alexander had come to the throne when barely out of his teens. He made short work of his foes. Once he was firmly seated in power, he launched a career of conquest. The roll call of his victories went on and on:

May 334: The Battle of Granicus, the capture of Miletus, and the reorganization of Asia Minor.

- 333: Onward to the Cilician Gates. The Battle of Issus, then southward through Phoenicia, scornful of Persian overtures for peace.
- 332: Byblos, Sidon, Tyre, Gaza captured. No compromise with Persia. Alexander crowned as Pharaoh at Memphis.
- 331: Alexandria founded. The Tigris crossed. Arebela falls. Susa occupied.
- 330: Persepolis sacked. Darius pursued via the Caspian Gates. Darius murdered and succeeded by Bessus. On with the war.
- 329: Surrender of Bessus. Revolt of Spitamenes. Annihilation of Macedonian detachment.
- 327: Capture of the Soghdian Rock. Alexander marries Roxane. The invasion of India begins.
- 324: Alexander returns to Persepolis. The Susa marriages. Alexander deified.
- 323: Alexander falls ill. Dies.

It was all as familiar to Paul as his Old Testament. But there was another side to the story. Greek religion! It was an obscene collection of old wives' fables, utterly degenerate and debilitating to national character. Just the same, although Paul deplored Greek morals, he admired the Greek mind. When he received the "Macedonian call," he wasted no time in launching his gospel expedition.

His conquest of Macedonia was as swift and as sure as Alexander's conquest of the ancient world. Philippi! Thessalonica! Berea! Three swift campaigns, and Macedonia was his. Athens! Corinth! Achaia! All his! And it took less than three years. He had kindled a light that would never go out.

And still Jerusalem called! Rome called! Spain called! Beyond that, Gaul called! The Germanic tribes called, and the tin islands of Britain called. The world called. Would Paul ever find time to go back to Macedonia? Not soon enough, he feared. So if he were too busy elsewhere to visit Macedonia, then he would write to the believers there.

Three of his letters were addressed to cities in Macedonia. Two of them, both addressed to the Thessalonians, rank among the earliest products of his pen. Alexander had brought Hellenism to the East; Paul brought the gospel to the West.

The two Thessalonian epistles share a common theme—the second coming of Christ. The first Thessalonian letter emphasizes the rapture of the church; the second letter emphasizes the rupture of the world. Both letters are tremendously relevant to the perilous times in which we live.

Exploring
1 THESSALONIANS

Complete Outline of 1 Thessalonians

PART 1: INTRODUCTION (1:1–2)

- A Paul and his companions (1:1a)
- B. Paul and his converts (1:1b–2)
  - 1. A word of greeting (1:1b)
  - 2. A word of gratitude (1:2)
    - a. Ceaseless praise (1:2a)
    - b. Ceaseless prayer (1:2b)

PART 2: THE LORD'S COMING: A SAVING TRUTH (1:3–10)

- A. The gospel in practice (1:3)
  - 1. Looking at the past (1:3a)
  - 2. Living in the present (1:3b)
  - 3. Longing for the prospect (1:3c)
- B. The gospel in perspective (1:4)
- C. The gospel in power (1:5)
  - 1. Paul's explanation (1:5a–b)
    - a. The power of the Holy gospel (1:5a)
    - b. The person of the Holy Spirit (1:5b)
  - 2. Paul's expectation (1:5c)
  - 3. Paul's example (1:5d)
- D. The gospel in person (1:6–7)
  - 1. What the Thessalonians discerned (1:6)
  - 2. What the Thessalonians displayed (1:7)

- E. The gospel in proclamation (1:8–9)
  - 1. The sphere of their witness (1:8a)
  - 2. The scope of their witness (1:8b–9a)
  - 3. The significance of their witness (1:9b)
- F. The gospel in prospect (1:10)
  - 1. A word about the Rapture (1:10a)
  - 2. A word about the Resurrection (1:10b)
  - 3. A word about the rescue (1:10c)

PART 3: THE LORD'S COMING: A STIMULATING TRUTH (2:1–20)

- A. The totality of Paul's commitment (2:1–2)
  - 1. Paul's coming (2:1)
  - 2. Paul's condition (2:2)
    - a. They saw his body (2:2a)
    - b. They saw his boldness (2:2b)
- B. The transparency of Paul's conduct (2:3–12)
  - 1. Paul's claim (2:3–4)
    - a. His integrity was undoubted (2:3–4b)
      - (1) The truth displayed (2:3)
        - (a) Free from anything deceitful (2:3a)
        - (b) Free from anything defiling (2:3b)
        - (c) Free from anything doubtful (2:3c)
      - (2) The truth declared (2:4a–b)
        - (a) A sacred trust (2:4a)
        - (b) A simple task (2:4b)
    - b. His integrity was undaunted (2:4c)
  - 2. Paul's conduct (2:5–9)
    - a. What he shunned (2:5–6)
      - (1) He shunned all guile (2:5a)
      - (2) He shunned all gain (2:5b)
      - (3) He shunned all glory (2:6)
    - b. What he showed (2:7–8)
      - (1) His love (2:7–8a)
      - (2) His life (2:8b)
    - c. What he shared (2:9)
  - 3. Paul's conscience (2:10)
    - a. He summons his witnesses (2:10a)
    - b. He searches his works (2:10b)

        4. Paul's concern (2:11–12)
            a. It was a fatherly concern (2:11)
            b. It was a fundamental concern (2:12)
    C. The triumph of Paul's converts (2:13–14)
        1. How they received the truth (2:13)
            a. In all its divine actuality (2:13a)
            b. In all its divine activity (2:13b)
        2. How they retained the truth (2:14)
            a. Who they followed (2:14a)
            b. What they faced (2:14b)
    D. The tragedy of Paul's countrymen (2:15–16)
        1. Their provocation (2:15a)
        2. Their presumption (2:15b)
        3. Their perversity (2:15c)
        4. Their prejudice (2:16a)
        5. Their punishment (2:16b)
    E. The tangibility of Paul's crown (2:17–20)
        1. Paul's earnest desire (2:17–18)
            a. The great hope he fostered (2:17)
            b. The great hindrance he faced (2:18)
        2. Paul's eternal delight (2:19–20)
            a. The reward he expected (2:19a)
            b. The return he expected (2:19b)
            c. The rejoicing he expected (2:20)

PART 4: THE LORD'S COMING: A STABILIZING TRUTH (3:1–13)
    A. Paul's concern (3:1–5)
        1. The place (3:1)
        2. The plan (3:2)
            a. The messenger chosen (3:2a)
            b. The messenger charged (3:2b)
        3. The plea (3:3–4)
            a. Suffering faced (3:3)
            b. Suffering foretold (3:4)
        4. The plot (3:5)
            a. The anxiety confessed (3:5a)
            b. The adversary confronted (3:5b)

- B. Paul's comfort (3:6–10)
  - 1. The tidings Paul received (3:6)
  - 2. The tenderness Paul revealed (3:7)
  - 3. The triumph Paul reviewed (3:8–10)
    - a. His life linked with theirs (3:8)
    - b. His life lived for them (3:9–10)
      - (1) His praise to God for them (3:9)
      - (2) His prayers to God for them (3:10)
- C Paul's compulsion (3:11–13)
  - 1. Paul and the Ruler of his life (3:11)
    - a. Who he saw (3:11a)
    - b. What he sought (3:11b)
  - 2. Paul and the reward of his love (3:12)
  - 3. Paul and the return of his Lord (3:13)
    - a. The review of the saints by the Lord (3:13a)
    - b. The return of the saints with the Lord (3:13b)

PART 5: THE LORD'S COMING: A STRENGTHENING TRUTH (4:1–18)

- A. Our mighty potential (4:1–2)
  - 1. What was committed to the saints (4:1)
    - a. The challenge received (4:1a)
    - b. The challenge repeated (4:1b)
  - 2. What was commanded of the saints (4:2)
- B. Our moral purity (4:3–8)
  - 1. Immorality is a sin against God the Father (4:3–5)
    - a. The need for sanctification (4:3)
      - (1) What is absolutely required (4:3a)
      - (2) What is absolutely rejected (4:3b)
    - b. The need for subjugation (4:4)
      - (1) The way to go (4:4a)
      - (2) The will to do (4:4b)
    - c. The need for separation (4:5)
      From the standard set by:
      - (1) Lustful passion (4:5a)
      - (2) Lost people (4:5b)
  - 2. Immorality is a sin against God the Son (4:6)
      - (1) The sin (4:6a)
      - (2) The sword (4:6b)

3. Immorality is a sin against God the Holy Spirit (4:7–8)
    (1) The rule involved (4:7)
    (2) The rebellion involved (4:8a)
    (3) The rejection involved (4:8b)

C. Our measured progress (4:9–10)
  1. Love taught (4:9)
  2. Love wrought (4:10)
    a. Love abiding (4:10a)
    b. Love abounding (4:10b)

D. Our manifest purpose (4:11–12)
  1. Toward temperamental things (4:11a)
  2. Toward temporal things (4:11b–12)
    a. A word about our work (4:11b)
    b. A word about our walk (4:12a)
    c. A word about our wealth (4:12b)

E. Our magnificent prospect (4:13–18)
  1. Those who are asleep (4:13–15)
    a. Our feelings reviewed (4:13)
    b. Our faith reviewed (4:14)
    c. Our future reviewed (4:15)
  2. Those who will arise (4:16)
    a. The revelation expanded (4:16a–c)
      (1) The shout for the church (4:16a)
      (2) The voice for the world (4:16b)
      (3) The trump for the Jews (4:16c)
    b. The Resurrection expected (4:16d)
  3. Those who are alive (4:17–18)
    a. Our promised rapture (4:17)
    b. Our present rest (4:18)

PART 6: THE LORD'S COMING: A SANCTIFYING TRUTH (5:1–22)

A. A word of explanation (5:1–11)
  1. Some significant contrasts (5:1–8)
    a. Regarding beliefs (5:1–6)
      (1) Saints are directed by Scripture (5:1–2)
        (a) Prior revelation (5:1)
        (b) Perfect revelation (5:2)

- (2) Sinners are deluded by Satan (5:3)
  - (a) The nature of their deception (5:3a)
  - (b) The nature of their doom (5:3b)
- (3) Saints are different in spirit (5:4–6)
  - (a) Their condition is different (5:4)
  - (b) Their character is different (5:5)
  - (c) Their conduct is different (5:6)

b. Regarding behavior (5:7–8)
- (1) A look at lost people (5:7)
  - (a) Their delusion (5:7a)
  - (b) Their destruction (5:7b)
- (2) A look at the Lord's people (5:8)
  - (a) Their arena (5:8a)
  - (b) Their armor (5:8b)

2. Some significant conclusions (5:9–11)
   - a. Our great escape from woe (5:9–10)
     - (1) What we shall escape (5:9)
     - (2) Why we shall escape (5:10)
   - b. Our great escape from worry (5:11)

B. A word of exhortation (5:12–22)
1. As to our values (5:12–13)
2. As to our virtue (5:14–15)
   - a. People to be helped (5:14)
     - (1) Those who are disorderly (5:14a)
     - (2) Those who are despondent (5:14b)
     - (3) Those who are dependent (5:14c)
     - (4) Those who are different (5:14d)
   - b. Principles to be held (5:15)
     - (1) What is to be prohibited (5:15a)
     - (2) What is to be pursued (5:15b)
3. As to our victory (5:16–22)
   - a. Praise (5:16)
   - b. Prayer (5:17–18)
     - (1) Access at all times (5:17)
     - (2) Acceptance in all things (5:18)
   - c. Presumption (5:19)
   - d. Prophecy (5:20–21)
     - (1) We are not to be disparaging of it (5:20)

(2) We are not to be deceived by it (5:21)

e. Propriety (5:22)

PART 7: CONCLUSION (5:23–28)

A. A parting intercession (5:23)
B. A parting proclamation (5:24)
C. A parting supplication (5:25)
D. A parting salutation (5:26)
E. A parting intimation (5:27)
F. A parting benediction (5:28)

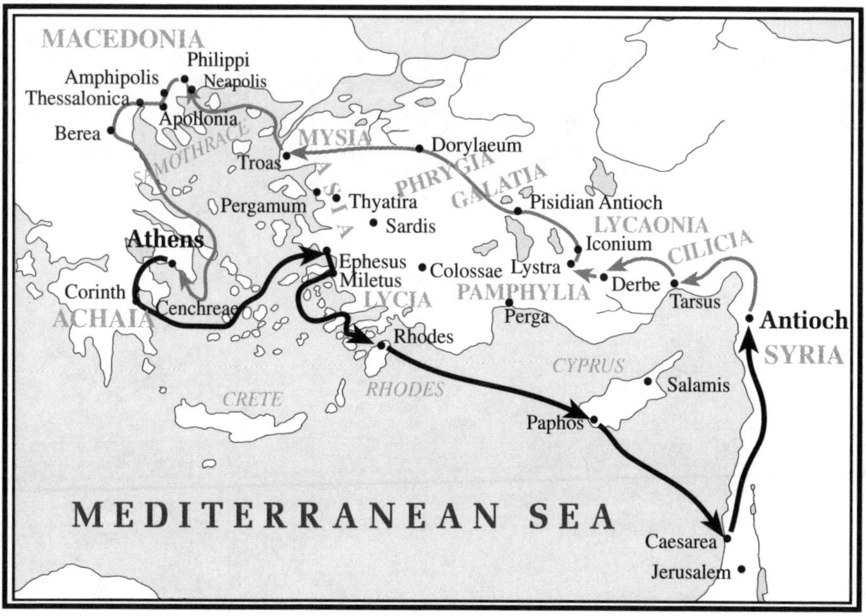

PART 1

Introduction

1 Thessalonians 1:1–2

Paul and Silas headed north from Antioch as Paul launched his second missionary journey. Tarsus, his birthplace, was the immediate target. Then came a swing through Galatia, visits to the churches that Paul founded on his first journey, and a steady westward march. More and more, the Holy Spirit hindered his plan for invading Asia Minor with the gospel. At last, he arrived at Troas (Acts 16:8), an important seaport not far from ancient Troy, a place to dream dreams and to see visions. Paul had his "Macedonian call" there. He knew at once that God had spoken, and he took a ship for Neapolis and planted his feet on the continent of Europe.

The sea voyage from Troas had been about 125 miles. Less than a dozen miles inland was the Roman colonial city of Philippi. Paul's first European contact was with a Jewess whom he met at a riverside prayer meeting. Lydia and her household responded to the gospel message at once. For the short but eventful time that Paul spent in Philippi, he seems to have been a guest in her home.

Events followed quickly. Paul cast an evil spirit out of a slave girl, was at once accused of interfering with the owners' business, and was hauled before the authorities. Both Paul and Silas were publicly flogged, imprisoned, and tortured by being locked up in the stocks. They sang! That night, an earthquake shook the prison, and their chains fell off. The other prisoners, now completely under Paul's spell, made no attempt to escape. The astonished jailor, who was about to commit suicide, became a believer instead. Then word came from the authorities that they could now be released.

Then Paul produced his trump card. He announced his Roman citizenship. By beating him, publicly no less, the magistrates had committed two serious offenses. Dire would be their punishment if Paul (and, presumably, Silas) made a federal case out of it. Meekly and abjectly, the guilty magistrates pleaded with the two missionaries. To their great relief, Paul not only chose not to press charges but also, magnanimously, agreed to leave town. Thus, the fledgling church was more or less guaranteed security from official interference. Paul and Silas moved on, leaving an infant church behind. More! Paul seems to have left his old friend, Luke, behind to help instruct the new believers. It is not at all impossible that Luke was that "man from Macedonia" of whom Paul had dreamed at Troas.

Paul's journey now took him to Amphipolis, a journey of thirty-three miles, then on to Apollonia, another thirty miles, and so on to Thessalonica, a final thirty-seven miles. Thessalonica had been founded in 316 B.C. and was named for a sister of Alexander the Great. It was a busy and important town with a mixed population of Romans, Greeks, and Jews.

It was situated on the *Via Egnatia,* the great highway that linked Rome with the whole region to the north of the Aegean Sea. Paul's strategic instinct quickly saw the value of planting a church on such a well-traveled interstate and in such a busy place as Thessalonica.

At Thessalonica, Paul preached both inside and outside the local synagogue. His rule was to go to the Jew first. He, Silas, and Timothy, a new young convert who had joined the missionary team at Lystra, first tried to win the Jews to Christ. They became guests of a Jew who bore the Greek name Jason (Acts 17:5, 7). For three Sundays, Paul accepted the customary invitation, extended to visitors, to address the synagogue congregation. From a note of Paul's to the church at Philippi, we learn that on at least two occasions while he was at Thessalonica Paul received financial assistance from that church (Phil. 4:16). The two cities were only a hundred miles apart.

In the synagogue at Thessalonica, Paul sought to prove to the Jews that it was necessary for the Christ to "have suffered, and risen again from the dead" (Acts 17:2–4). The few Jews who did believe were soon well nigh swamped by the vast host of Gentile "God-fearers" who believed along with a considerable number of high-ranking women.

The Jewish religious authorities greatly resented this and stirred up the rabble. A mob stormed Jason's house and he and some of the other new Christians were hauled before the authorities. The charge was serious enough. Paul, the accusers said, was proclaiming the advent of some other king than Caesar, one Jesus by name. The magistrates, all too familiar with the touchiness of the Jews in matters of religion, played down the whole affair. They contented themselves with taking security from Jason and the others and released them. The security probably was a pledge that Paul would leave town quietly, a pledge that Paul might well not have signed had he been present. Still, the pledge was given, so Paul packed his bags and prepared to leave.

He left behind him a new but virile church. Some of its members are named, Aristarchus and Secundus, for instance (Acts 19:29; 20:4; 27:2; Col. 4:10; Phil. 24). Its members were chiefly Gentiles, mostly slaves and artisans. Paul seems to have visited Thessalonica, too, on his third missionary journey (Acts 20:1–3). Meanwhile, he was deeply concerned about having to leave these new converts so soon, especially since they were exposed to the active malice of their enemies. Just as Paul left Luke at Philippi, it seems likely he left Timothy at Thessalonica.

It was some forty or fifty miles to Berea, the next city that Paul intended to invade with the gospel. The Jews at Berea were greatly interested in Paul's message and actually searched the Scriptures daily to see if Paul's teaching was true.

But, before long, spiteful Thessalonian Jews showed up, determined to stir up trouble again. Paul was obliged to leave. He seems to have been escorted by some of his converts to the port of Dium, some sixteen miles away. At Dium, he took ship for Athens, some 250 miles away. He was now alone and doubtless spent his time aboard ship praying for his converts and for guidance when finally he arrived at fabled Athens, the great university city of his day.

Athens greatly interested Paul. Much of its illustrious history he doubtless knew by heart. The roll call of scientists and philosophers who had graced the city would, of course, have been familiar to him. He missed his companions. Timothy was in Thessalonica and Silas was somewhere in Macedonia. Both were diligently running Paul's errands.

Unable to sit still, Paul wandered the streets of Athens, noting with every darting glance the gross idolatry of this fabled capital of learning. Mere sights and scenery did not move him much. What he wanted was souls. He began to challenge the Jews in the synagogue and the pagans in the marketplace. Eventually, he was summoned to Mars' Hill to give account of his teaching. The hearers mocked him. He moved on, alone.

As Athens was the seat of Greek culture, so Corinth, which Paul visited next, was the seat of commerce. It was fifty miles west of Athens and stood on an important isthmus. It had two ports, Corinth itself and Cenchrea. The city stood astride the central maritime route between Rome and the East. It was the Vanity Fair of the ancient world, a godless and vile place to live. Paul, however, planted one of his largest and most gifted churches in this strategic city.

In time, both Silas and Timothy showed up. Timothy's news was so good (3:6), Paul felt the urge to write a letter to the believers at Thessalonica. Some think that this was Paul's first apostolic epistle. He seems to have written it from Corinth, sixteen years after his own conversion when he was about forty-six years old. One interesting fact about this letter is that it does not contain a single Old Testament quotation. The imminence of Christ's return is its predominant theme.

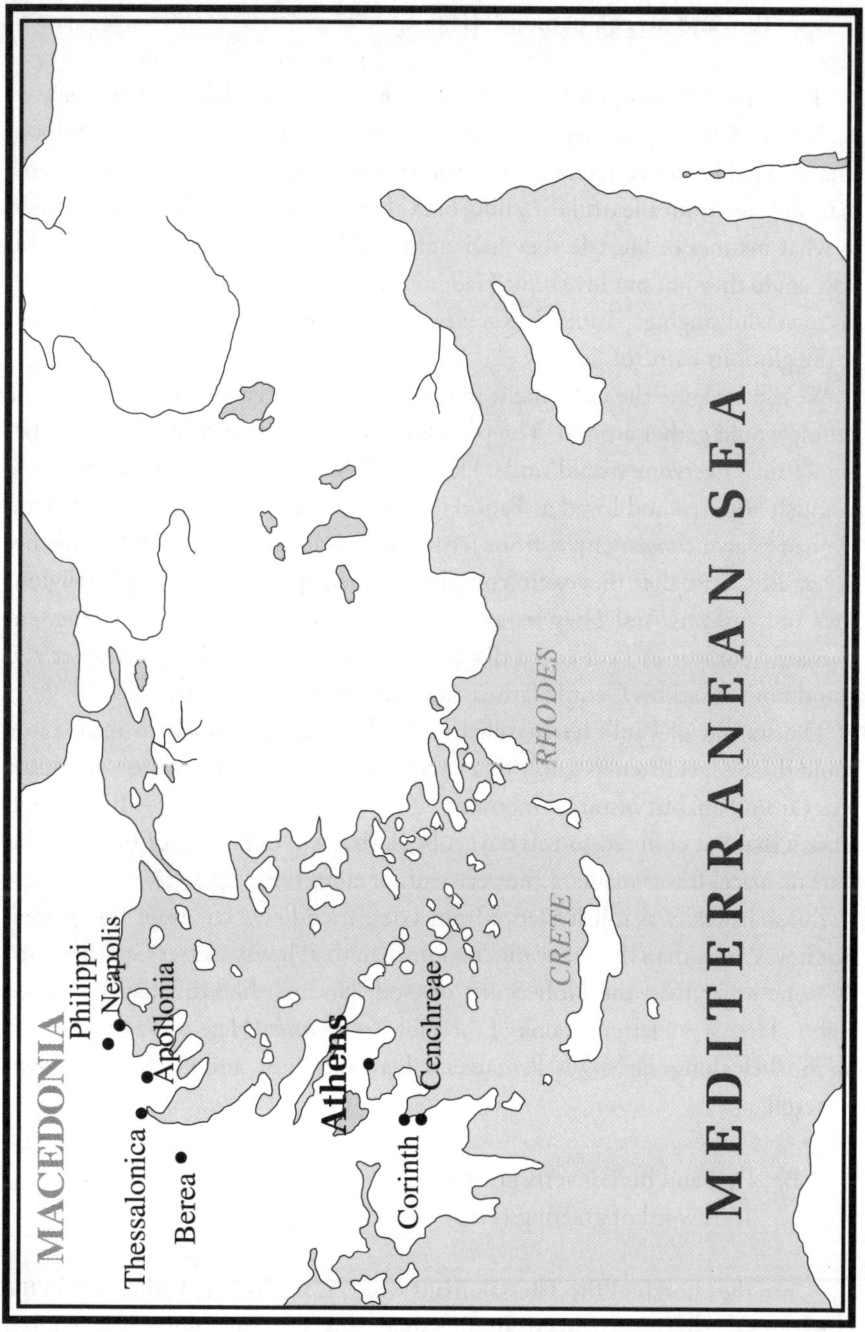
MACEDONIA
Philippi
Neapolis
Thessalonica
Apollonia
Berea
Athens
Corinth
Cenchreae
RHODES
CRETE
MEDITERRANEAN SEA

A. Paul and his companions (1:1a)

"Paul, and Silvanus, and Timotheus." Thus, the letter begins. Paul feels no need to add the customary words *an apostle* here. He was writing to beloved friends. Had he not risked his life to bring them the gospel? Had they not seen a man still sore from a fearful thrashing back there at Philippi? When they thought of what manner of lifestyle they had embraced before Paul led them to Christ, how could they not but love him? Had not the greetings that they sent to him set his own soul singing? "Paul!" It was a name that was almost as precious to them as the glorious name of Jesus.

We can imagine the excitement in the church when Paul's letter arrived. The people would gather around. The presiding elder would open the scroll and begin: "Paul!" Everyone would smile. Dear Paul! "And Silvanus!" Beloved Silas was as much admired and loved as Paul. He had once been a prophet in Jerusalem. He had been a chosen envoy from Jerusalem, commissioned to tell Gentile believers in Christ that they were completely emancipated from Jewish religious laws and customs. Yes! They remembered Silas and Timotheus, the young, enthusiastic convert of Paul and a disciple. Timothy, with his Jewish mother and grandmother and his Gentile father. They remembered Timothy!

The stanzas of Paul's letter rolled on as the elder continued to read. Little could these eager listeners know that they were listening to Scripture—not just a letter from Paul but inspired, inerrant, infallible truth, a brand-new Bible book, a book that has endured to this day! A book that will outlast all of the suns and stars of space! It was made of the very stuff of eternity!

But so it was. Was it just a letter from a dear friend now far away? Yes, indeed. But it was more than that, very much more than that! It was a letter God-breathed by none other than the Holy Spirit of God. Nothing like this had happened before. Here was a letter, a book of the Bible for *Gentiles!* Here was a book to put on the shelf alongside Moses' Pentateuch, David's psalms, and Daniel's apocalyptic scroll.

B. Paul and his converts (1:1b–2)

1. A word of greeting (1:1b)

"Unto the church of the Thessalonians which is in God the Father and in the Lord Jesus Christ." What an astounding statement! The Thessalonians, of course, were familiar enough with the word *church*. The Greek word *ekklesia* was a thoroughly secular word. It was the name used of the citizens of a Greek town when they assembled to conduct their governmental affairs. The Jews had adopted the word and used it in the Septuagint to describe the nation of Israel (Deut. 18:16; Neh. 13:1).

It was Jesus Himself, however, who seized the word and appropriated it to His own use. He said to Peter, "Upon this rock I will build my *church*" (Matt. 16:18). He was speaking prophetically of *the church universal,* which was to be brought into being on the Day of Pentecost. He used the word again later to describe *the church local* (Matt. 18:17). The Holy Spirit took over the sacred use of the word. We read that "the Lord added to *the church* daily such as should be saved" (Acts 2:47).

In addressing the Thessalonian church, Paul gives it two addresses. It was "the church of the Thessalonians," the address of the church local. It was also the church "which is in God the Father and in the Lord Jesus Christ," its address as part of the church universal.

No wonder the gates of hell cannot prevail against the church! Satan may attack and disrupt a local church at times, but he is impotent to harm the universal church that is as terrible to him as an army with banners. No wile of Satan, no wickedness of men, no attack of the world, and no work of the flesh can harm *that* church. It is "in God the Father and in the Lord Jesus Christ." And, in the end, God overrules even all of Satan's seeming triumphs over a given local church and makes them to advertise His wisdom, love, and power.

The church at Thessalonica was a case in point. Paul had been forced to leave town, leaving an infant church to face an outbreak of persecution and all of the malice of the Evil One. No doubt, Satan congratulated himself on winning such a swift and spectacular victory. If so, he was speedily disillusioned. True, Paul's presence would have been a great comfort to the Thessalonian church. After all, Paul was an old hand at facing persecution. But his physical presence was not nearly as important as his ability to wage war from afar, which is just what he did. He seized his pen and, under the direct inspiration and illumination of the Holy Spirit, wrote an apostolic epistle, a letter that would outlive all of the suns and stars of space.

The church at Thessalonica was God's *ekklesia.* It was uniquely united with both God the Father and the Lord Jesus Christ. It might look small, vulnerable, and even contemptible to the world, but it is a formidable foe to the powers of darkness. They see it as a called-out company, glorious, invincible, without spot, without wrinkle, and without any such thing. God has set it in the heavenlies, where it is feared by all of Satan's principalities and powers, by the rulers of this world's darkness, and by wicked spirits in high places (Eph. 6:10–20).

Paul's opening statement reminds the Thessalonians that Jesus is coeternal, coequal, and coexistent with the Father. We sometimes forget that fact. Satan never does. He is reminded of it at every twist and turn as he fights the church at all times, in all places, by all means, and with all of his might.

Satan fears and fights the Word of God. His first attack upon Eve in the Garden of Eden centered on the Word of God (Gen. 3). He faced her with a *doubt* ("Yea, hath God said?" Gen. 3:1), with a *denial* ("Ye shall not surely die," Gen. 3:4), and with a *delusion* ("ye shall be as gods," Gen. 3:5). Satan has watched with dismay and despair as, century after century, God added book after book to the Bible. Then the canon was closed. Satan must have breathed a sigh of relief. Thirty-nine books were headache enough!

Now, foolishly, by driving Paul out of Thessalonica, he had opened another floodgate. Paul began to write. Soon, another twenty-seven books would be added to God's Word, including some fourteen epistles from Paul's powerful pen. Well might Satan tremble!

2. A word of gratitude (1:2)

"We give thanks to God always for you all, making mention of you in our prayers." "Always!" "All of you!" How like Paul! How like Jesus! Next to the sight of a believer pondering the sacred page, the Devil must be terrified at the sight of one of God's people kneeling in prayer.

What a bulging book it must have been—well-worn and filled with names, addresses, cryptic entries, specific reminders, and all sorts of other information—Paul's prayer book! To Paul, it was as natural to pray as it was to breathe. In all places, at all times, under all circumstances, and in matters great and small, Paul prayed. It was an activity that he practiced, it was an attitude that he cultivated, and it was an asset that he exploited.

And, as its twin, he developed the power of thanksgiving and praise. All of Paul's letters, with the exception of Galatians, begin with a word of thanksgiving.

PART 2

The Lord's Coming: A Saving Truth

1 Thessalonians 1:3–10

A. The gospel in practice (1:3)

The cardinal theme in this epistle is the second coming of Christ. It is a vital truth of the gospel. After all, it was barely twenty years since Christ conquered death, took possession of the keys of death and hades, and ascended to heaven with the unequivocal promise of His coming again. The promise was as reliable as it was recent.

Paul reviews, first, the three tenses of the gospel. He begins with *the past.* The gospel has its roots in historical events, in things that actually happened and were still common knowledge when Paul wrote this book.

The Son of God, who entered into human life by way of a virgin's womb, invaded our planet from outer space. The event took place in Bethlehem of Judea. Both angelic and human witnesses saw the newborn babe. He grew up in a well-known town that the cultured population of Jerusalem, the capital city of His land, despised. His coming was announced by the greatest preacher of the day, who boldly proclaimed Him to be the nation's promised Messiah. He lived an impeccable life under the constant scrutiny of God and man. He performed countless amazing but well-accredited miracles. He taught great truths in a particularly pungent and unforgettable way. He was both loved and hated. In His life and death, He fulfilled, literally, many Old Testament prophecies.

His enemies were victorious. In the end, they succeeded in their efforts to get rid of Him by means of crucifixion. Despite the continuing machinations of His enemies, He was buried in a rich man's tomb. Three days later, He arose from the dead. Shortly afterward, before many witnesses, He ascended bodily into heaven. These are all historical facts. The doctrine of salvation cannot be divorced from them.

So Paul begins by noting "your work of faith," which put each Thessalonian believer into the family of God. The Old Testament believers looked forward by faith to these monumental truths. We look back to them.

The believer, however, does not live in the past. He lives in *the present.* Paul mentions their "labour of love." Love is essentially what the Christian faith is all about. Love brings things down to earth and up-to-date. The life of Christ can be summarized in one word—*love!*

Some time ago, I asked a friend of mine, who pastors a thriving "megachurch," how he accounted for the astonishing and continuing growth of that church. He said, "Our people love the Lord Jesus. Our people love each other. Our people love lost people."

Moreover, the believer longs for *the prospect* set before him of the second coming of Christ. So Paul mentions their "patience of hope." The great hope of the church is the Rapture, what Paul calls our "blessed hope" (Titus 2:13). He keeps this hope before the Thessalonians throughout his letter.

The Thessalonians were practicing faith, love, and hope in the light of the Lord's expected return and "in the sight of God and our Father." His benevolent eye rests upon us. He loves us with an everlasting love, a love that suffers long and is kind, a love that will not let us go. Our enemies may well be eyeing us, but there is One watching over us who is Love Himself.

B. The gospel in perspective (1:4)

"Knowing, brethren beloved, your election of God." The word for "election" here is *eklogē*. The Lord Himself used the word when He sent Ananias to visit the newly reborn Saul of Tarsus in that house on Straight Street in Damascus. Ananias objected. Saul was a dangerous man. He had wrought great evil to the Jerusalem church. And there in Damascus he was the agent of the Jewish religious establishment of Jerusalem, expressly commissioned to arrest all of the believers in the city. Ananias seems to be well informed. But he was simply telling the Lord things that the Lord already knew! And he was eloquent about it too. But the Lord knew what Ananias did not know; Saul of Tarsus was now a believer. Indeed, Ananias must do what he was told because as for Saul, "he is a chosen vessel [*eklogē*] unto me, to bear my name before the Gentiles, and kings, and the children of Israel" (Acts 9:15).

God makes choices. So do we. The Holy Spirit makes perfectly clear that divine election is based solidly on God's foreknowledge (1 Peter 1:2). Our lives are conditioned by the fact that we live in a space, time, and matter universe. We express our mode of being in three tenses of time—"I was, I am, I will be." God is not thus confined. He lives and moves and has His being in eternity. He expresses His mode of being, however, as existing in the eternal present tense—"I AM" (Exod. 3:14). When challenged, Jesus maintained His deity in the same way. He said, "Before Abraham was, I am" (John 8:57–59). God gathers all time into the present tense. Thus, the exact moment we choose Christ is the same exact moment God chooses us. As far as God is concerned, the two acts are simultaneous.

We cannot say that God has endowed us with a will and then say that we cannot exercise our will in relation to our decision for Christ. God created people, not puppets, and people have wills of their own.

C. The gospel in power (1:5)

"For our gospel came not unto you in word only, but also in power, and in the Holy Ghost, and in much assurance; as ye know what manner of men we were among you for your sake." The gospel is always "in word." Essentially, it is a message from heaven. It deals with facts. It reveals truth about God and man. It extends an invitation, it woos, and it warns. People need to be told. The gospel is in word.

But it is not in word only. Talk is cheap. "Ye have wearied the LORD with your words," Malachi told the Jews (Mal. 2:17). Paul had not walked all of the way from Philippi to Thessalonica with a bleeding back just to talk. His message was in power; the word used is *dunamis*—untrammeled, unequaled power. When Paul came to town, he did not merely conduct a few meetings, collect his honorarium, and leave town. He fully expected that things would happen. Souls would be saved, lives would be changed, and churches would spring up. People would get angry. The Devil would stir up opposition.

Thus, when he approached Thessalonica, he expected the high explosive of the gospel to stir things up there just as it had at Philippi. It never occurred to Paul that he should come to town, preach, and go on his way without people knowing that a man of God had been in their midst.

Paul, however, did not rely on his excellent hermeneutics, his knowledge of homiletics, his first-class education, his mastery of the original languages, his natural eloquence, or his powerful personality. It was not his outlines, his illustrations, or his sincerity that produced such spectacular results as always followed in the train of his preaching. It was the Holy Spirit. From start to finish, everything about Christianity is supernatural. No wonder we have to rely on the Spirit of God.

Between Passover and Pentecost, the Lord's disciples gathered in the Upper Room and enjoyed each other's fellowship. They had a lot to talk about. They could discuss the past and anticipate the future. They could pray and determine what made a man an apostle. But they were powerless to witness. The Holy Spirit had to come. Preaching has to be "in power and in the Holy Spirit."

Paul's preaching was also "in much assurance." Paul preached for three Sabbaths. Countless people were saved. When George Whitfield preached, hardened men wept. Moody could talk to vast congregations, and each individual felt as though he was talking just to him. Billy Graham could preach to tens of thousands in the pouring rain, stating gospel truths almost unadorned with illustration, with practically no discernible outline, speaking with a total lack of oratory or passion, give a matter-of-fact invitation, and hundreds would come forward to receive Christ. When Finney preached, the agony of conviction that fell on people was excruciating. At times, his mere appearance at a factory would cause people to fall down beside their machines, crying out in horror for their sin. When Jonathan Edwards preached his famous sermon "Sinners in the Hands of an Angry God," people fell in the aisles, smitten of God. He did not even preach it; he read it. Copies of it are still in circulation. The only explanation of such results is the Holy Spirit.

Thus, Paul marched into Thessalonica filled and anointed with the Spirit of God. Paul was as confident that God would produce spectacular results in Thessalonica as Elijah was when he called down fire from above; as Moses was when he stood before Pharaoh, staff in hand; and as Joshua was when he commanded the sun to stand still.

D. The gospel in person (1:6–7)

"Ye became followers of us, and of the Lord," Paul said (1:6a). We note *what the Thessalonians discerned.* There was no difference between the Christ whom Paul preached and the Christianity that he practiced. To follow Paul was to follow Christ because Paul himself so closely followed Christ. Paul had so learned how to live the Christ life that he could actually encourage his converts to follow him.

The Lord Jesus set before us a day-by-day, audiovisual, full-color demonstration of what God is like. We should set before others a day-by-day, audiovisual, full-color demonstration of what Jesus is like. Paul's colleagues did the same. The Christ life was not just for the Pauls of this world; it is for the Timothys and the John Marks as well.

The Thessalonians "received the word in much affliction, with joy of the Holy Ghost" (1:6b). They recognized the fact that Christianity is alien to this world. The world is our enemy. It murdered God's Son. It persecutes the church. Persecution of the church is endemic in all human society. From time to time, persecution becomes epidemic, and when that happens a holocaust occurs. In Paul's day, Christians had to confront raw paganism, Greek intellectualism, Roman totalitarianism, and Jewish intolerance.

The Thessalonians responded to persecution just the way Paul and Silas had responded to it at Philippi—they sang (Acts 16:22–25)! The Thessalonians sang "with joy of the Holy Ghost." Joy is the second fruit of the Spirit (Gal. 5:22). It is not simply happiness. Happiness depends on what happens; joy is rooted in God. Throughout the ages, Christian martyrs sang in the arena and when burned at the stake.

We note also *what the Thessalonians displayed:* "So that ye were examples to all that believe in Macedonia and Achaia" (1:7). The word *examples* is *tupos.* It means literally "types." It is used of the print of the nails in the hands of Jesus (John 20:25), which, Thomas said, would alone convince him that Jesus was indeed bodily alive from the dead. The word suggests a mold, a pattern, a model. Jesus had been Paul's model. Paul had been their model. They became model believers, the true pattern for all believers in Greece. Incidentally, Paul sent this letter from Corinth, the chief city of Achaia, to Thessalonica, the chief city of Macedonia. Every believer should so live Christ that others can point to him or her as a true Christian type, a model for everyone.

One reason Christianity was able to conquer the Roman Empire was because it was so obviously genuine. Pagans were faced by neighbors, friends, loved ones, workmates, masters, and officials whose lives had been radically changed by the gospel. Licentious people became pure, dishonest people became trustworthy, and cruel people became kind. The pagans did not just see people who had turned over a new leaf and were trying to live better lives. They saw people who were regenerated by the Holy Spirit, born from above, made loving and joyful—at peace with God, themselves, and everyone they met, friend and foe alike. They saw people who were now patient, gentle, good, meek, self-controlled, and full of the highest kind of faith. They saw a radical, permanent, and miraculous transformation of character. They saw people who were triumphing over temptation, and people who were undeterred by the most savage persecution, people whose lives adorned their doctrine. Paul saw the Thessalonian Christians setting the pace for all of greater Greece.

E. The gospel in proclamation (1:8–9)

Paul now tells us how the Thessalonians were spreading the gospel. He speaks first of *the sphere of their witness:* "For from you sounded out the word of the Lord not only in Macedonia and Achaia, but also in every place your faith to God-ward is spread abroad" (1:8a). The word for "sounded out," *exēcheomai,* occurs only here and refers to the sounding of a herald's trumpet. Such was the boldness of their witness in a hostile world! They did not hide timidly behind closed doors and whisper the gospel into the ears of their most trusted friends. They shouted it from the housetops. They preached the Good News loudly in the marketplace. They told it to everyone. Everyone sat up and took notice. What they had discovered in Christ was too good to be kept to themselves.

They were sounding out "the word of the Lord." This expression, which occurs more than two hundred times in the Old Testament, stands for the revealed truth of God. Ezekiel was particularly fond of the expression (Ezek. 1:3). He uses it to indicate the secondary divisions of his book. The Jews had "the word of the Lord," but they kept it jealously to themselves. If a Gentile wanted to hear it, he had to go to the synagogue and become a proselyte of Judaism. The Christians received the Word of the Lord, amplified as it was by New Testament revelation, and took it out of the synagogue, out from behind the closed doors of Judaism, and into the marketplace and onto the city streets. They trumpeted the message where they worked and where they lived. They told everyone. They became fearless ambassadors for Christ and earned the resentment and active malice of the Jews as a result.

We can imagine the resentments that the Jews nurtured against the Christians. The truth of God had been the exclusive preserve of the Hebrew people for two thousand years. If God had anything to say, He said it in Hebrew. He spoke to a Jew. For centuries, the Jews had been the recipients and custodians and sole proprietors of the Word of God. If a Gentile wanted to know the truth of God, he had to go to a Jew.

Pentecost put an end to all of that. After Pentecost, if God had anything to say, He said it in Greek. He spoke in a Gentile language that most people could understand. The New Testament was written in Greek because God was now speaking to the world, and Greek was the *lingua franca* of that world. It was being preached and proclaimed to Gentiles and by Gentiles in ever-increasing numbers.

The Jews did not like that. They did not want the gospel themselves, and they did not want the Gentiles to have it. They bitterly resented this massive movement of the Holy Spirit that was bypassing the rabbinical schools, the synagogue, traditional Judaism, and entrenched Jewish traditions. They hated Paul, Christ, Christianity, and they hated to see Gentiles preaching "the word of the Lord."

How could these Gentiles know the Word of the Lord? They had not spent years of arduous study in the schools of the rabbis. They had not learned to read the Hebrew Bible. They had not been brought up in the synagogue. What did these upstart Gentiles know? They had a few weeks' teaching from a renegade rabbi named Paul, a hodgepodge of proof texts, and an absurd story about a crucified Christ, and they set themselves up as Bible teachers! And, as if that was not bad enough, people were flocking to their meetings and joining their movement by the thousands. The Jews rose up in wrath to stamp out this pestilential cult. But the more they persecuted it, the more it spread.

Timothy had brought the good news to Paul at Corinth. But, by the time Paul came to write this letter, he was hearing the same story from everyone. All of Macedonia and Achaia were ablaze. The Thessalonian believers were setting the world on fire! The gospel was sweeping across the heartland of Greece like a prairie fire driven by the wind. The Holy Spirit was at work, and no amount of persecution was going to put a stop to His work.

So Paul goes on to describe *the scope of the witness:* "Your faith to God-ward is spread abroad; so that we need not to speak any thing. For they themselves show of us what manner of entering in we had unto you . . ." (1:8b–9a). Paul had worked himself out of a job! Instead of him going to others with the gospel, they were coming to him because they had already heard it from the Thessalonian believers! *That* is revival! The gospel and its impact was being gossiped all of the way from Thessalonica to Corinth. It had become a general topic of conversation.

We note, too, *the significance of their witness:* "How ye turned to God from idols to serve the living and true God" (1:9b). Obviously, most of the converts in this mighty moving of the Holy Spirit had been pagans and idolaters. The Greek pantheon of fabled gods gave the Thessalonians many gods from which to choose. At Athens, Paul saw that great city wholly given over to idolatry. The Romans sarcastically said that it was easier to find a god than a man at Athens. The pagan world of Paul's day was grossly superstitious and idolatrous. The gods of the East, such as Artemis of the Ephesians, rubbed shoulders with the gods of Egypt, such as Issis. The gods of Greece—Zeus, Hermes, Neptune, and Aphrodite—were worshiped everywhere. Gods and goddesses were available to suit everyone's tastes. Much that passed for worship was the grossest immorality. It was more than superstition. Demons lurked behind the idols, eager to enslave the minds and souls of devotees. Powerful priesthoods served the gods and enslaved the masses. Most thoughtful Gentiles were weary of this wholesale, senseless mockery of their deep longing to find and know God.

Then Paul came, preaching Christ and proclaiming "the living and true God." The Gentiles, by the thousands, were eager and ready to turn to God from idols. The truth seized their hearts, minds, and wills with great power. Here, at last, was the reality for which they had longed. Some of them had turned hopefully toward the Jews, only to be repulsed, treated as unclean, and faced with demands that they be circumcised and adopt the Jewish dietary codes along with rabbinical shibboleths, traditions, and rules. The arrogance, narrowness, and hypocrisy of many Jews turned them off and kept many on the outer fringe, drawn and repulsed at the same time.

Paul exposed idolatry and its attendant evils. Judaism, with its dead rules, was pushed aside. The truth of God in Christ—proclaimed in all of the mighty convicting, converting power of the Holy Spirit—had taken their hearts by storm. By the thousands, they—"turned to God from idols to serve the living and true God." *That* is genuine conversion. It always involves a complete about-face. The word for "serve" here means "to serve as a bondsman." They became the willing bond slaves of Jesus Christ.

F. The gospel in prospect (1:10)

Paul now brings us to the central truth of this epistle, the truth toward which he has been moving throughout the first chapter. The Lord's coming is *a saving truth.* Paul brings to a climax his praise for their glorious conversion experiences and for the evangelistic zeal of the Thessalonians. He states three magnificent truths.

He mentions *the Rapture:* "Ye turned to God from idols," he says, "to serve the living and true God; and to wait for his Son from heaven" (1:9b–10a). The word for "wait" is *anamenō.* It occurs only here in the New Testament. A word of close kind *(perimenō)* makes its sole appearance in the Lord's last words to His disciples before His ascension into heaven. He said that they were not to depart from Jerusalem "but *wait* for the promise of the Father" (Acts 1:4), wait for the coming of the Holy Spirit.

The word used here is used in the Septuagint to describe a servant's eager waiting for his wages (Job 7:2). It is used to describe the longing of an afflicted person for deliverance (Isa. 59:11). It can be translated "wait up." The Thessalonians were saved, and they were *waiting up* for God's Son from heaven. What a homey picture, that is!

When I go away on my many itineraries across the United States, I sometimes fly and sometimes drive. Sometimes when I drive, I'll call my wife and say, "I'm coming home on Thursday. The service will be over at eight o'clock. It's only about 250 miles. I'll be home about twelve o'clock. I can't give you an exact time. But, give or take half an hour, I'll be home at midnight." At that point, my coming is announced. Sometimes my wife will decide to wait up. Of course, she has been waiting ever since I went away, but now my coming is imminent. She expects me at any moment. She waits up. It is a heartwarming sight to drive around the last bend in the road and see the house all lit up. As I pull into the driveway, activate the garage door opener, and pull to a stop, there she is!

The Thessalonians had been taught the truth of the Rapture, the truth of the imminent coming of the Lord Jesus. They were expecting Him at any moment. They were waiting up for Him. That is how real the truth of the Rapture was to the Thessalonians. It spurred them on to win souls to Christ. They wanted to be found active in His service, in the center of His will, waiting up for Him when He came.

At this point, it is important to distinguish between the two comings of Christ. The Jews of Jesus' day failed to recognize the fact that their Old Testament Scriptures foretold two comings. The rabbis recognized seemingly conflicting Scriptures. They read the glowing promises of the prophets of a sovereign Messiah and looked for a Messiah who would crush their enemies, make Jerusalem the capital of a new world empire, and reign from the river to the ends of the earth. They looked for One who would beat swords into plowshares, make the desert blossom as the rose, and cause the lion to lie down with the lamb. That kind of a Messiah they would have welcomed with open arms.

But they read, too, of a suffering Messiah. They read of One who would be despised and rejected of men. They read of One who would be betrayed by a friend and sold for the price of a slave. They read of One whose hands and feet would be pierced, who would be given vinegar mingled with gall to drink, and One for whose vesture people would cast lots. They read of this One who would be abandoned by God. However, this One would be buried in a rich man's tomb, and His body would be preserved from corruption.

The rabbis puzzled over these seemingly conflicting Scriptures. Their solution was to postulate two messiahs, One who would be a sufferer and one who would be a savior. They were wrong in their conclusion. There were not to be two Christs; there were to be two comings.

Many professing Christians make a similar mistake regarding the Lord's return. Some Scriptures portray the return of Christ as imminent. Other Scriptures make evident that many things must happen before the Lord's return. Some

Scriptures point to the date of the Lord's return as the best secret in the universe (Matt. 24:36). Other Scriptures point to the Lord's return as being very specifically dated. Attempts to reconcile these seemingly conflicting Scriptures have resulted in a bewildering array of conflicting positions. We have premillennialists, postmillennialists, and amillennialists. We have those who hold to a pretribulation rapture, those who espouse a midtribulation rapture, those who believe that the church will go home before the Tribulation begins, those who think that the church will be raptured halfway through the Great Tribulation, and those who think that the church will go through the terrible "time of Jacob's trouble." As a result, some people have given up any attempt to understand Bible prophecy. They are content to hold a vague, general belief that the Lord will come again.

It is important that we at least try to untangle this knotted skein. There are to be *two* comings of Christ. The Lord is coming first in the air to receive His own to Himself. Later, He is coming to the earth to set up His millennial kingdom. He is coming first *for* His saints; He is coming later *with* His saints. His coming *for* His saints we call *the Rapture.* His coming *with* His saints is called the *return.* The coming of the Lord *for* His saints is an imminent, undated event, something that can take place at any moment. This coming is for the church, and it is the coming that predominates the eschatology of Paul's first Thessalonian letter. The coming of the Lord *with* His saints is a dated event. Certain things have to happen before it can happen. The Antichrist, for instance, must come and briefly rule the world. This coming has to do primarily with Israel and the world and is the coming that predominates the eschatology of 2 Thessalonians.

There is no point in "waiting up" for an event that, right from the start, is a long time off. But every reason exists to wait up for an event that could take place at any time.

God has always set dates for predicted future events that concern the nation of Israel. When He promised to give Abraham a land that would stretch all of the way from the Nile to the Euphrates, He told him, from the start, that it would not be in his lifetime. On the contrary, four hundred years would elapse before the fulfillment of the promise could be expected. Abraham's descendants would be persecuted in a foreign land, and they would be emancipated in the fourth generation (Gen. 15:13–18). A biblically literate Hebrew in the Egyptian ghetto could have known for sure that Moses was the Emancipator and that the date foretold was at hand. Moses represented the fourth generation! Levi, Kohath, Amram, Moses . . . four generations. God set a date, circled it on His calendar, and kept it.

When the Babylonian captivity loomed on the Judean horizon, God set another date. The captivity would last for seventy years (Jer. 25:11; 29:1, 10). When Darius the Mede entered Babylon in the wake of Cyrus, whose coming had been foretold much earlier even by Isaiah (Isa 44:28; 45:1), Daniel realized that the time of the Exile was over. It was time for God to act. Daniel gave himself to prayer (Dan. 9:1–19). God sent an angel to assure Daniel that things were proceeding according to plan. The seventy-year captivity was about to end. It was time to reveal to Daniel a new cycle of time that was soon to commence. There would be a period of seventy sevens—a period of 490 years. After sixty-nine of those sevens (i.e., 483 years), Messiah would be cut off. The remaining period of seven years was left in suspension, awaiting events and further revelations (Dan. 9:24–27). A starting date was given for the commencement of this new period of seventy sevens. A biblically literate Jew, living in the time of Christ, could have set the date of the Crucifixion to the day. Sir Robert Anderson has shown that the period of 483 years expired the day Jesus rode in triumph into Jerusalem.[1]

It is the same with the return of Christ to the earth, *with* His saints, to set up His millennial kingdom. The pending final seven years of Daniel's prophecy now comes into focus. The Antichrist will sign a seven-year treaty with the nation of Israel that will signal the beginning of the final countdown to the return of Christ. Halfway through the period, the Antichrist will tear up his treaty, occupy Jerusalem, seize the rebuilt Jewish temple, and set up his image within. He will promulgate his terrible laws demanding worship for his image, for Satan, and for himself. He will inaugurate that fearful time of persecution known as "the Great Tribulation," and as "the time of Jacob's trouble." At this point, exactly 1,260 days will be left until the visible return of Christ to put an end to these horrors, judge the earth, and set up His kingdom (Rev. 11:1–3). The biblically literate Jew living in those days of terror will be able to do a day-by-day countdown to the return of Christ.

Setting dates has to do with the nation of Israel, not with the church. The coming of Christ for the church is an undated, imminent event, the actual time of which is a secret known only to God (Matt. 24:33–36). The Thessalonians were not looking for the return of the Lord to reign; there was no point in "waiting up" for that event. The Lord had indicated in various parables that a considerable delay would occur before He would come back and claim His kingdom (Matt. 24:48; 25:14–15; Mark 12:1–9; Luke 20:9). Peter also indicated that it would be a long time before the final judgment (2 Peter 3:3–10). Although there

1. Sir Robert Anderson, *The Coming Prince* (Grand Rapids: Kregel, 1984), 126–29.

was no point in waiting up for the return of Christ to set up His kingdom, there was every reason to "wait up" for the Rapture.

Having thus mentioned the Rapture, Paul mentions *the Resurrection,* which is closely connected with the Rapture—"to wait for his Son from heaven, whom he raised from the dead, even Jesus . . ." (1:10b). His resurrection is the guarantee of our resurrection (1 Cor. 15). The truth of resurrection is unfolded in the New Testament under the figure of a harvest. The Jewish harvest was in three stages. First came *the firstfruits* dedicated to God and waved before Him. When the Lord Jesus rose from the dead, He brought the "wave-sheaf" (Lev. 23:9–14) with Him (Matt. 27:52–53). After the firstfruits came *the main harvest.* The main resurrection harvest will be at the time of the Rapture, when the Lord takes His beloved church to be with Himself. Paul develops this truth later in this letter (4:13–18). After the harvest came *the gleaning.* The poor were allowed into the field to gather what remained. The gleaning anticipates the various subsidiary resurrections of kingdom-age believers at various times. The rapture of the church and the resurrection of God's saints are closely associated truths.

Finally, Paul mentions *the rescue:* "even Jesus," he continues, "which delivered us from the wrath to come" (1:10c). The word *delivered* is in the present tense. The word itself *(rhuomai)* carries predominantly the idea of rescue. The present tense here ("rescues us") is linked, as is often the case in Scripture, with a future meaning (e.g., Matt. 26:2; John 14:3; 2 Cor. 13:1). In other words, our salvation not only takes care of our past sins and our present needs but also embraces our rescue from the coming wrath of God yet to be poured out on this planet.

The word for "wrath" is *orgē,* which is often used to depict God's purposes in judgment (Matt. 3:7; Luke 3:7; Rom. 1:18; Eph. 2:3; Col. 3:6). The wrath mentioned here is closely associated with rapture and resurrection. It refers to the coming time when God will visit this world with judgment. Right now, we are living in the age of grace. The terrible crime of Calvary remains unavenged because God is actually making the blood that was shed on the cross of Christ the very instrument of His saving grace (Col. 1:20). Scripture assures us that the age of grace will eventually give way to the day of God's righteous judgment. His wrath will be unleashed in judgment upon Jews and Gentiles alike.

The word *orgē* is used five times in the Apocalypse to depict the Great Tribulation. The people living on the earth when the seal judgments are unleashed will cry in terror to the mountains and rocks, saying, "Fall on us, and hide us from the face of him that sitteth on the throne, and from *the wrath* of the Lamb" (Rev. 6:16). They will add, "For the great day of his wrath is come" (Rev. 6:17).

When the Antichrist finally consolidates all power into his hands and triumphs over the two witnesses, a terrible earthquake heralds the translation of the two martyrs to heaven. The time arrives for the sounding of the last trumpet that signals, among other things, the actual outpouring of the vials of God's wrath. Thanksgiving in heaven is matched by rage on earth. We read, "And the nations were angry, and *thy wrath* is come, and the time of the dead, that they should be judged, and that thou . . . shouldest destroy them which destroy the earth" (Rev. 11:18).

The word is used to describe the overthrow of Babylon, the coming economic capital of the Antichrist's empire, the terrible Vanity Fair of the post-Rapture world, and the home of all wickedness during the Antichrist's brief reign: "And the great city was divided into three parts, and the cities of the nations fell: and great Babylon came in remembrance before God, to give unto her the cup of the wine of the fierceness of *his wrath*" (Rev. 16:19).

When the Lord returns with His saints, at the end of the Great Tribulation, to meet the Antichrist and the marshaled millions from both the East and the West massed at Megiddo, it will be to make a swift and summary end of His foes: "And out of his mouth goeth a sharp sword, that with it he should smite the nations: and he shall rule them with a rod of iron: and he treadeth the winepress of the fierceness and *wrath* of Almighty God" (Rev. 19:15).

There is another word for "wrath" that also occurs five times in the Apocalypse—the word—*thumos,* which indicates the outburst of wrath rising from God's indignation. The word is used to describe God's anger against all of those who succumb to the Antichrist's demand that all men everywhere receive his mark in their forehead or in their right hand. God sends an angel to warn the world: "The same shall drink of the wine of the *wrath* of God, which is poured out without mixture into the cup of his indignation; and he shall be tormented with fire and brimstone in the presence of the holy angels, and in the presence of the Lamb" (Rev. 14:10). It would be hard to find a more terrible warning in the entire Bible than this.

When God's final judgments are about to be visited on this planet, an angel will be sent to gather in the vintage of this world's wickedness: "And another angel came out from the altar, which had power over fire; and cried with a loud cry to him that had the sharp sickle, saying, 'Thrust in thy sharp sickle, and gather the clusters of the vine of the earth; for her grapes are fully ripe.' And the angel thrust in his sickle into the earth, . . . and cast it into the great winepress of the *wrath* of God. . . . and blood came out . . . even unto the horse bridles, by the space of a thousand and six hundred furlongs" (Rev. 14:18–20). This is evidently another reference to Armageddon.

No sooner has the preceding announcement been made than the stage will be set for the outpouring of the seven bowls of God's wrath. John says, "And I saw another sign in heaven, great and marvellous, seven angels having the seven last plagues; for in them is filled up the *wrath* of God" (Rev. 15:1).

This solemn assembling of God's agents of destruction is followed by worship in heaven. The heavenly hosts are thrilled that, at long last, God is about to put an end to man's wickedness on earth. The angels of wrath come out of the temple, armed and ready to accomplish God's final judgments: "And one of the four beasts gave unto the seven angels seven golden vials [bowls] full of the *wrath* of God, who liveth for ever and ever" (Rev. 15:7).

The heavenly temple is suddenly filled with smoke (Rev. 15:8). No man will now be able to enter that temple. It will be out of bounds until after the outpouring of the bowls. Prayer time is over. John adds, "And I heard a great voice out of the temple saying to the seven angels, Go your ways, and pour out the vials of the *wrath* of God upon the earth" (Rev. 16:1). As a result, the Antichrist's power structure will be broken; the eastern half of his global empire will break away. The nations of the East will unite, mobilize against him, cross the Euphrates, and march to Megiddo. God's final judgment will fall there.

From all of this the church is to be delivered (1 Thess. 1:10). But, coming back to the Thessalonians, certain false teachers had tried to persuade them otherwise—but this only called forth Paul's second letter to them in which he re-emphasizes the pretribulation rapture of the church. We are delivered, rescued from all of these coming horrors by the Rapture.

PART 3

The Lord's Coming: A Stimulating Truth

1 Thessalonians 2:1–20

A. The totality of Paul's commitment (2:1–2)

Paul pauses for a moment and then goes back to recent history. He reminds the Thessalonians once again of *his coming:* "For yourselves, brethren, know our entrance in unto you, that it was not in vain" (2:1). Paul had sent Timothy back to help and to encourage the new Christians. He was afraid that his new converts, under the pressure of persecution, might compromise or even give up altogether. He was afraid that his labor might, after all, have been in vain. Undoubtedly, opposition to the gospel, instigated and fomented by the Jews, had been running high when he had been forced to leave town. The arrival of the same Jewish enemies in Berea had confirmed his fears. The enemies of the gospel were not about to give up. No wonder Timothy's tidings had warmed his heart. His coming to Thessalonica had not been in vain.

He reminds them of *his condition* at the time of his arrival at Thessalonica. "But even after that we had suffered before, and were shamefully entreated . . . at Philippi, we were bold in our God to speak unto you the gospel of God with much contention" (2:2). He had come marching into Thessalonica bearing in his body what he described to the Galatians as the "stigmata," the slave brands of Jesus Christ. Not that stripes and imprisonment could deter men like Paul and Silas. They were made of sterner stuff than to be turned aside from their mission by beatings and bonds. Men who could sing in the stocks with bleeding backs, cramped muscles, and an uncertain future were not the kind of men who would give up.

Such men baffle Satan. Beat them to within an inch of their lives, and they sing for pure joy because they have been counted worthy to suffer persecution for Christ. Lock them up in prison, and they pray.

Paul, under house arrest in Rome, wrote three of his most magnificent Christ-exalting epistles. These letters have stimulated faith, stirred hearts, won souls, blessed believers, and transformed homes for nearly two thousand years. He also wrote a memo that struck the ultimate death knell of slavery.

Turn such men loose, and they evangelize the world. Set men like Paul at liberty, and they will march into city after city with the gospel, shaking Satan's kingdom to its foundation. They will strengthen churches, win souls, disciple converts, and engage in missionary work to the end of time.

Kill such men, and you only promote them to glory. You give them a martyr's crown and a triumphant entry into heaven to receive a resounding welcome home.

Thus, Paul and Silas had come to Thessalonica. "We had suffered!" Paul reminds the Thessalonians. He did not make demands on them that he was not prepared to impose upon himself. The modern Israeli army expunged the words *Forward march!* from its vocabulary and replaced them with the words *Follow me!* Soldiers who are not prepared to *lead* their men into battle are not considered suitable officer material. Paul felt the same way. He was prepared to face any hardship, any insult, any suffering, and any injury in a cheerful spirit. His converts knew that. No wonder they were prepared to follow him.

The word for "shamefully entreated" is *hubrizō,* which means both to be insulted and to suffer bodily abuse. Paul and Silas had suffered both types of mistreatment at Philippi. Although they were Roman citizens, and therefore exempt from being scourged, they accepted such treatment at the hands of the unjust magistrates, probably to protect young Timothy and to secure the future well-being of the infant church. The Philippian magistrates were horrified when they learned that the two people whom they had mistreated were Roman citizens. They were fearful of official reprisals from Rome should their outrageous behavior be reported. Presumably, they consequently adopted a hands-off policy toward the Philippian church.

"We were bold," Paul reminds the Thessalonians. The word *bold* is used a number of times in the New Testament, always in connection with preaching the gospel. It is used of the boldness of Saul of Tarsus when he preached the gospel at Damascus right after his conversion (Acts 9:27). It is used of his equal boldness in disputing with the Hellenist Jews in Jerusalem (Acts 9:29) It is used to describe the boldness of Paul and Barnabas in Pisidian Antioch when, realizing that the Jews were adamant in their rejection of Christ, they announced that henceforth they would go to the Gentiles (Acts 13:46). It is used of the boldness of the missionaries at Iconium when, faced with the active animosity of the Jewish community, they settled down in the city for a long stay with total disregard for the opposition (Acts 14:3). It is used of the boldness with which Apollos preached the gospel to the Jews in the synagogue at Ephesus (Acts 18:26) and of the boldness of Paul in the same city where, for three months, he disputed and persuaded in his efforts to win Jews to Jesus (Acts 19:8).

The word *boldly* includes the idea of speaking without reserve. Paul would never dream of diluting the message. His boldness was intellectual as well as physical. The word (translated "freely") is used to describe the boldness, for example, with which Paul bore testimony before King Agrippa. He was unintimidated by the pomp and ceremony by which he was surrounded. He was undeterred by his chains and his uncertain future. He was unperturbed by the scornful and slanderous outburst of the Roman governor Festus. He boldly confronted the king with his own need of Christ (Acts 26:26). This boldness came from prayer (Eph. 6:18–20). As he reminds the Thessalonians, "we were bold in our God to speak unto you the gospel of God. . . ."

Paul's boldness came from God. It was not just natural boldness. We learn that Paul had arrived in Corinth (not long before writing this letter to the Thessalonians) "in weakness, and in fear, and in much trembling" (1 Cor. 2:3). This behavior was doubtless a reaction. He had been manhandled and mauled, he had been hounded out of city after city, he had been beaten by his own Jewish kinsmen, and he had been abused by authorities who were supposed to uphold Roman law. He had been laughed out of court by the intellectuals at Athens. He was lonely and discouraged—"knocked down but not knocked out," as he put it himself later.

The coming of his colleagues, however, had put new heart into him (Acts 18:5). About this time, too, God gave him a vision to encourage him (Acts 18:9). The Lord, knowing the limits of this His most intrepid servant, deliberately restrained the malice of the Corinthian Jews. Paul cheerfully acknowledged that his courage came from God.

B. The transparency of Paul's conduct (2:3–12)
  1. Paul's claim (2:3–4)
    a. His integrity was undoubted (2:3–4b)
      (1) The truth displayed (2:3)

When he came to Thessalonica, his transparent honesty as to motive, method, and message was evident.

"For our exhortation was not of deceit, nor of uncleanness, nor in guile," he says. His sole purpose had been to win souls to Christ. His life had been totally free from anything deceitful, defiling, or doubtful.

The Thessalonians were all too familiar with the utter vileness of pagan religion and with the trickery, lust, greed, and dishonesty of many pagan priests. What had first attracted them to Judaism had been the purity of the doctrine that the Jews proclaimed; what had repelled them had been the hypocrisy of many of the Jews. What now attracted them to the gospel was the sublime message of love, joy, peace, holiness, forgiveness, and new life in Christ. What made them eager and willing converts was the transparent integrity of its messengers.

In the sixties, the United States and many other Western countries were inundated by social upheaval, religious apostasy, and cultural decay. Rock and roll became the drumbeat of a new age. Flower power was the "in" thing. The counterculture spawned a generation of hippies dedicated to drugs, dirt, and decadence. Countless thousands of young people dropped out of society, thumbed their noses at their parents, and plunged into a weird world of religion, rock, and revolution. They shoved aside all of society's norms. People from both the slums and the suburbs plunged into an exotic world of lust and lawlessness.

The major driving force behind the abandonment of morality, decency, and religious sanity came from the new rock-and-roll music world. Another strong allure came from Hinduism, imported into the United States and elsewhere by an obscure Hindu guru, A. C. Bhaktivedanta Swami Prabhupada. His total capital when he arrived in New York City in 1965 was seven dollars, but the assets of his weird religious cult, upon his death in 1977, were fabulous. The Hare Krishna movement that he founded owned more than two hundred temples and farms in sixty countries. It commanded millions of dollars. Its devotees and adherents were numbered in the tens of thousands.

The god that the gurus proclaimed was the Hindu Krishna, a handsome, flute-playing "little boy blue," supposed to be the omnipotent, omnipresent God of the universe—a "god" who was also very fond of stealing butter and hanging around with beautiful girls. He wore flowers and feathers and went barefoot. The form of "worship" to which the bright-eyed dupes were introduced was purely and simply idolatrous. They groveled before graven images. They were called upon to render abject submission to gurus. They engaged in endless and mindless chanting and repetition of hypnotic religious formulas. Every morning, the idols were dusted and washed in a "holy" brew of milk, rose water, and cow's urine. When these ablutions were finished, the devotees drank the rest. The idols were then arrayed in lavish robes and offered food. Vegetarianism (a common mark of all demonic cults) was required of all devotees.

The man who imported this brand of Hinduism into the West had once been an Indian businessman, husband, and father. His devotion to Krishna became an obsession. He became so busy chanting and studying that he neglected his business to the point that it failed. His wife was driven to steal one of his religious books and sell it to buy something to eat. Her husband, Prabhupada, simply abandoned her, walked out never to return—to become a holy man! His idea of holiness was to chant repeatedly (sixty-four rounds of it every day) the hypnotic religious formula that he taught to his followers and that so captivated the Beatles that they turned it into a best-selling record. As he chanted, he counted the repetitions on his *japa-mala* beads, the Hare Krishna rosary. This stern, religious ascetic introduced this Hindu cult to the disillusioned dropouts of Western society. The Western gurus whom he appointed picked up the formulas, made converts, ripped off a gullible public, and wedded Hinduism to drugs, sex, and crime.

The full story has been told in a book titled *Monkey on a Stick,* written by a couple of newspaper reporters, both of whom have covered the Hare Krishna movement and done painstaking research into its sordid underworld. They have revealed a world of child abuse, sadistic torture, prostitution, drug peddling, arson, gunrunning, and murder. It is a story of "faith and betrayal, money and power, murder and madness. . . ."[1]

No religion can rise higher than its source. Sadly, Christianity has often been corrupted in its stream, but Hinduism is corrupted at its fountainhead. The man who introduced Hare Krishna to the West was a severe, cold, and calculating ascetic who was able to wield terrible power over those who were deluded by his outward robe of Olympian calm. He brought his followers to a polluted stream and made them drink. He was not above using worldly means to achieve his purpose—the introduction of his followers to religious, mental, and moral slavery.

The Thessalonians were all too familiar with such religious gurus. The world of their day was full of them. Paul himself had encountered them (Acts 13:6–12). The message that he preached was different. It was not one of asceticism. It was not one that condoned sin. It did not introduce people to a lustful god. Paul preached Christ in all of His wisdom, holiness, love, and power. He introduced people to One who is mighty to save and able to cleanse, regenerate, and fill people with the Holy Spirit. The Christ whom Paul preached is able to transform our lives and to make drunken men sober, profligate women pure, crooked men straight, and bad people good.

"Our exhortation was not of deceit, nor of uncleanness, nor in guile," Paul reminds the Thessalonians. The word *exhortation* is *paraklēsis,* which means "to call aside" or "to appeal to" (by means of exhortation, entreaty, comfort, or instruction). Incidentally, this was the nickname that the Jerusalem apostles gave to Paul's former colleague, Barnabas. They called him "the son of consolation" *(paraklēsis),* or "the son of exhortation," as the word also translates (Acts 4:36).

1. John Hubnes and Lindsey Gruson, *Monkey on a Stick* (New York: Penguin Books, 1988). Note: this book is very graphic and unexpurgated.

Paul had evidently profited much from his friendship with Barnabas. The Thessalonians knew firsthand how sincere Paul and Silas had been and how pure and straightforward was the gospel that they preached.

(2) The truth declared (2:4a–b)

Paul viewed the gospel as *a sacred trust:* "But as we were allowed of God to be put in trust with the gospel. . . ." The word for "allowed" here is *dokimazō*. It means to be approved or tested.

The three missionaries were not novices. Paul had been saved for some ten years before Barnabas first sought him out at Tarsus (Acts 11:25–26). Some of that time he had spent alone in Arabia. He had to sort himself out after his traumatic conversion experience. He needed to think through the Old Testament in light of Calvary. His encounter with the risen, ascended, glorified Christ called for a radical new approach to everything. Three years later, he had returned from the desert. He had gone to Damascus and then on up to Jerusalem. From Jerusalem he had gone back home to Tarsus. He spent time in Syria and Cilicia and evidently planted a number of churches there before Barnabas invited him to join him at Antioch (Acts 15:41). In Antioch, he had made full proof of his ministry.

Similarly, Silas had made such a good account of his ministry in the Jerusalem church that he was actually called an apostle and was counted among the chief men of the church (Acts 15:22; 1 Tim. 3:13). Paul had been so impressed with him that he had invited him to become his colleague on his second missionary journey.

Timothy, too, though young, had proved himself. He had won the earnest commendation of his fellow Christians in both Lystra and Iconium. He had a godly mother and grandmother and was well versed in the Scriptures. He was one of Paul's own converts. That fact in itself, however, would not have been sufficient recommendation for Paul to include him in the missionary party. Paul still had indignant memories of John Mark's defection and was not about to choose another quitter. Moreover, Paul was familiar, by now, with the pattern of praise and persecution that marked his missions. They could test any man's mettle. Timothy, however, had made such proof of his trustworthiness that Paul had not hesitated to take him along on his second missionary journey. He had, however, applied one test—he had demanded that the young man, already half-Jewish, be circumcised. It was a good test of Timothy's obedience, flexibility, and willingness to endure suffering and hardship as a good soldier.

The gospel ministry is a trust. It is beset with perils and pitfalls. It is no sphere for the novice.

Paul viewed the ministry, furthermore, as a *simple task:* "even so we speak," he said. That was and is the essence of the whole business: to speak. The evangelist, the pastor, and the teacher are speakers. They speak out of a sense of the greatness of both the message and the mission. God Himself has put the preacher "in trust with the gospel." The preacher is an ambassador of heaven. He is responsible not only to tell the tidings but also to adorn the gospel with his life. His character, convictions, conduct, conversation, career, and commitment are all parts of a whole. It must never be said of him that "what you are speaks so loudly that we cannot hear a thing you say."

b. His integrity was undaunted (2:4c)

Paul's integrity in the gospel was undoubted; it was also undaunted. He says that he and his colleagues preached "not as pleasing men, but God, which trieth our hearts." The pulpit must never be intimidated by the pew. The preacher must always be courteous, but at times he is honor bound to say things that will likely offend someone who holds a different view or who is guilty of some particular sin. That is not his primary concern. He is to speak the truth in love. So often the truth is trimmed because it might upset a rich benefactor, an influential deacon, or a prominent and powerful citizen. John preached against Herod and Herodias at the cost of his life. Jesus denounced the religious establishment, and it never stopped plotting against Him until it had Him dead and buried in His tomb.

Paul's testimony to the Thessalonians was that when he preached in their city, he was not concerned whether his message pleased men. His preaching was such as could stand the test of God's examination. His recent experience at Philippi might well have so frightened him that, at Thessalonica, he would try not to upset anyone. Compromise, so beloved by the politician, has no part in the gospel. The gospel is not presented to us in the New Testament in accommodating shades of gray; it is presented in stark black-and-white. People are either saved or lost. We are going either to heaven or hell. Something is either true or false, right or wrong, of the flesh or of the Spirit, good or bad. Jesus is *the* Way, not just *a* way. The gospel is concerned with the truth; anything that contradicts the gospel is a lie.

Throughout the ages, men have dared to stand up and speak the truth, careless of whether they were pleasing men. Those men, not compromisers, have moved the world. Shadrach, Meshach, and Abednego gave Nebuchadnezzar the lie to his face when he tried to persuade them to prostrate themselves before his golden image. They refused to bend, to bow, or, when it came to the torment of the fiery furnace, to burn!

Martin Luther defied the assembled might of papal Rome and refused to retract a single word of what he had written. When his friends warned him that he was walking into a trap by going to the city of Worms, he remained unmoved. He was going there, he said, even if every tile on every house was a demon sent to oppose him.

John Knox was cut from the same piece of cloth. At one time in his stormy career, he was a galley slave on a French ship. The ship's priest came down the aisle where the unfortunate victims of tyranny toiled at the oars. Behind him came the slave master with a whip. The priest had in his hand a painted image of the Virgin. He presented it to each of the rowers in turn, demanding that they, blasphemous heretics indeed, kiss the mother of God. At length, he came to John Knox and made the same demand of him.

"Mother?" he cried. "Mother of God? This is nothing but a piece of painted wood, more fit for swimming than worship," and he flung it overboard! No wonder Mary Queen of Scots said that she was more afraid of John Knox than all of the armies of England!

Truth is truth. Error is error. We have no mandate to water down the truth to please men. Bold men in fields other than the ministry have dared to speak the truth at all costs. Galileo declared that the earth moved around the sun. The pope considered that view to be heresy. Galileo was arrested and handed over to the Inquisition. Pope Urban VIII made a papal announcement, speaking *ex cathedra,* as "the Vicar of Christ." He was supposed to be infallible. He declared it to be an absolute article of faith that the sun revolves around the earth. Galileo must recant! He did so. After all, the Inquisition had terrible powers of persuasion. But, even as he declared himself to be in error in saying that the earth moved around the sun, Galileo was heard to say, under his breath, "Nevertheless, it *does* move."

Truth is truth. Paul, "put in trust with the gospel," had little concern whether his message pleased man. Nor was he the kind of man to affirm truth in whispers under his breath. He aimed to please God, "which trieth our hearts," he said. Paul was sometimes accused of trimming his sails to suit the wind, of being "all things to all men" in a bad sense. Paul here indignantly repudiates such a charge.

"God tries our hearts!" Paul said. The word is the same as that translated "allowed" in the first part of the verse. Here it means to examine or test. Paul invoked God to be the witness to his integrity. With so many religious charlatans and quacks around, Paul was always careful to make his motives transparent and pure.

2. Paul's conduct (2:5–9)

Paul now tells the Thessalonians *what he shunned:* "For neither at any time used we flattering words, as ye know, nor a cloak of covetousness; God is witness: Nor of men sought we glory . . ." (2:5–6a). He shunned all *guile,* all *gain,* and all *glory*—the three things that religious deceivers most commonly seek.

The Thessalonians themselves were called to bear witness that Paul and his colleagues never resorted to flattery. We use flattery when we insincerely tell people pleasurable things about themselves. The word that Paul used here refers to using insincere words as an instrument of policy, the hope being that the person so manipulated will do what is wanted of him.

Tertullus, the lawyer whom the Jews hired to press charges against Paul before Felix, the Roman governor, used flattery. He began his speech thus: "By thee we enjoy great quietness, and . . . very worthy deeds are done unto this nation by thy providence: We accept it always, and in all places, most noble Felix, with all thankfulness." (Acts 24:2–3). Paul scorned to use such fawning words in his reply. He was sincere when he said that he was pleased that his case was being tried by a man who had been "many years a judge unto this nation" (Acts 24:10). That was the simple truth. A newcomer could not be expected to know the intricacies and nuances of Judaism versus Christianity, nor appreciate the vindictiveness of the Sanhedrin toward Christians generally and Paul particularly. At least Felix had been around long enough to have some feel for the special difficulties in a case involving Jewish religious prejudice.

There is a great deal of difference between genuine praise and insincere flattery. I have often received sincere words of praise. One unique instance was when a fellow preacher introduced me to an assembly of preachers thus: "You all know John Phillips. You all have his books. I'll tell you what I do with mine—I put a Bible cover on them and take them into the pulpit and preach them!" That was genuine praise.

Flattery, however, is usually counterproductive, especially if the person being flattered can see through it. A man once used these flattering words: "Your generosity overwhelms me and is only exceeded by your personal charm." The person who received this flowery accolade replied, "You seem to be intoxicated by the exuberance of your own verbosity!" So much for flattery!

Moreover, Paul had no ulterior motives. He did not use flattery to get money from people. Covetousness, which Paul avoided like the plague, was the sin that slew him in his unconverted days. "I had not known lust," he said, "except the law had said, Thou shalt not covet" (Rom. 7:7). Young Saul of Tarsus, secure in his religious armor, could run his eye down the Decalogue and claim, like the rich young ruler who came to Christ (Matt. 19:20), that he had kept every demand of the law. He had never had any God but the true God, nor had he bowed to a graven image. He had never taken the Lord's name in vain or ever profaned the Sabbath. He had always honored his parents. He had never killed, stolen, committed adultery, or borne false witness. However, when he came to the tenth commandment—"Thou shalt not covet" ("Thou shalt have no evil desire")—the law smote him. We do not know what young Saul of Tarsus coveted. Possibly he coveted a seat in the Sanhedrin, or even the place and palace of the high priest. The tenth commandment, however, probed his inner life, and he wilted before it. His boasted morality and integrity collapsed in ruins.

As a Christian, with his inner life now controlled by the Holy Spirit, he set a special guard against covetousness, the one prevailing sin of his unregenerate days.

But what is covetousness? William Barclay defines it as the sin of the person who gives full play to lawless appetite, of the person who thinks that his desires, appetites, and lusts are the most important things in the world. The covetous person treats other people as though they were mere things to be exploited. Such a person has no god but himself and his desires.[2] No wonder the Holy Spirit defines covetousness as idolatry (Col. 3:5).

There is a great temptation for the preacher to covet, to cast an avaricious eye on what belongs to somebody else—especially when some of his converts or followers are wealthy, attractive, or influential. Paul had long since crucified such evil desire, and it never tainted his ministry.

Paul's conduct was beyond all reproach. He not only shunned guile and gain as motivating forces in his life but also another snare of the popular preacher—the desire for glory: "Nor of men sought we glory, neither of you, nor yet of others, when we might have been burdensome, as the apostles of Christ" (2:6).

Apostles! No greater office ever existed on earth than that held by an apostle. In the Old Testament, the office of prophet was greater than that of either priest

---

2. William Barclay, *A New Testament Wordbook* (London: SCM Press, 1955), 99.

or king. A prophet such as Samuel could step into the priest's office, something that no king dared do, and offer sacrifices and minister directly from God to man. A prophet such as Nathan could rebuke even a king such as David. No priest of Israel could be a king, and no king could be a priest, but a prophet could be a king or a member of the royal family, as Daniel was, and he could be a priest, as Jeremiah and Ezekiel were. Or he could be a nobody, as Amos was. When a prophet stepped onstage in Old Testament Israel, all other actors stepped back.

In New Testament times, the gifts of the evangelist, the pastor, and the teacher are all excellent gifts. The gift of a prophet was even greater, but no gift compared with the gift of the apostle. Moreover, no apostle compares with Paul. To be an apostle of the Lamb was an honor indeed. There have been only a few such men. Their names will be eternally immortalized in the foundation of stones of the New Jerusalem (Rev. 21:14). No secular office can compare with this high and holy calling. No king, president, caesar, emperor, church dignitary, conquering general, artist, scientist, engineer, no political pundit, or business tycoon ever had an office such as "the apostles of Christ" held. They were unique, a chosen handful. They had gifts and a calling that set them apart from all others. They were the aristocracy of heaven, the Lord's own chosen friends, His "sent ones," His special messengers. If any man could have glorified in his apostleship, it was Paul. But Paul said, "God forbid that I should glory, save in the cross of our Lord Jesus Christ, by whom the world is crucified unto me, and I unto the world" (Gal. 6:14).

Once, in defense of his apostleship, Paul was driven to express something akin to glorying. He wrote,

> Seeing that many glory after the flesh, I will glory also. For ye suffer fools gladly. . . . Are they Hebrews? so am I. Are they Israelites? so am I. Are they the seed of Abraham? so am I. Are they ministers of Christ? (I speak as a fool) I am more; in labours more abundant, in stripes above measure, in prisons more frequent, in deaths oft. Of the Jews five times received I forty stripes save one. Thrice was I beaten with rods, once was I stoned, thrice I suffered shipwreck, a night and a day I have been in the deep; in journeyings often, in perils of waters, in perils of robbers, in perils by mine own countrymen, in perils by the heathen, in perils in the city, in perils in the wilderness, in perils in the sea, in perils among false brethren; in weariness and painfulness, in watchings often, in hunger and thirst, in fastings often, in cold and nakedness. Beside those things

> that are without, that which cometh upon me daily, the care of all the churches. Who is weak, and I am not weak? who is offended, and I burn not? If I must needs glory, I will glory of the things which concern mine infirmities. (2 Corinthians 11:18–19, 22–30)

It was not like Paul to glory. In his unconverted days, he had gloried in his race, religion, and righteousness (Phil. 3:4–6). But one glimpse of the face of the glorified Christ put an end to all of that.

"Yea doubtless," he said, "and I count all things but loss for the excellency of the knowledge of Christ Jesus my Lord: for whom I have suffered the loss of all things, and do count them but dung, that I may win Christ" (Phil. 3:8).

"Nor of men sought we glory," Paul reminds the Thessalonians. "We might have been burdensome to you," he adds. The word for "burdensome" is *baros* ("a weight"), a physical burden (Matt. 20:12) or something that makes a demand upon one's resources. That seems to be the sense here. Paul had bent over backward not to take advantage of his apostolic gift and its accompanying power and authority to acquire either wealth or adulation from his grateful converts. Moreover, he had even repudiated lawful and legitimate claims. The Bible declares, "Thou shalt not muzzle the ox when he treadeth out the corn" (Deut. 25:4; 1 Cor. 9:9). Paul had every right to be reimbursed for his labors in the gospel. But he would have preferred to starve rather than give anyone the impression that he was in the ministry for money or that he coveted praise. Paul's Jewish upbringing would help reinforce his own natural independence. Jewish rabbis were expected to work and support themselves, not live off their congregation.

Having reminded the Thessalonians of what he had shunned, Paul now reminds them *what he showed*—his love and his life (2:7–8). "But we were gentle among you, even as a nurse cherisheth her children" (2:7). He had shown his *love* to them. Paul loved people.

Paul seems to have had all of the gifts. He was a superb scholar and a first-class theologian. He had a giant intellect. He loved to study. Books were an important part of his life. People who are like that are often neglectful of people. Paul was also an able organizer, a capable manager, and a strategic planner. Often, those who have such talents use people. But Paul loved people. He loved lost people, which is what made him a gifted evangelist and an unsurpassed missionary. He loved saved people, and that trait made him a warmhearted pastor. His companions, Silas and Timothy, were the same.

Far from having any desire to exploit his converts, Paul was gentle toward them, like a nurse cherishing her own children. The word for "gentle" is *ēpios,* a word that the Greeks used to describe the kindness displayed by parents toward their children. The word for "nurse" is *trophos.* As it is used here, the word probably refers to a nursing mother and the children whom she cherishes as her own. The word for cherishing is *thalpō,* which means literally "to warm." In the Septuagint, the word is used of a bird's nestling its young beneath its feathers (Deut. 22:6). The whole picture is one of tender, loving care. Far from exploiting his converts, as is usually the case with the propagators of religious cults, Paul looked out for only the protection, development, nurture, and well-being of his converts.

Moreover, he showed his *life* to them: "So being affectionately desirous of you, we were willing to have imparted unto you, not the gospel of God only, but also our own souls, because you were dear unto us" (2:8). That is how sincere he was. He would have died for them. The word here rendered "souls" denotes lives. A mother will defend her children to the doors of death itself.

Years ago, a missionary in Africa was walking down a forest path where, some while before, a fire had blazed. He saw beside the pathway the charred remains of a nest and a mother hen. Idly, he nudged aside the carcass. To his astonishment, out from beneath the burned fragments ran some baby chicks. Mother love had taught that hen to give her life for her brood. That was exactly how Paul was toward his babes in Christ. He would have given his life for them. The love of a mother hen toward her chicks, after all, is merely creature love; the love that Paul had for his converts was Calvary love.

If he had brought them only the gospel, that would have made them his lifelong debtors. The "gospel" is very good news indeed. Here, Paul speaks of the gospel as "the gospel of God." Various gospels are referred to in the Bible. First, there is the gospel of the grace of God. It is described in various ways in the New Testament. It is called "the gospel of Christ" (2 Cor. 10:14) because it is based on His redemptive work. It is called "the gospel of your salvation" (Eph. 1:13) because it is by believing it that we enter into salvation. It is called "the glorious gospel" (1 Tim. 1:11) because it tells of One who came from glory, is now in the glory, and is bringing us all home to glory. It is called "the gospel of the uncircumcision" (Gal. 2:7) because it saves us apart from the rules and requirements of religion. It is called "the gospel of peace" (Eph. 6:15) because it gives us peace with God and imparts to us the peace of God. Paul calls it "my gospel" (Rom. 2:16) because it includes revelations of divine truths and mysteries imparted by God through Paul—especially in his epistles to the Ephesians and the Colossians.

But two other gospels also have their place in the New Testament. There is "the gospel of the kingdom" (Matt. 24:14), the good news concerning the coming kingdom. This gospel will be preached after the rapture of the church. Those to whom this gospel will be preached will be saved, but they will not be in the church—the church will be already raptured to heaven—but they will be in the kingdom (Rev. 7). The kingdom and the church are two separate entities in God's dealings with mankind. Failure to distinguish between "salvation" truth and "kingdom" truth leads to many errors.[3]

Then, too, there is "the everlasting gospel" (Rev. 14:6–7) entrusted to an angel. This gospel is to be preached to men just before the outpouring of God's wrath upon this planet. It is the gospel stripped to its bare essentials. It contains no mention of Christ, no mention of the blood, and no mention of any of the elements that we normally associate with the gospel. It is simply a call upon men to acknowledge God as the Creator and to fear and glorify Him. It is just the kind of gospel that we would expect God to proclaim to the heathen who have no knowledge of Christ and no time to learn. It is similar to what we have in Romans 1:18–23. It is God's last attempt to save some souls before the judgment falls.

Here, Paul calls the gospel "the gospel of God." It is another description of the gospel of the grace of God. He calls it the gospel of God because that was exactly what it was to the Thessalonians, most of whom had been raw pagans when first they heard it. What a motley collection of gods these old Greeks and Romans had! And what a riotous crew they were who crowded the pantheon: what a scheming, lustful, quarrelsome, warring, vengeful, malicious dynasty of deities! What good news it was that God was not like that at all! The true and living God was a God who "so loved the world, that he gave his only begotten Son, that whosoever believeth in him should not perish, but have everlasting life" (John 3:16). Nor was God like the god imagined by the Jews, a god mostly concerned with circumcision; Sabbaths; dietary restrictions; animal sacrifices; and endless rules, rituals, and requirements. The "gospel of God" swept aside all such false notions of God. The good news about God is that He is a loving heavenly Father who is eager, able, and willing to forgive, cleanse, justify, regenerate, and save to the uttermost!

The Thessalonians would have been forever in Paul's debt if he had just *told* them that, but he did more. He was a living incarnation of the gospel that he preached. His love and his very life was theirs. He not only imparted the gospel

3. See John Phillips, *Bible Explorer's Guide* (Grand Rapids: Kregel, 2002), 85–87.

of God to them but also put his life on the line—"Because ye were dear unto us," he adds.

Then, too, Paul reminds them of *what he shared:* "For ye remember, brethren, our labour and travail: for labouring night and day, because we would not be chargeable unto any of you, we preached unto you the gospel of God" (2:9). Paul liked to pay his own way. When he was short of funds, he resorted to the trade that he had learned when he was young, the skilled trade of the tent maker. He would get a job and work rather than give anyone grounds for saying that he took money from his converts. No doubt, too, he saw his sphere of secular employment as an ideal place to make friends, spread the gospel, and win people to Christ. People are often far more receptive to one of their workmates than they are to a professional preacher.

I found that point to be true years ago when I lived in a town in northern Canada. I helped start a church in that town and was obliged to do nearly all of the preaching and most of everything else connected with it, too. At the same time, I worked as an accountant. Many indeed were the contacts made, and spiritual conversations were opened up around the coffee table in a local restaurant with people in the business and workaday world. People who would never have dreamed of talking to a minister often talked to me. I seemed more like one of them. I rubbed shoulders with them in the marketplace.

Paul had remembered the Thessalonians and their "work of faith" and "labour of love" (1:3). Now he reminds them of their labor and travail. The word for "labor" is *kopos.* The word means to beat, as, for instance, the beating of the breast. It suggests the weariness of laborious toil. It suggests work that results in weariness. The word for "travail" is *mochthos.* It carries the idea of painful effort, tiring labor. The root word suggests difficulty. Taken together, the words make clear that the missionaries had worked hard. They had not just done token work. They went to bed tired—when they went to bed at all. Paul says that they labored "night and day." Paul had no use for laziness in the Lord's work.

This seems to have been Paul's customary policy. He wrote this letter from Corinth, where he was, at that very time, working for his support (1 Cor. 4:12; 2 Cor. 11:9). He did the same at Ephesus (Acts 20:34). So then he shared with the Thessalonians, most of whom had to work hard. Paul shared their daily toil.

3. Paul's conscience (2:10)

"Ye are witnesses, and God also, how holily and justly and unblameably we behaved ourselves among you that believe." Paul's behavior was transparent to not only the eyes of men but also to the eye of God, who alone can read our motives.

Paul and his companions behaved *holily.* The word used means to be pure from all crime, religiously observant of every duty, careful to fulfill every obligation. Particularly, the word has to do with the discharge of one's duties toward God.

The word *justly* is *dikaios,* and it carries the idea of straight dealing. It has to do with the careful discharge of our duties to men.

Paul states the idea of unimpeachable conduct positively, "holily and justly." Now he states it negatively—"unblameably." The word is *amemptōs.* They were faultless; nothing could be said against them. If someone were to bring a charge against the missionaries, the allegation would never get off the ground. The entire body of believers would testify to their blameless conduct. Nothing less will do in those who serve the Lord.

4. Paul's concern (2:11–12)

Paul had a twofold concern for his converts. First, he had *a fatherly concern:* "As ye know how we exhorted and comforted and charged every one of you, as a father doth his children" (2:11). Paul was not content simply to win people to Christ. He recognized his responsibility to his newborn babes in Christ. As short as had been his stay at Thessalonica, as hard as he had been called upon to work, as zealous as he had been in preaching the gospel in street and synagogue, and as severe as had been the obstacles that his enemies put in his way, he had found time to lay a firm foundation for their faith in each person whom he had led to Christ.

He had "exhorted" them. The word used means "to call aside," "to appeal to." The ideas of exhortation, entreaty, and instruction are all incorporated in this word. Paul would call various ones to his side. After asking a few penetrating questions, he would know at what stage his companion was in the spiritual life. He would build on that. His great aims were to impart doctrine, to develop Christian character, to teach the principles of new life in Christ, and to encourage submission to the will of God.

Paul "comforted" his Thessalonian converts. They had been called upon, very early in their Christian experience, to face persecution, active dislike, and open hostility. Paul knew all about that. Some converts would suffer physical abuse. Family and friends had already ostracized some of them. Others had suffered financial loss. Paul knew how to comfort them. He would put an arm around the shoulder of this one and listen sympathetically to his or her tale of woe and weep with the person. The word he used here is also used in connection with the death of Lazarus: "And many of the Jews came to Martha and Mary, to *comfort* them concerning their brother" (John 11:19). The word *comfort* means "to speak tenderly."

The word for *charged* means "to testify," "to bear witness." Paul could talk to his converts out of his own knowledge and his rich, varied, and personal experience.

A conscientious father will take his children aside to encourage them, instruct them, console them, and point out to them the good and right way. Paul was so much more experienced than his converts were. He knew the perils and the pitfalls of the spiritual life. Moreover, he knew the characters, abilities, strengths, weaknesses, talents, and handicaps of his converts. Paul talked to them "as a father doth his children."

His concern, moreover, was a *fundamental* concern: "That ye would walk worthy of God, who hath called you unto his kingdom and glory" (2:12). Paul had a high view of the Christian life. The church is not the kingdom, but it is *in* the kingdom God's people are sons of God, heirs of heaven, citizens of glory, and joint heirs with Christ, the very aristocracy of the universe.

The story is told of a French count who was reduced to poverty by the spendthrift ways of his forebears. He dwelt in a common lodging house. His companions were harlots and thieves who urged him to join in their nefarious practices. But he held himself aloof. He excused himself. "You will excuse me, gentlemen. I am a French count. *Noblesse oblige.* Privilege has its responsibilities. If I were to do as you say, I should dishonor the great name I bear. I pray you, have me excused."

How much more should the child of God walk worthy of God, who has so signally blessed him. We have been lifted from the gutter to the glory—"from the guttermost to the uttermost," as the old-time preachers used to put it—and God expects that we will walk worthy of the high honor bestowed upon us.

C. The triumph of Paul's converts (2:13–14)
   1. How they received the truth (2:13)

Paul was proud of his Thessalonian converts. He was thankful to God for them. He says, "For this cause also thank we God without ceasing, because, when ye received the word of God which ye heard of us, ye received it not as the word of men, but as it is in truth, the word of God . . ." (2:13a). They received the truth at its face value *in all of its actuality* as God's inspired and inerrant Word. They never doubted what Paul preached. It was not some religious philosophy that he had evolved. What he preached had the ring of truth and the ring of authority about it. It was not man's word; it was, in very truth, the Word of God.

The Word of God is like the word of man in that it reveals the one who speaks and partakes of his nature, character, and personality. By listening to someone's ordinary conversation, we can tell if that person is educated or illiterate, good or bad, moral or immoral, cultured or profane, pure or vile, virtuous or vicious, and saved or lost. The Word of God, as revealed to men, contains a perfect blend of the human and the divine. The Lord Jesus is described as "the Word." He was there "in the beginning." He was with God. He was God. He became "flesh, and dwelt among us" (John 1:1–3, 14). God's revealed Word (the Bible) is the same. We detect the differing personalities, styles, and vocabularies of the various human instruments. At the same time, everything they said was "God-breathed" (2 Tim. 3:16) so that every word bears the imprimatur of God. Every "jot and tittle" is God-breathed (Matt 5:18).

The Word of God has a fivefold quality, however, that the word of man does not have. First, the Word of God is *inspired*—"God-breathed" is the Holy Spirit's own description of it. The word that He uses is *theopneustos.* As a trumpeter breathes into his instrument and his fingers control the flow of his breath through the tubes, so God breathed His words through His instruments and controlled the very parts of speech that they used—without in any way violating the freedom of the human composer of the psalm, or narrative, or letter being penned. Often, the human author did not know why he had written the words that he saw on the scroll before him (1 Peter 1:10–12). As they wrote, the thoughts came and the very words leaped readily to mind. They wrote as they were "moved by the Holy Ghost" (2 Peter 1:19–21). The word here is *pherō,* "to bear," or "to carry." The human authors were borne along, impelled by the Holy Spirit. They did not write what their own unaided wills or understanding might have suggested. They expressed God's thoughts in words that the Holy Spirit brought into their minds. Peter uses the same word in the same context to describe the voice that spoke on the Mount of Transfiguration: "He received . . . honour and glory, when there *came* [*pherō,* 'was borne'] such a voice to him from the excellent glory, This is my beloved Son, in whom I am well pleased" (2 Peter 1:17). The Word of God is unique, therefore, in its source. It is inspired. God has spoken.

Second, the Word of God is also *inerrant.* The original autographs are miraculously free from all error. God's Word in its original documents contains no absurdities, no mistakes, no inaccuracies, and no contradictions. God has sovereignly and sublimely revealed to men the truth about all subjects to which He speaks. When God speaks about creation, for instance, He speaks authoritatively. Any theory of origins that contradicts the Bible story of creation is false no matter what the "scholarship" or how great the reputation of the one who advocates it. When God speaks about Adam and Eve, the Fall, the Flood, or the origin of languages, that settles it. The theory of evolution is wrong; the Bible is right. God's Word is true. As the Holy Spirit says, "Let God be true, but every man a liar" (Rom. 3:4). After all, the Holy Spirit was there when these things happened and was an eyewitness to them all.

Seeming errors and contradictions in the Bible arise from poor translations, wrong interpretations, a partial grasp of the whole, human ignorance, bias, and fallibility. A god who cannot write a book without making mistakes is not the God of the Bible. Such a god is no god at all.

Third, the Word of God is *infinite;* it is without measure or end. It conveys some truths (about the Trinity, for instance) that transcend our own powers of thought or comprehension. David says, "Thy thoughts are very deep" (Ps. 92:5). The Holy Spirit says, "As the heavens are higher than the earth, so are my ways higher than your ways, and my thoughts than your thoughts" (Isa. 55:9). In one of his doxologies, Paul, who had one of the keenest minds in the world, declared, "O the depth of the riches both of the wisdom and knowledge of God! how unsearchable are his judgments, and his ways past finding out! For who hath known the mind of the Lord? or who hath been his counsellor" (Rom. 11:33–34).

The Word of God is an inexhaustible mine of wonder and truth. Who can ever say the last word, for instance, on Psalm 23; John 3:16; Isaiah 53; or any other passage of Scripture? People can spend their whole lives studying the Scriptures, then someone will come along, make a comment, and their reaction will be, "Why didn't *I* see that!" Or after years of puzzling over some obscure statement, another verse, in a different part of the Bible, will suddenly stand out to them, and the whole puzzling mystery will be resolved.

The Word of God is made of the very stuff of eternity. Jesus said, "Think not that I am come to destroy the law, or the prophets: I am not come to destroy, but to fulfil. For verily I say unto you, Till heaven and earth pass, one jot or one tittle shall in no wise pass from the law, till all be fulfilled" (Matt. 5:17–18). Later, He added, "Heaven and earth shall pass away, but my words shall not pass away" (Matt. 24:35). Throughout the endless ages of eternity, we shall continue to find new depths and wonders in God's infinite Word.

Fourth, the Word of God is *incisive.* It has the power to penetrate our thoughts, move our hearts, quicken our consciences, and conquer our wills. "For the word of God is quick [*zaō,* 'living'], and powerful [*energēs,* 'energetic,' possessed of strength put forth from within], and sharper than any twoedged sword, piercing even to the dividing asunder of soul and spirit, and of the joints and marrow, and is a discerner of the thoughts and intents of the heart" (Heb. 4:12).

The word for "discerner" is *kritikos.* It occurs only here. God's Word is a critic. Once, and once only, has God used this word *kritikos,* confining its use to His Word as the critic of all who live on earth. Yet, so-called "higher critics" dare to sit in judgment on the Word of God. They invent phony authors for the Bible's various books. They debunk men such as Moses, Jonah, and Daniel and substitute their own imagined authors. They deny this truth and explain away that truth. They come up with a hodgepodge of supposed documents from which the Bible was somehow patched together. And all the time it is God's Word that is the critic. It stabs and pierces and divides and discerns. It penetrates into the very depths of our being. It exposes our thoughts and our desires and motives. It can do its work deep within, where the mysterious boundary line exists between soul and spirit.

The Word of God is the instrument that the Holy Spirit uses to bring about conviction of sin and to make those who are "dead in trespasses and sins" suddenly alive to their lost condition, their peril, and their doom. Like living seed, it goes down into the soil of the soul. It germinates. It regenerates. "Being born again," Peter says, "not of corruptible seed, but of incorruptible, by the word of God which liveth and abideth for ever" (1 Peter 1:23).

Fifth, the Word of God is *inescapable.* Jesus said, "He that rejecteth me, and receiveth not my words, hath one that judgeth him: the word that I have spoken, the same shall judge him in the last day" (John 12:48). The word for "judge" here is *krinō,* which is used of a legal decision in a court of law. Men treat God's Word lightly. They ignore and set aside the claims and teachings of Christ. Nevertheless, the day will come when the books will be opened, and men will be judged "out of those things which were written in the books, according to their works" (Rev. 20:12). One of the books that will be opened is the Word of God.

In his booklet *The Reason Why,* Robert Laidlaw pictures a man from England arrested in the United States for driving his car on the wrong side of the road. He is brought before the judge, who hears his plea: "Your honor, I live in England. In England, we always drive on the left-hand side of the road."

The judge replies, "Sir, you are not being judged by the laws of England but by the laws of the United States. The law in the United States is that you drive on the right-hand side of the road. Your plea is inadmissible. *You are responsible to acquaint yourself with the law by which you will be judged.*"[4]

Ignorance of the law is no excuse. We are expected to know the law. How foolish is the person who ignores the inescapable Word of God, which contains in very truth the law by which he ultimately will be judged.

Such is the Word of God. When Paul preached, the Thessalonians recognized the voice of authority with which he spoke. They heard, recognized, and believed the Word of God. They recognized it in all of its actuality; it actually is the Word of God. They received it as such without cavil and without question. Nobody had ever spoken to them like that. They had heard the priests of the various pagan religions. They had heard the oracles speak in tongues with the voice of demons. They had heard the rabbis. But Paul, like Jesus, spoke with authority and not as the scribes. When he spoke, they heard, recognized, and understood, for the first time in their lives, the Spirit-inspired, God-breathed Word.

Moreover, they received the truth *in all of its divine activity.* They received it, as Paul put it, "as it is in truth, the word of God, which effectually worketh also in you that believe" (2:13b). The expression "effectually worketh" can be rendered "the word of God that is *made energetic* . . . in you that believe." It is "a power in the lives" of those that believe. The words are in the present continuous tense. What they had heard was alive; it was living seed. It worked away in the believer's life, effecting a change of character. The Spirit of God energizes the Word of God and so transforms the child of God. God's Word is a hammer to devour, a fire to burn, a mirror to reveal, a light to dispel darkness, and a sword to pierce the foe (Ps. 119:105; Jer. 23:29; Eph. 6:17; James 1:23–25).

There is wonder-working power in the Word of God. In the early dawn of time, God had only to say, "Light, be," and light was (Gen. 1:3) Such is the power of God's Word. He had only to speak, and a hundred billion galaxies sprang into being. He had only to speak, and life arose and multiplied itself in a billion forms. He had only to speak, and the seas swarmed with life, and the hills clothed themselves with meadows and forests. When the Word was made flesh, one word from Him, and demons fled, leprosy vanished, and the dead arose. That is the *energeō* of His Word. All of that omnipotent power resides in His written word like the explosive force that lies in a stick of dynamite.

The word rendered "worketh" here is nearly always used in the New Testament to denote some form of supernatural activity. Usually, it denotes divine

4. Robert Laidlaw, *The Reason Why* (South Plainfield, N.J.: Bridge, 1994), 15.

activity (1 Cor. 12:16; Phil. 2:13), although occasionally it is used to refer to satanic activity (Eph. 2:2). It is used to describe the activity of faith (Gal. 5:6) and the effectiveness of prayer (James 5:16). It is used to describe the activity of death and life in our souls (2 Cor. 4:12) as well as the activity of sin (Rom. 7:5). Here, Paul emphasizes to the Thessalonians that their transformed lives were the result of divine power, the power latent within the Word of God, and not the result of any power this world might offer.

2. How they retained the truth (2:14)

The transforming power of the Word of God in the lives of the believers made them some natural enemies. It also enabled them to face the bitter hostility that arose around them. "For ye, brethren, became followers of the churches of God which in Judaea are in Christ Jesus: for ye also have suffered like things of your own countrymen, even as they have of the Jews" (2:14).

Paul knew whereof he spoke. In the early days of Christianity, he had been the Sanhedrin's chief accredited agent to spread death and destruction far and wide among Jewish believers in Christ. Indeed, it was the violence of the persecutions he instigated that led to the spread of the original church in Jerusalem throughout all Judea, Galilee, and Samaria (Acts 8:1). Nor had Jewish persecution of Jewish Christians ceased. It had died down following the conversion of Paul, but it had flared up again not long before Paul wrote this letter. In A.D. 48, Ventidius Cumanus arrived in the country as the new Roman procurator of Judea. About the same time, the Zealots instigated an outbreak of persecution. They launched a campaign to force circumcision on those who had neglected that rite. They targeted particularly the Jewish Christians in Judea and the churches in Antioch and Galatia.

A similar thing had happened at Thessalonica. The persecutions of the Christians was originally instigated by the Jews (Acts 17:5). When Timothy came back from Thessalonica with up-to-date news of what was happening there, he also must have brought with him news that the persecution of the church was continuing and that now it was the Gentiles themselves who were harassing the church. "Ah well!" says Paul. "You are in a noble tradition." Indeed, persecution is the natural lot of those who embrace Christianity. "Blessed are ye, when men shall revile you, and persecute you," Jesus said (Matt. 5:11). When Paul was daily expecting his own martyrdom at the hands of Nero, he reminded Timothy, "Yea, and all that will live godly in Christ Jesus shall suffer persecution" (2 Tim. 3:12). The history of the church has been one long story of persecution. The roll call of the martyrs will take long to complete "in the crowning day that's coming by and by."

It was, of course, the energetic activity of the Word of God in the hearts and lives of the Thessalonians that enabled them to face persecution with equanimity.

D. The tragedy of Paul's countrymen (2:15–16)

The mention of persecution, and the remembrance of how that persecution first took such firm and virile root in Jerusalem, turns Paul's thoughts, for a moment, to the tragedy of the Jewish people. Their bitter hostility to Christ and Christianity never ceased to amaze him, although he himself had been one of the most zealous Jewish opponents of the gospel years earlier. Paul discussed the theological implications of all of this in Romans 9–11. Here, however, he just mentions it in passing as he thinks about the sadness of it all. Briefly, he reviews the persistent opposition to the gospel by the Jews.

He mentions *their provocation:* "who both killed the Lord Jesus, and their own prophets, and have persecuted us . . ." (2:15a). No charge could be more terrible: "They killed the Lord Jesus." This is the only place where Paul expressly charges the Jews with the murder of their Messiah. They would have liked to have had Him privately assassinated, but they were foiled by the Lord's popularity with the Jewish masses (Matt. 21:46). A public trial in their own courts would not have produced the desired result because the Romans refused the Sanhedrin the right to execute anyone. So they had resorted to a politician's trick—a trumped-up political charge (Luke 23:2). Then off to Pilate with Him, and pressure was on the Roman governor. The wily procurator had seen through their trickery and had been disposed to dismiss the charges—until the Jews had found a way to force his hand. If he let this man go, then he would not be Caesar's friend, for this man claimed to be a rival king. Thus, the actual execution had been carried out by the Romans and the opprobrium of it was attached to Pilate. Such political juggling does not deceive God. Here, all pretense is stripped away.

"The Jews," Paul says, "killed the Lord Jesus," who had done them nothing but good. He had healed their sick, cleansed their lepers, and raised their dead. He had fed their hungry multitudes. He had loved them, taught them, reasoned with them, pleaded with them, wept over them, and warned them. And they killed Him. They whipped up the mob. They chose Barabbas over Jesus when the frustrated Pilate had offered them a choice. They had gathered around the cross to mock Him as He died. They had killed the Lord Jesus, the Son of the living God, God manifest in flesh. No crime could be greater than that.

Nor had their insane hatred stopped there. They ignored the abundant evidence of the Resurrection and of His ascension into heaven. They had ignored the coming of the Holy Spirit on the Day of Pentecost. Then, as soon as the new movement had begun to take root, they had dug in their heels and launched a campaign of persecution against it.

"They persecuted us," Paul says. One would have thought that the spectacular conversion of their chief agent would have given them pause. Not a bit of it! They had persecuted him as they had James and Peter. Nor was it only the Jews of Jerusalem who had become so bitterly opposed to the gospel. Everywhere he went, Paul always went first to the synagogue. Everywhere he went, the Jews first listened politely, then, as soon as some of their number embraced Christianity, they turned on him in fury.

All of this was in line with Jewish history. They "killed . . . their own prophets," Paul explains. "Which of the prophets have not your fathers persecuted?" Stephen asked the Sanhedrin. "They have slain them which showed before of the coming of the Just One; of whom ye have been now the betrayers and murderers" (Acts 7:52). We know with what murderous rage the Jewish authorities had turned on Stephen in response to his blunt charge.

The Old Testament is largely silent regarding the deaths of the prophets, but the stories passed into Jewish history. Isaiah, the Jews believed, was sawn asunder by order of wicked King Manasseh. Jeremiah, after being forcibly abducted to Egypt by the recalcitrant Jews, was then stoned to death.

So the Jews provoked God. Yet they still prided themselves to be true children of Abraham and God's chosen people. Which brings Paul to *their presumption:* "They please not God," Paul says (2:15b). For nearly two thousand years, since their murder of their Messiah, the Jews have persisted in their unbelief. When the Romans, under Vespasian and Titus, destroyed Jerusalem and the temple, the Jews took that in stride. They took refuge in rabbinical Judaism and in the burgeoning Talmud. Down through the centuries, they have become bitter and intolerant in their opposition to Christianity and their rejection of Christ. The concrete of unbelief that the first-century rabbis poured over the nation has now set hard into a fixed attitude of unbelief. They blame Gentile anti-Semitism, but God recognizes no such excuse, although He judges the nations that foster it. "They please not God," says Paul, himself once a trained rabbi and bitterly hostile to Christ.

"They please not God." God is not pleased with a Judaism that rejects Christ. He is not pleased with Gentile unbelief either. The Jews remain the object both of His love and pity and of His displeasure. They were the ones who, in the face of unique privilege (Rom. 9:1–5), spat in the face of Jesus, moved heaven and earth to get Him crucified, delighted in His sufferings, urged Pilate to seal His tomb, invented a falsehood to explain away His resurrection, rejected the Holy Spirit, thrashed the apostles, applauded Herod for murdering James, hired Saul of Tarsus to stamp out Christianity, martyred Stephen, threw Paul out of every synagogue he entered, hounded him to his death, and invented the Talmud to replace the Torah. They frequently blaspheme the name of Jesus in their writings; and, by and large, they stubbornly resist all efforts to win them to Christ. "They please not God," Paul says.

Next, Paul mentions *their perversity:* "And are contrary to all men," he continues. The word for "contrary" is *enantios,* which means antagonistic. Matthew uses the word to describe the predicament in which the disciples found themselves after the feeding of the five thousand. The Lord sent them on across the lake. Suddenly, a storm arose, and "the ship was now in the midst of the sea, tossed with waves: for the wind was *contrary*" (Matt. 14:24) The word means "over against." It also can be translated "opposite."

Paul testified to King Agrippa that, in his unconverted days, he himself thought that he "ought to do many things *contrary* to the name of Jesus of Nazareth" (Acts 26:9). The kindred word *apenanti* occurs in Luke's account of Jewish opposition to Paul at Thessalonica itself. Having first used the mob to set the city in an uproar, the people seized Jason, Paul's host and convert, and hauled him before the magistrates. "These that have turned the world upside down are come hither also," they said, "whom Jason hath received: and these all do *contrary* to the decrees of Caesar, saying there is another king, one Jesus" (Acts 17:6–7). Paul now uses their own word against them. "They are contrary to all men," he says.

God called the Hebrew people apart from the rest of the world for Himself (Num. 23:9, 21). His plan was to reveal Himself to them, redeem them, reign over them, and make them a model of His goodness, greatness, glory, and grace. He set them in the midst of the nations, in a land where three continents (Europe, Africa, and Asia) meet astride the busy highways of the Gentile world. The nations of the world would come into contact with the nation of Israel and they would be blessed (Gen. 12:1–3; 22:16–18; Jer. 4:1–2).

They failed. First Israel, then Judah, plunged into an apostasy and idolatry worse than that of the surrounding nations. They became besotted with the vile and vicious gods of the pagans.

The Babylonian captivity cured them of that, but they returned to the Promised Land to develop a spirit of sanctimonious superiority, exclusiveness, and bitter dislike of the Gentiles. The more the rabbinic form of Judaism took hold, the more intolerant the Jews became of the Gentiles. Their synagogues, scattered throughout the world, fostered their contrariness toward the Gentiles. They despised the Gentiles' idolatry, shuddered at the thought of entering a Gentile home and eating Gentile food, and considered their touch a contamination. They called them "dogs" and regarded them as unclean as wild animals.

No wonder the Gentiles, worldwide, have turned on them and persecuted them age after age in country after country. To this day, anti-Semitism is endemic in all Gentile societies. From time to time, it becomes epidemic and gives rise to a holocaust. The liberation of the countries of Eastern Europe from the shackles of communism has been accompanied by a new wave of anti-Semitism. The Jews have been blamed for communism (Karl Marx, Trotsky, and many Bolsheviks were Jews) and for the economic mess in which many nations found themselves once communism collapsed. One day, when the Antichrist comes, anti-Semitism will become pandemic, and persecution will become global (Matt. 24:15–26)

Then, too, Paul mentions *their prejudice:* "forbidding us to speak to the Gentiles that they might be saved, to fill up their sins always . . ." (2:16a). This dog-in-the-manger attitude of the Jewish people toward the gospel was a constant problem to Paul in his crusades. The Jews did not want the gospel themselves, a fact that they made very obvious. But neither did they want the Gentiles to have it.

They obstructed the gospel at Pisidian Antioch (Acts 13:45, 50), at Iconium (Acts 14:1–5), and at Lystra (Acts 14:19) on Paul's first missionary journey. They hindered him at Berea (Acts 17:13), at Thessalonica (Acts 17:5–10), and at Corinth (Acts 18:12) on his second missionary journey. They constituted themselves his bitterest enemies and hounded him to imprisonment and death. They did not want Gentiles to be saved. They did everything in their power to prevent Paul from evangelizing them.

"To fill up their sins alway," (2:16b) Paul adds to explain why judgment had not yet fallen on them for their stubborn wickedness. As Shakespeare observed, there are tides in the affairs of men. God permits men to pursue their wicked ways for a long time before He acts in judgment. He is patient. He gives time for repentance. He waited for many centuries before sending the judgment of the Flood (1 Peter 3:20; 2 Peter 3:9). He withheld His hand for four hundred years in the case of the Amorites (Gen. 15:16). By the time judgment does fall upon a nation, it is often obvious, even to men, that it is long overdue and that it is just and well deserved.

In Paul's day, God was still waiting patiently for the Jews to "fill up the measure of their sins." The Jews of the homeland had already gone almost to the limit. They had not yet added to their sins the arrest and attempted murder of Paul, but they were well on the way. The Jews of the Dispersion were also well advanced in their rejection of Christ, but, as yet, they had not poured the final load of talmudic concrete over their Christ-rejection. That would not happen until after the fall of Jerusalem. So God waited and held His hand, and the Jews, secure in their fantasy that they were God's chosen people and therefore safe from wrath, persisted in their supreme sin of rejecting Christ.

Finally, in this digression, Paul mentions the Jews and *their punishment:* "For the wrath is come upon them to the uttermost" (2:16b). The question arises as to how and in what sense the wrath "is come" to the uttermost upon the Jews. God's wrath had already overtaken them, but its execution was still pending. Time was running out. The full measure of their sins was already counted out in heaven. Paul was so sure that the Jews were under God's judgment that he used the aorist tense. It can be rendered "came" upon them. The certainty of their punishment was such that the prophetic past could be used to describe it. The wrath of God upon unrepentant Israel embraces past, present, and future. The background is that terrible catalog of curses that were so very much a part of the Palestinian covenant (Deut. 28:15–68).

The Jews learned nothing from their history. The ten tribes were carried away into captivity by the Assyrians and disappeared. The remaining kingdom of Judah persisted in its sins. The Babylonians came, destroyed Jerusalem and the temple, and deported the bulk of the nation. The Jews rather enjoyed their exile once they settled down in it. When Cyrus opened the door for their return, only a handful responded. The majority had fallen in step with the ways of Babylon and had cultivated the art of making money and getting on in the world. They spread far and wide throughout the Gentile empires and called themselves the Diaspora. Religiously, the Babylonian and Palestinian Jews were absorbed by the budding Talmud and settled down to substitute man-made tradition for revealed truth.

Then came Antiochus Epiphanes. The Jews were given their first taste of full-fledged Gentile hatred and persecution. So severe were the persecutions of Antiochus that he stands to this day as the outstanding type of the Antichrist.[5]

5. See John Phillips, *Exploring the Book of Daniel* (Grand Rapids: Kregel, 2004), 129–30.

Then the Romans had come, and the Promised Land was held in a subjection from which there was no escape. No small part of the bitterness that the Jews nursed against Jesus lay in the fact that He had not proven to be the kind of Messiah they envisioned and desired. Barabbas was more to their taste. So, later, was Bar Kochba, the Jews' first false messiah. So the Jews crucified their Christ.

But the first great war with Rome, foretold by Jesus (Matt. 23:33–24:2), was on the horizon. It would be fought from A.D. 70, resulting in the destruction of Jerusalem and the temple, and would be finished in A.D. 135, when Bar Kochba's fierce rebellion was finally crushed. The Romans eventually built a temple to Jupiter on the site of the Jewish temple, changed the name of Jerusalem to Aelia Capitolina and the name of the country itself to "Palestine" in honor of the Philistines, hereditary enemies of the Jews, and banished all Jews from the country on pain of death. For two hundred years, Jerusalem passed into oblivion. When Paul wrote to the Thessalonians, however, all of this was in the future. In time, the majority of Jews became reconciled to the Diaspora and settled contentedly into talmudic Judaism, a form of Judaism that effectively quarantined the majority of Jews from faith in Christ.

The long centuries of their dispersion have been full of peril for the Jews. In the various lands of their exile, they have suffered discrimination, segregation, persecution, and expulsion. The very expression "wandering Jew" became proverbial. They have been regarded as Shylocks, blamed for the ills of the world, accused of horrible atrocities, held responsible for the Black Death, and made the scapegoats for every failed enterprise. "His blood be on us, and on our children," they said to Pilate when they clamored for the crucifixion of Christ (Matt. 27:25), and it most certainly has been. Their history shows how tragically and terribly their self-imposed curse has haunted them.

And the end is not yet because the wrath is by no means over. The Jews have not yet repented nationally for the crime of Calvary. So "the time of Jacob's trouble" awaits them (Jer. 30:7), the terrible time that Jesus Himself calls "the great tribulation" (Matt. 24:15–22). One of these days, the Jews will sign a seven-year treaty with the Antichrist. The Bible calls it "a covenant with death, and with hell" (Isa. 28:14–21). Halfway through the period of the treaty, the Antichrist will break it, seize the rebuilt Jewish temple in Jerusalem, defile it, and launch a global onslaught against the Jews. It will be a holocaust unparalleled in all of their long and tragic history (Dan. 9:27; Rev. 12:16). All of this is bound up in this statement here concerning the wrath of God. It will have its climax in the coming universal day of God's wrath.

E. The tangibility of Paul's crown (2:17–20)
  1. Paul's earnest desire (2:17–18)

Paul now returns to the present and the Thessalonian believers who were so dear to his heart. We note *the great hope he fostered:* "But we, brethren, being taken from you for a short time in presence, not in heart, endeavoured the more abundantly to see your face with great desire" (2:17).

They were all familiar, of course, with the circumstances that forced him to leave them in such a hurry. The arrest of Jason and his release on bail all added up to the same thing. Paul would have to leave. Regardless of whether Jason had given security to this end, the result was the same. As long as Paul was around, the Jews would foment trouble. The fact that they did, indeed, follow him on down to Berea, demonstrates their determination to get rid of him one way or another. If it had been left up to Paul, and if it had been only *his* life that was at stake, he probably would have stayed at Thessalonica, but circumstances had taken the matter out of his hands. His heart, however, was with them all.

He never stopped trying to get back. "We . . . endeavoured the more abundantly" he says, "to see your face." Quite clearly, Paul did not take his expulsion from the city sitting down, but he was overruled. Perhaps the new believers, apprehensive of persecution intensifying against them, urged him to leave, at least for a while. It was about five years before he was able to come back (at the end of his third missionary journey), but of that visit we have only Luke's barest note (Acts 20:1–3).

Paul, however, assured his converts that he wanted to be back with them in person "with great desire." The word is *epithumia.* It means "a craving." It is the word that the Lord Jesus used when He told His disciples, "With desire I have desired to eat this passover with you before I suffer" (Luke 22:15). It is the word that Paul uses when he is in prison at Rome to describe his heartache for heaven: "For I am in a strait betwixt two, having a *desire* to depart, and to be with Christ; which is far better" (Phil. 1:23). The word is translated "lust" some thirty times in the New Testament. That is how great was his longing to see them.

He mentions, however, *the great hindrance he faced:* "Wherefore we would have come unto you, even I Paul, once and again; but Satan hindered us" (2:18). On Paul's second missionary journey, the Holy Spirit had hindered him from staying in Asia Minor and had flung open the door of opportunity to Europe (Acts 16:6–9). Now Satan hindered him. Paul knew the difference between the restraining ministry of the Holy Spirit and the restricting opposition of the Evil

One. Paul very likely recognized the personal activity of Satan behind the rioting that had driven him out of Thessalonica.

Paul had no trouble believing in Satan as a personal, malicious, and active enemy. His name means "adversary." The word occurs thirty-six times in the New Testament. He personally tempted Christ. He has about a dozen names. He is called "the Devil," that is, the accuser or slanderer. He is called Beelzebub, that is, lord of the dunghill. He is called the great dragon and the old serpent. He is called the tempter, the Evil One, the Enemy. He is called the ruler of this world, the prince of the power of the air, and the god of this world. He is called Belial, the worthless one.

As great, powerful, and terrible as he is, however, he is still only a created being. He was once "the anointed cherub." He was known as Lucifer, son of the morning, and had his place in heaven with "the sons of God" (Job 1:6). Pride was his downfall (1 Tim. 3:6). He is not to be trifled with (Jude 9). Still, he is no match for the Holy Spirit.

We are not told exactly how Satan hindered Paul's repeated attempts to return to Thessalonica. Ramsay is sure that Satan was behind the ruling of the magistrates in Thessalonica, putting it into their minds to demand such security from Jason as would ensure that Paul left town permanently. Certainly Satan has his hand in every governmental pie, either directly or through fallen angelic delegates who are loyal to him (Dan. 10:12–13, 20–21).

Paul wanted his beloved Thessalonians to know how greatly he missed them and longed to be back with them.

In the last two verses of the chapter, he returns to his favorite theme in this letter—the second coming of Christ. It is seen as a stimulating truth. It raises thoughts of the judgment seat of Christ; and that, surely, should stimulate all believers to holy living and godly zeal.

2. Paul's eternal delight (2:19–20)

We notice, first, the *reward* he expected: "For what is our hope, or joy, or crown of rejoicing? . . . ye" (2:19a). The word for crown is *stephanos,* the victor's crown, the crown that was given to the winner in the games. It is a favorite symbol for a reward or a prize. What greater anticipation or joy could Paul have than to see his converts stepping forward at the judgment seat of Christ to receive their reward? Apart from anything else, that would crown the apostle's own efforts. Oh! how he was going to rejoice. The word for "rejoicing" can be translated "exultation." As proud parents exult in the achievements of their children, so Paul, a proud father, was already anticipating the joy of seeing his Thessalonian converts winning their rewards. What greater reward could he want than that?

The judgment seat of Christ is closely related to the second coming of Christ (Matt. 16:27; Luke 14:14; 1 Cor. 4:5; 2 Tim. 4:8; Rev. 22:12). The judgment seat of Christ is inescapable for the believer. It is a time of reward and rebuke. It will be possible for believers to suffer conscious loss at the judgment seat although their works, not their persons, will be judged there. Our lifework since we became Christ's will be weighed. Paul elsewhere warns that what is "wood, hay, and stubble" will be burned. He encourages us, too. All that is "gold, silver, and precious stones" will be rewarded. It is tragically possible for a believer to have a saved soul and a lost life. The judgment seat will determine our place and power in the coming kingdom.

The judgment seat of Christ is to be feared. It is not going to be a Sunday school picnic. It is not a mercy seat but a judgment seat. Thankfully, there is a mercy seat; it is called "the throne of grace" (Heb. 4:16). We can flee to it at any time, in any place, and under any circumstance (Heb. 10:19–22), and we can find "grace to help in time of need" and obtain cleansing (1 John 1:8–10) and power. But that is for the here and now. It will be too late to change our earthly lifestyle once we cross Jordan and are summoned to appear before the Lord upon His throne.

The judgment seat of Christ, which is closely associated with the Lord's return, adds a somber hue to the canvas of His coming. It is intended to make the anticipated return of Christ a stimulating truth. Paul sets teaching about the judgment seat in the same passage that warns us that we are indeed our brother's keeper (Rom. 14:10). In a similar context, he adds, "Knowing therefore the terror of the Lord, we persuade men" (2 Cor. 5:11).

So, then, Paul emphasizes the reward. He was confident that he had rewards coming to him. He had earned one crown at least—a crown of rejoicing and exultation; the triumph of his dear Thessalonians assured him of that fact. Now he underlines *the return:* "Ye!" he exclaims, "in the presence of our Lord Jesus Christ at his coming" (2:19b).

The word for "coming" here is *parousia.* It is the first of seven occurrences of this word in these two epistles (3:13; 4:15; 5:23; 2 Thess. 2:1, 8–9). The word occurs twenty-four times in the New Testament. Its first occurrence is in the prelude to the Lord's Olivet discourse. The disciples asked Him, "What shall be the sign of thy coming?" (Matt. 24:3). The complete list is as follows: Matthew

24:3, 27, 37, 39; 1 Corinthians 15:23; 16:17; 2 Corinthians 7:6–7; 10:10; Philippians 1:26; 2:12; the seven Thessalonian occurrences as listed above, and James 5:7–8; 2 Peter 1:16; 3:4, 12; 1 John 2:28). In everyday secular life, the word was used as a technical expression for the arrival of a king, or of some other person in authority. Literally, the word means "presence."

The word is not used exclusively of the Lord's coming. Paul speaks, for instance, of his *parousia* (his "presence") at Philippi in contrast to his *apousia* (his "absence") from Philippi (Phil. 2:12). The word is always connected with a period of time, whether short or long. It draws attention to the stay and what happens once the arrival has taken place. Some translators think that instead of translating the word as "coming" every time it occurs in connection with the Lord Jesus, it should simply be transliterated and left to stand as *parousia.*

When the word is used in the New Testament in connection with the Lord, it refers to a specific period. For instance, Peter used it to describe the brief moment when the Lord was transfigured and he and his friends were "eyewitnesses of his majesty" (2 Peter 1:16; see also Matt. 17:1–8).

When this word is used in a prophetic sense, it covers a very specific period of time. The word *parousia* refers to a future period that will begin with the Rapture, the arrival of the Lord in the air (1 Thess. 4:16–17), and that will end with His return, with His unveiling of Himself in power and glory to the world.

During this interim period, the *parousia* of the Lord in the air (and the rapid development on earth of the mystery of iniquity), we shall appear before the judgment seat of Christ (1 Cor. 4:1–5; 2 Cor. 5:10). Here, in this epistle, Paul anticipates that event with a great deal of eagerness, thanks to the victorious lives of his Thessalonian converts. Both Peter and John convey much the same thought (1 Peter 5:1–4; 1 John 2:28).

W. E. Vine says, "The *parousia* of the Lord Jesus is thus a period with a beginning, a course, and a conclusion. The beginning is prominent in 1 Thess. 4:15; 5:23; 2 Thess 2:1; 1 Cor. 15:23; James 5:7–8; 2 Peter 3:4; the course here in 1 Thess. 2:19; 3:13; Matt. 24:3, 37, 39; 1 John 2:28; and the conclusion in 2 Thess. 2:8; Matt. 24:27."[6]

Finally, Paul mentions the *rejoicing* that he was both currently experiencing and anticipating at the Lord's return: "For ye are our glory and joy," he says (2:20). What people glory and rejoice in reveals their character and their spiritual condition. Solomon lost a kingdom, an empire, and a crown because he wanted

6. C. F. Hogg and W. E. Vine, *The Epistles to the Thessalonians* (Grand Rapids: Kregel, 1959), 88.

this earth's tinsel glory, and because he loved wealth, women, and this world and allowed these things to cloud his judgment and affect his decisions. For all of his outward show and flamboyance, Solomon was no match for his father, even taking into consideration David's sins. David used things and loved people; Solomon loved things and used people.

Paul loved people. He lived for people. He spent his life winning people to Christ and building them up in the faith. His glory and joy was to see people saved and established in the things of God. His ambition was to see them, at last, as crowns and trophies to put at Jesus' feet.

PART 4

The Lord's Coming: A Stabilizing Truth

1 Thessalonians 3:1–13

A. Paul's concern (3:1–5)

These visions of a rosy future end abruptly, and Paul comes back down to Earth. He recounts some recent history to illustrate to his friends at Thessalonica how greatly he was concerned about them. First, he mentions *the place:* "Wherefore when we could no longer forbear, we thought it good to be left at Athens alone" (3:1). Although the chronology is not cut-and-dried, it seems that Paul sent Timothy back to Thessalonica from Athens. Paul seems to have sent Silas back to Macedonia on some other errand. They were to meet him back at Athens or, if he had left, at Corinth.

There was plenty to see at Athens, if Paul had a mind to go sightseeing. What he saw disgusted him. There were idols everywhere, dedicated to every conceivable kind of god. The famous Athenians were religious imbeciles. Paul's spirit was stirred within him. He was mad! The word Luke uses to describe his anger is *paroxunomai* (Acts 17:16), which gives us our word *paroxysm*. It is one of Luke's medical words.

He couldn't hold his peace. Soon he was in hot debate with the disciples of pagan philosophies. Luke mentions particularly the Epicureans and the Stoics. The Epicureans were followers of Epicurus (342–279 B.C.), who taught that pleasure was what life was all about. The Stoics (the name is derived from the porch *[stoa]* where they met) were disciples of Zeno (about 270 B.C.), who taught that virtue was the supreme good. According to them, a man should be free from passions and should be moved by neither joy nor grief, pleasure nor pain. Soon, Paul was seeking to win both groups to Christ.

His speech on Mars' Hill gave him access to the intelligentsia of the Greek world. They listened politely—until he proclaimed the resurrection of Christ. Then they laughed in his face. One or two of them sought out Paul and responded to the gospel. But Paul could see that Greek sophistication and intellectual snobbery, wedded as it was to gross religious superstition, was no congenial soil for the gospel. He left Athens and went on to Corinth, where, presumably, his colleagues later joined him.

"We thought it good to be left at Athens alone," Paul says in this note. Alone! It is probably that Paul never was lonelier than he was at Athens. The crowds milled all about him. He wandered the city streets.

As a young man, I left my native land and arrived in the great city of Vancouver,

Canada. Vancouver is a beautiful city. The Pacific Ocean lies at its foot, and in the background tower the mountains. Two of them resemble lions. They are majestic and often touched with snow. The city has beautiful parks, magnificent shops, museums, fairgrounds, and places of amusement and entertainment. But I was lonely. I was thousands of miles from home. I worked for a large bank and liked my fellow employees, but their interests were not my interests. I went to a church where the people were friendly, but they had very separatist views. I was lonely. I can still remember those days. I lived for letters from home. I wandered the streets and the stores. I had no one to talk to and nowhere to go. I was poor and lonely. The city was filled with people, hurrying here, there, and everywhere. Faces would loom up ahead. Cool stares would be exchanged. The people vanished back into anonymity. All about me were people, throngs of people—and I was lonely. I would whisper to the Lord, as I wandered those downtown department stores, filled with things that I couldn't afford to buy, rubbing shoulders with people who didn't care whether I lived or died. "Oh, Lord," I would say, "I'm lonely. And there's not even a letter from home."

"We thought it good to be left at Athens alone," Paul says. Underline that word *alone.* Picture for yourself what it is like to be left alone in a foreign country surrounded by strangers, your heart aching for those whom you have left behind. There was no news from home for me just as there was no news for Paul from Thessalonica. If he wanted to talk to someone, he had to accost someone on the street, one of the idlers standing around gawking at the sights or arguing with a fellow on a soapbox in the market.

Well, the apostle had one Friend, the same Friend I had. He had a Friend who knows all about being lonely. Many were the long talks that Paul had with that Friend "that sticketh closer than a brother." But, doubtless, Paul, being human after all, felt as I felt in those desperately lonely days in that foreign country, alone. He enjoyed his communion with the Lord, but he longed for someone with a face and a heart, too. As for Paul, sick to death of Athens, he went on to Corinth—where he soon made many friends.

Meanwhile, he wandered the streets of Athens, alone. He was a gregarious man; he liked people. But he endured the loneliness for the sake of his beloved Thessalonian babes in Christ.

There was, then the place. There was also the *plan:* "And sent Timotheus, our brother, and minister of God, and our fellowlabourer in the gospel of Christ, to establish you, and to comfort you concerning your faith" (3:2). In the book of Acts, and throughout Paul's letters, we always seem to be bumping into Timothy.

He was one of Paul's converts and a young man whom Paul not only loved as a son but also in whom he had the most implicit confidence. He was always entrusting him with responsible missions. He sent him to Thessalonica. He sent him to Corinth (1 Cor. 4:17; 16:10) and to Philippi (Phil. 2:19). "I have no man likeminded," Paul told the Philippians, "who will naturally care for your state . . . [Timothy], . . . as a son with the father, he hath served with me in the gospel" (Phil. 2:20, 22). That is high praise, indeed, from the great apostle.

Timothy's commission was clear. He was to "establish" the Thessalonian believers. The word is *stērizō.* It means to set fast or to make fast, to fix firmly.

An illustration is found in Israel's war with Amalek (Exod. 17). Joshua was down in the valley in the thick of the battle. Moses, Aaron, and Hur (the son of Caleb) were on the hilltop. As long as Moses kept his hands upraised, Israel won. But when his arms grew tired and dropped down, Amalek won. Prayer is the most tiring work there is. There was only one solution. Moses sat on a stone, and his two companions "stayed up" (*stērizō* in the Septuagint) his hands. It took a prophet (Moses), a priest (Aaron), and a prince (Hur), all anointed ministers, to guarantee Israel's victory. Jesus—as prophet, priest, and king—now sits in the seat of power on high, our Advocate with the Father Himself, our guarantee of victory down here.

Timothy was sent to—"fix firmly" the faith of the Thessalonians. He was to teach them more of God's Word. He was to visit in their homes, pray with them, tell them more about Jesus, and enable them to draw upon the illimitable resources of the Holy Spirit.

He was to "comfort" them. The word used means "to call aside," or "to appeal to" (by means of entreaty, comfort, and instruction). The persecution facing the new believers at Thessalonica did not cease when Paul was smuggled out of town. It went on for a long time. Six years later, Paul could still speak of the churches of Macedonia enduring "a great trial of affliction." He could speak of "the abundance of their joy" and of "their deep poverty" out of which they gave, with almost supernatural generosity, to the Lord's work abroad (2 Cor. 8:1–5).

Perhaps one reason why the Thessalonians were so steadfast in the face of suffering and persecution lay in the fact that Paul had foretold it: "That no man should be moved by these afflictions: for yourselves know that we are appointed thereunto. For verily, when we were with you, we told you before that we should suffer tribulation; even as it came to pass, and ye know" (3:3–4). Here we have *the plea.* They could face suffering because it had been foretold. Paul preached no cheap gospel. He never watered down the cost of being a Christian.

"That no man should be *moved,*" says Paul. The word is *sainō,* which means "to wag the tail," "to fawn," or "to flatter." The sense is that nobody should be deceived or deluded, in the midst of persecution, by someone who comes along with tail-wagging suggestions, even though he might pose as a well-wisher. Some scholars have translated it "Don't be perturbed," others, "We did not want any of you to lose heart" or "Don't be shaken."

Paul was determined to leave no stone unturned. His converts must stand firm despite their sufferings. He hoped that the sufferings, far from shaking them, would only strengthen their faith.

In New Testament times, suffering and persecution were taken for granted. It was part of the price of being a Christian. For three hundred years, starting with Nero and ending with Diocletian, the church went through a continuing baptism of blood and fire. In many non-Christian lands, to this day, the price for becoming a believer is persecution. After all, we are in enemy territory. This world scourged, murdered, and derided the Christ of God, so we cannot expect it to have any liking for His people. That is why Paul continued emphasizing the second coming of Christ. It is believers' sure and certain hope throughout these chapters even as it has been the hope of the church throughout history. It is a stabilizing truth. The enemy cannot win in the end. And, meanwhile, his worst persecutions develop character, strengthen faith, produce courage, and ensure for many believers a martyr's crown.

Paul next exposed *the plot:* "For this cause, when I could no longer forbear, I sent to know your faith, lest by some means the tempter have tempted you, and our labour be in vain" (3:5). It was one thing to warn the new believers what they could expect. It was one thing for him to show them the scars of many an old wound in his own body. It was one thing for him to level with them from the start, for him to tell them tales from his own experiences as Saul of Tarsus and as the Grand Inquisitor of the Sanhedrin, tales of unbelievable heroism and fortitude, even unto death. It was one thing for him to tell them of Stephen's martyrdom and how his triumphant death plunged the flaming arrow of conviction into his own obdurate and unbelieving heart. It was one thing for him to tell them how he was once stoned and left for dead, and how he was caught up into the third heaven, how he saw things impossible to translate, how, ever after, he coveted martyrdom. It was one thing to tell them that he and Silas, and even young Timothy, counted themselves as sheep for the slaughter. It was one thing to warn and encourage them. But how would they take it when it happened to them? That was what now concerned him.

He could bear the suspense no longer. He acted. "Off you go, Timothy, back to Thessalonica; stiffen their resolve, teach the Word, be their example." Paul well knew the wiles of the Devil. He is a dirty fighter. He knows all of the lowdown tricks. Paul knew, only too well, how Satan would tempt the Thessalonians to purchase peace with the world at the unacceptable price of apostasy. Later, at the height of the imperial persecutions, immunity from further harassment could be purchased just by putting a pinch of salt on the altar of a pagan god. That was all. But it was everything. It was the price of a soul. The mania of persecution had not yet reached the terrible heights it would attain when Nero burned Rome and blamed the church. Even so, the temptation to abandon Christianity to purchase exemption from persecution was already very real. Paul was on tenterhooks while he awaited Timothy's return.

He knew that the tempter was at large and busy, driven by his malicious hatred of God and His people. Paul had only just referred to the tempter, and that by name (2:18), as the one who had put obstacles in his way to prevent his own return to Thessalonica. Satan habitually overreaches himself. He did himself a great disservice in thus hindering Paul. Had Paul been able to go back to Thessalonica himself, he would have given his friends there the comfort and instruction they needed and would then have proceeded on his way. That would have been that. Instead, he wrote them these two magnificent letters packed with truth and practical advice. These letters have not only added greatly to our knowledge of the second coming of Christ but also unmasked some of Satan's most secret plans. Moreover, they have become part of the inspired Word of God and a source of blessing, enlightenment, and encouragement to believers for the rest of time!

Paul remained anxious, however, because he knew that Satan was a very real being and that he was doing everything in his vast power to destroy the infant church at Thessalonica. If the faith of the Thessalonians collapsed, his labor in their city would indeed have been in vain. Paul hoped that Timothy would be able to prevent that. But Timothy, although loyal and capable, was young. Moreover, Satan was using fierce persecution as his weapon against the new believers. Paul was thankful that he had warned them what to expect. The Lord had suffered, so we can expect to suffer, too. A believer must learn to "glory in tribulations" (Rom. 5:3). Had the Thessalonians learned that lesson? Had they met the fury of the adversary with a triumphant faith in the Advocate? That was what Paul did not know—until Timothy returned with the glorious news. Yes, indeed! The Thessalonians were "more than conquerors."

B. Paul's comfort (3:6–10)

1. The tidings Paul received (3:6)

Paul records his joy: "But now when Timotheus came from you unto us, and brought us good tidings of your faith and charity, and that ye have good remembrance of us always, desiring greatly to see us, as we also to see you." Such was the bond of love and affection that Paul and Silas formed with their converts.

Here was no artificial evangelism—a high-powered message; a high-pressured invitation; everyone eager to leave for food, fun, and fellowship as soon as they can decently escape the crowds; and the counseling of those responding to the invitation turned over to others.

No indeed! Paul loved people. He was eager to meet those who responded to the gospel invitation and anxious to get to know them; to visit in their homes; to meet their relatives; to instruct them in the first steps in the Christian faith; to teach them—"the apostles' doctrine and fellowship, and in breaking of bread, and in prayers" (Acts 2:42); and to see them baptized and growing in grace and increasing in the knowledge of God. Paul did not consider evangelism to be worthy of the name if it divorced itself from a heart-and-soul love relationship with those who were led to the Lord through his ministry. No wonder they desired greatly to see him again! He was not just the man under whose preaching they had been led to the Lord; they had come to know him personally. They had sensed his love, warmth, and sincere interest in them individually. He was their friend. They were his friends. He had been a guest in their homes. He remembered their names. He loved them.

So Timothy returned to Paul, brimming over with the good news. The Thessalonians were doing well. Satan had been unable to shake their faith. Their love was triumphant. What a good thing it was that Paul had not preached the false "name it-claim it" message that is so popular today: "God wants you to be healthy and wealthy." The so-called "prosperity gospel" of the "charismatics" would not have taken the Thessalonians through the onslaught of the persecution that burst upon them soon after they were saved. "Possibility thinking" was no foundation for a faith that was to be tested by temptation. What they needed was a faith based on realities. "The power of positive thinking" and all other such psychological gospels ignore the stark reality of Calvary and the bottomless hatred of this world toward God.

2. The tenderness Paul revealed (3:7)

The Thessalonians had been going through it. Paul had been going through it, too. His deep concern for them was only part of it. By the time Timothy caught up with him, Paul was already launched on his gospel crusade in nearby Corinth. He arrived in that city in "weakness and much fear and trembling." He had been mauled at Philippi, and he had been mocked at Athens. In Corinth, too, before Gallio afforded him his protection, Paul had been exposed to much persecution and danger. The Jews had thrown him out of the synagogue (Acts 18:6). Attempts against him had finally broken out in insurrection, and Paul was dragged before the authorities. No wonder Paul, having been chased out of one city after another, possibly began to consider whether he had misread God's guidance that he must evangelize Europe (Acts 16:10). His concern for the converts at Thessalonica was another of his concerns, what he himself later described as "the care of all the churches" (2 Cor. 11:28).

3. The triumph Paul reviewed (3:8–10)

Again Paul dipped his pen in the ink to assure his converts that *his life was linked with theirs:* "For now we live, if ye stand fast in the Lord" (3:8). He could enjoy life again! The *if* here was not intended to question their stability; it was simply a reminder to them that his peace of mind depended on their bold stand for Christ.

All evangelists could take a leaf out of Paul's notebook on the care and follow-up of converts. Converts are not just statistics to be reported triumphantly in the next prayer and support letter. No, indeed! Paul's converts were a vital part of his life. He loved them and lived in them. Did someone try to lead them astray? Paul was outraged. Did someone attack them? Paul leaped to their defense. Were they suffering persecution? Paul's heart ached for them! He wept with those who wept. He rejoiced with those who rejoiced. He wrote to them. He kept in touch with them. As far as was humanly possible, Paul involved himself in their affairs. Think, for instance, of the catalog of names that are such an integral part of Paul's letters. Nor are the inspired New Testament epistles in our hands the only letters that Paul wrote. We can be sure that he conducted a voluminous correspondence with churches and individuals all over the world.

Then, too, *his life was lived for them* (3:9–10): "For what thanks can we render to God again for you, for all the joy wherewith we joy for your sakes before our

God" (3:9). Praise! Praise to God for the wonder of His work in their hearts. Prayer! Prayer to God for a future reunion: "Night and day praying exceedingly that we might see your face, and might perfect that which is lacking in your faith" (3:10).

Paul had received good news from Thessalonica, but he did not relax his disciplined prayer life on their behalf on that account. Instead, he redoubled his efforts because they had flaws in their faith. A margin of error existed in their understanding of the second coming of Christ. Some of the Christians did not have a belief that behaved. Paul would deal with these issues, as far as possible, by mail. However, another visit to them was clearly desirable. That would be the best way for him to break down Satan's obstructionist tactics (2:18). As it turned out, Paul did get back to Macedonia on his third missionary journey (Acts 20:1–4). Meanwhile, this letter was an invaluable help to the Macedonian churches.

C. Paul's compulsion (3:11–13)
   1. Paul and the Ruler of his life (3:11)

As much as Paul was moved by his emotions, he remained clear in his thinking and resolute in his decisions. He never allowed himself to be ruled by his intellect, his emotions, or his will. He made decisions on a deeper level. His decisions were spiritual, ruled by the indwelling Holy Spirit: "Now God himself and our Father, and our Lord Jesus Christ, direct our way unto you." This close linking of the Father with "our Lord Jesus Christ" is an acknowledgment of the deity of the Lord Jesus. Paul's first epistle to the Thessalonians is one of the earliest of the New Testament writings. It gives us valuable proof of the way the early church accepted and taught the deity of Christ. The Lord Jesus is here united with the Father in terms of His deity but separated from the Father in terms of His person.

W. E. Vine says, "The Greek verb translated 'direct' is in the singular number notwithstanding that two names form its subject. Thus the simple grammatical law, that a verb must agree with its subject in number, is set aside in order that the unique relationship existing between the persons may be indicated."[1]

Paul wanted his return visit to Thessalonica to be directed by the overruling providence of God, without detours or deviations. God can make straight paths for our feet (Ps. 5:8; Matt. 3:3). As it turned out, Paul was able to go there, quite

1. Hogg and Vine, *The Epistles to the Thessalonians,* 105.

naturally, when, at the end of his third missionary journey, he was driven out of Ephesus. A tour of Greece and Macedonia fitted smoothly into his plans—just enough time, indeed, to visit these churches. Brief though that visit was, Luke recalls in his memoirs that Paul gave the Macedonians "much exhortation" (Acts 19:1–2).

Generally speaking, three factors figure in the equation of divine guidance. Circumstances play a part, constituting the *outward* indicator. Often, events that happen to us seem to indicate a change. With Elijah, the brook dried up (1 Kings 17:2–7). He had been divinely directed to that brook by "the word of the Lord." How long he remained there is uncertain. We do know, however, that, for that particular period in his life, he was in the center of God's will—doing nothing! We live in an age of feverish activity. We think that we are wasting precious time and neglecting privileges, opportunities, and responsibilities if we are not actively engaged in some form of Christian work in every spare moment. "Go hide thyself," God said to Elijah. The prophet needed time for rest, reflection, and realizing God's daily provision of care and protection from the malice of Jezebel. But "the brook dried up." It was evidently time for a change—unless, of course, God indicated that He intended to provide him water to drink as miraculously as He had provided him food to eat. Elijah came face-to-face with a decision forced on him by his circumstances. Faced with a dry brook and the imminent prospect of a miserable death by thirst, Elijah pondered his next move. He waited, however, for God to speak.

Circumstances alone do not constitute clear leading from the Lord. Circumstances can be deceptive. On Paul's journey to Rome, Luke tells us, "When we had sailed slowly many days, and scarce were come over against Cnidus, the wind not suffering us, we sailed under Crete, over against Salmone; and, hardly passing it, came unto a place which is called The fair havens . . ." (Acts 27:7–8). So far, so good. They had found a port. The circumstances, as represented by contrary winds, drove them into that haven.

They spent some time there, but soon a decision had to be made. It was really too late in the season to hope for a safe voyage down the Mediterranean to Rome. However, the master and the owner of the ship had a financial interest in pressing on. Paul remonstrated. He had been shipwrecked before. He knew the danger of the treacherous Mediterranean Sea. The centurion in charge of the expedition listened carefully to Paul but, in the end, "believed the master and the owner of the ship" (Acts 27:11). After all, the master was the expert. As much as the centurion admired Paul, and as much as he was willing to defer to him, Paul was only a preacher, after all. The captain, however, was a trained seaman. It was a natural decision, especially when the captain explained how inconvenient and poorly situated Fair Haven was to ride out the winter storms. Besides, they would go only as far as Phenice on the western end of the island; that was a much more commodious harbor. Then, to cap it all, "the south wind blew softly" (v. 13). That decided them. They ignored Paul's urgent warnings. "Supposing that they had obtained their purpose, . . . they sailed" (Acts 27:13). Luke spent the rest of that long chapter chronicling the difficulties and disaster that followed.

Beware the south wind blowing softly! Circumstances, however seemingly favorable, do not, in themselves, constitute sufficient proof of guidance.

Besides, Satan can, and doubtless often does, manipulate and exploit circumstances. He used circumstances in the temptation of the Lord Jesus Himself to try to beguile Him into making a wrong move. Not until after the Lord, in the will of His Father and led by the Holy Spirit, had fasted for forty days and "was afterward an hungered" did the tempter come to Him with the suggestion, "If thou be the Son of God, command that these stones be made bread" (Matt. 4:1–3). Surely it could not be God's will for Jesus actually to starve to death in that wilderness, especially when the Lord had the means to take matters into His own hands and relieve His distress! But that was the very essence of the first temptation—to act independently of God, to respond to circumstances alone.

The second factor in guidance is the *inward* indicator our own thoughts and feelings about the matter. After all, God has given us brains. When considering God's will, common sense (as we call it) is not necessarily to be set aside. God does want us to act rationally. The majority of our daily decisions we can make by far on the basis of our own thoughts and feelings. Moreover, just because something appeals to our reason, temperament, secret desires, or instinctive impulses does not necessarily mean that a proposed move must be suspect on that account. Paul used his plain common sense, based on wide experience, when he advised the centurion not to risk launching out to sea at that time of the year.

It was plain common sense for Paul to escape from Damascus by the way of a basket lowered over the wall, especially when all of the gates were being watched so his enemies could catch and kill him (2 Cor. 11:32–33). God does not usually perform miracles, especially when a little thought can suggest an alternative. Our own logical deductions may lead us to the right conclusion. There is a place in all of this for consulting others, for getting all of the facts. Our own feelings can be consulted, too, especially if we ensure that they are pure. All of the ordinary means that we habitually use for making thousands of decisions every day are part of the process when we try to decide the good, acceptable, and perfect will of God.

But here again the *inward* indicators can sometimes lead us astray just as much as can the *outward* indicators. Paul confessed to King Agrippa that, in his unconverted days, he "verily thought with [him]self, that [he] ought to do many things contrary to the name of Jesus of Nazareth" (Acts 26:9). Contrast the "Behold, I thought . . ." of Naaman the leper in 2 Kings 5:11 with his later "Behold, now I know . . ." (2 Kings 5:15).

Joshua thought that it was a good idea to sign a treaty with the Gibeonites, but he was wrong. He was unduly influenced by what seemed to be good, solid evidence. He was wrong—as God would have told him had he consulted his Bible (Josh. 9:3–27; Exod. 23:27–33).

Lot thought that he had excellent reasons for choosing the well-watered plains of Jordan (Gen. 13:10–11), but he was wrong. Had he sought the Lord's mind on the matter, he never would have gone (Gen. 13:13).

Eve listened to what she believed to be the voice of reason and common sense when Satan tempted her (Gen. 3:1–5). Likewise, Adam foolishly and disastrously followed the voice of his heart (Gen. 3:6) and plunged the human race into sin. Both the mind and the heart are vulnerable to wrong impressions. We should particularly suspect clamoring pressure, impulses that would force us into an immediate decision without taking time to inquire of the Lord.

The third factor in securing divine guidance is the *upward* indicator. God ultimately makes His will clear to us by means of His Word. Even here we must be careful. Flinging the Bible open at random, plunging a finger on a text, and seeking thus to obtain guidance is insulting alike to God and our own intelligence! The story has often been told of the man who tried that "method" when faced with an urgent decision. His finger landed on the text, "Judas went out and hanged himself." He decided that he must have made a mistake, so he tried again. This time, the text he obtained read, "Go thou and do likewise!" He dismissed that "guidance" also, and he tried again. The text upon which his finger finally landed read, "What thou doest, do quickly." Playing that kind of Russian roulette with the Holy Scriptures is foolish.

We must read the Bible steadily and systematically. We must meditate on verses in their context and keep an open mind for the "still small voice" of God to speak to our inner man. God can reinforce a word, a phrase, a text, a passage, and a truth. We must say with little Samuel, "Speak, LORD; for thy servant heareth" (1 Sam. 3:9). Then, sooner or later, God will speak directly to our need and reveal His mind clearly and beyond all ambiguity. But that takes time and receptiveness to the mind of the Spirit. It also calls for a willingness to do what God says when He does make a course of action clear.

A traveler aboard ship, approaching Belfast harbor, asked the pilot how he knew when he was in the right channel. The pilot pointed to three lights ahead of the vessel. "What I have to do, as I approach the port," he said, "is get those three lights lined up one behind the other. When they are in line, I know I can sail the ship safely in."

We obtain divine guidance in much the same way. When our circumstances, our inward convictions, and our reading of the Word of God all line up, we are usually on a safe course. So Paul waited for the Lord's leading: "Now God himself and our Father, and our Lord Jesus Christ, direct our way unto you," he said (3:11). He preferred to be sure rather than sorry.

2. Paul and the reward of his love (3:12)

Meanwhile, while Paul waited for a favorable opportunity to return to see the Thessalonians, he had some good advice for them: "And the Lord make you to increase and abound in love one toward another, and toward all men, even as we do toward you."

Love! *Agapē* love! More *agapē* love! Abounding *agapē* love! Abounding *agapē* love toward all believers! Abounding *agapē* love toward all men! That was the kind of abounding *agapē* love that they themselves had experienced from him!

We can never have too much of that kind of love. We can have too much money. Too much money is a fruitful source of abuse. Barbara Hutton had too much money. She was the granddaughter of F. W. Woolworth. At the age of twelve, she inherited $25 million (worth very much more than that today). Her money did not make her happy. Nor did her seven husbands. She was plagued with sickness and died of a heart attack. Her last years were spent as a recluse, often bedridden, and when she died, she weighed barely eighty pounds. The newspapers called her "the poor little rich girl." We can have too much money.

We can have too much power. Alexander the Macedonian had too much power. In the end, he wanted to be worshiped as a god. Nero, Napoleon, Hitler, and Stalin had too much power. Lord Acton said, "Power corrupts, and absolute power corrupts absolutely." Power is heady stuff. It is more intoxicating than wine. People with power think that they can do and be and have whatever they want. Few things are more self-corrupting, more ego-inflating, more soul-destroying than power. Some

Christians are forever asking God for power, but God is too wise to grant their request. Instead, He gives us His Holy Spirit—the One who is the Spirit of power (2 Tim. 1:7). Only the Holy Spirit can be trusted with such power.

We can have too much education. All of the education in the world does not necessarily make a person wise. Never in history have men had more knowledge and less wisdom than they have today. There are millions of clever people in the world, and most of them are too clever to come to Christ. We can have too much education. Many a young person goes off to college to sit at the feet of diabolically clever, humanistic professors who systematically strip him of his faith and throw him back into the world as an educated moron, hopelessly adrift; without spiritual anchor, compass, or rudder; and driven before the winds of this godless age.

But we can never have too much *agapē* love, the highest kind of love in the universe, the love that beats in the very heart of God (John 3:16). It has no explanation outside of God Himself. God loves us, in all of our wretchedness and lostness, with a love that passes all understanding. In trying to explain to the children of Israel why God loved them, Moses finally resorted to this explanation: "He loved you because He loved you" (see Deut. 7:7–8). It is simply God's nature to love. That love was incarnate in Christ (2 Cor. 5:4; Eph. 2:4). As the poet Thomas Kelly (1769–1854) wrote,

Love that no tongue can teach,
Love that no thought can reach,
No love like His!
God is its blessed source,
Death ne'er can stop its course,
Nothing can stay its force,
Matchless it is.

This kind of love in the Christian is the direct fruit of the Spirit (Gal. 5:22). Paul loved lost people and saved people alike with this kind of love. Love seeks the well-being of all. It is no respecter of persons, it keeps no running account of injuries suffered, and it is marvelously kind. It works no ill to any but seeks out opportunities to do good to all. Christian love is far more than mere affection *(phileō)*. Love may, and often does, involve the emotions, but *agapē* love is commanded and, therefore, is as much an action of the will as it is of the emotions and intellect.

The Thessalonians were enduring fierce persecution at the hands of their enemies, particularly at the hands of the Jews (2:14). They must have been tempted to retaliate. Many of them might have nurtured desires for vengeance and harbored active dislike toward their enemies. "Win them by love" was Paul's advice. To respond bitterly to persecution is self-defeating and destructive of character. God reserves all vengeance to Himself as His own prerogative (Rom. 12:19). Here again, the Lord Jesus is our supreme example.

Nor was the apostle Paul far behind his Lord in setting the example of *agapē* love toward all men! Paul was first brought under conviction of sin by the sight of a man with an angel face. That man was Stephen. As Saul of Tarsus, Paul had tried debating Stephen to convince him that Jesus of Nazareth was a blasphemous impostor and that Christianity was a heretical cult (Acts 6:8–9). He joined with other young hotheads "of the synagogue of Cilicia" (the province of Asia Minor of which Tarsus was the capital), likely in suborning men to accuse Stephen of blasphemy and in hiring false witnesses to testify against him before the Sanhedrin (Acts 6:13–15). Undoubtedly, Paul was present at Stephen's trial and "saw his face as it had been the face of an angel" (Acts 6:15). Doubtless, he heard Stephen announce to the maddened assembly that he could see "the heavens opened, and the Son of man standing on the right hand of God" (Acts 7:55–56). He was certainly present when Stephen was stoned. He heard him cry with a loud voice as the stones were beating him down, "Lord, lay not this sin to their charge" (Acts 7:60). The face of Stephen haunted him ever afterward. He as good as tells us so in giving his own testimony before the Sanhedrin (Acts 22:19–20).

3. Paul and the return of his Lord (3:13)

Again Paul comes back to his major theme—the second coming of Christ. He wanted the Thessalonians to emulate his example in view of the Lord's return: "To the end he may stablish your hearts unblameable in holiness before God, even our Father, at the coming of our Lord Jesus Christ with all his saints." The word for "coming" here is *parousia.*

We have already seen that the word refers to the Lord's presence, specifically, in a prophetic context, to the Lord's coming in the air (4:16–17) and to our appearing before Him at the judgment seat of Christ before we accompany Him back to earth to deal with His foes.

Three words are associated with the second coming of Christ: the *parousia,* which has to do with the fact of the Lord's being present; *epiphany,* which has to do with the Lord's manifestation of Himself, first to the church (1 John 3:2; 2 Tim. 4:8) as part of the *parousia* in the air, and then, later, to the world (2 Thess. 2:18), which is delayed until the *apocalypse,* the unveiling of the Lord's glory (2 Thess. 1:7). We have a picture type of this fact in the story of the boy-king Joash, who was first secreted in the temple for seven years and there revealed to the priests and nobles within the secret and sacred precincts of the temple. He was then brought forth and shown where every eye could see him (2 Chron. 23:3, 11). Thus, Joash had what our Lord will have—two epiphanies.

The first great act in the coming end-times drama is the *parousia.* The word refers not only to the coming of the Lord Jesus but also to His actual presence. It refers to the Lord's immediate presence in the proximity of this planet to His arrival "in the air" surrounded by the clouds. The psalmist prophetically refers to it: "He bowed the heavens also, and came down: and darkness was under his feet. He made darkness his secret place; his pavilion round about him were dark waters and thick clouds of the skies" (Ps. 18:9, 11).

It is the first phase of the Second Coming. The Lord descends the stairways of the sky. He enters the environs of our planet. He shouts, and the dead in Christ arise and the living saints ascend with them toward the sky. They meet in the clouds of heaven (Acts 1:9–11), and the Lord arranges His judgment seat in a pavilion of cloud. The *parousia* is a secret meeting of Christ and His church. The psalmist saw it as "secret" (His hiding place), stationary ("his pavilion"), and invisible (in "darkness"). The Lord ascended visibly before the astonished gaze of His disciples on the brow of Olivet. Then He was wrapped around with clouds, and they saw Him no more. He is to "so come in like manner" (Acts 1:11). The process is reversed. First, the Lord will descend, invisible to the eyes of men, hidden in the clouds; later, He will burst upon the astonished eyes of men, and they will see Him whom they pierced visibly, bodily descending toward the earth's surface accompanied by His saints (Rev. 1:7; 19:11–21) to deal with His foes. The period in between is the *parousia.*

The *parousia* is an important interlude indeed. The raptured saints meet the Lord in the air, encompassed with clouds (4:17). This is our reunion. It is not in heaven and not on earth but in the air. The Old Testament prophet caught a fleeting, wondering glimpse of it: "Who are these that fly as a cloud, and as the doves to their windows?" (Isa. 60:8).

In a sense, the *parousia* is our ark, our shelter in the time of storm. The psalmist wrote, "Thou shalt hide them in the secret of thy presence from the pride of man: thou shalt keep them secretly in a pavilion from the strife of tongues" (Ps.

31:20). This is the heavenly hiding place of the true church, where we will be kept safe from the judgments of the Apocalypse. Against this hidden refuge, the Antichrist will rave and revile: "And he opened his mouth in blasphemy against God, to blaspheme his name, and his tabernacle, and them that dwell in heaven" (Rev. 13:6).

The Lord's presence in the cloud signals the opening of His court. He begins that review of the lives of His own, which we associate with the judgment seat of Christ (Rom. 14:10; 1 Cor. 3:10–15; 2 Cor. 5:10). Indeed, judgment begins, in very truth, at the house of God (1 Peter 4:17). At this great arraignment, the works of the Lord's people will be reviewed, to be rewarded or rebuked as need be. Some believers will appear before Him empty-handed and will see their life deeds go up in smoke as wood, hay, and stubble. Others will have gold, silver, and precious stones to lay at His feet. All of the blemishes, spots, and wrinkles of the Bride will be removed. Rewards will be given, and each one's position in the coming kingdom will be determined. Remember that this is a judgment seat, not a mercy seat. It will be a sobering event. And it is inescapable for every believer.

The duration of the judgment seat review is not revealed. Nor are we told the process. The parable of the pounds (Luke 19) shows that it cannot be instantaneous, but it might be speeded up miraculously. Otherwise, it would have to go on for a very long time, considering the millions who will be involved. Time, especially as it relates to God, moves on quite a different plane than it does with us. For one thing, God dwells in the eternal present tense (Exod. 3:14), whereas we live our lives one moment at a time.

To some extent, at least, the *parousia* of Christ runs simultaneously with the *parousia* (2 Thess. 2:9) of the Antichrist. While we are being prepared for the coming kingdom, antedeluvian and sodomite wickedness will come to a head on earth (Luke 17:26–37). A rising tide of lawlessness will meet God's outpoured judgments descending from on high. The Antichrist will appear, seize control of Europe, revive the Roman Empire, sign his seven-year treaty with Israel, nod approval at the building of the Jewish temple in Jerusalem, confront Israel's foes, seize the world, inaugurate the Great Tribulation, and march to Armageddon. All of this will take time.

Meanwhile, the *parousia* in the sky will continue. The judgment seat will give way to the marriage supper of the Lamb, even as the stage is set on earth for the Battle of Armageddon. Both *parousias* will end. The clouds will part, and every eye will see the blazing glory of the returning Christ. "For as the lightning cometh out of the east, and shineth even unto the west; so shall also *the coming* [*parousia*] of the Son of man be" (Matt. 24:27). He will paralyze the Antichrist, "consume him" *(analiskō),* indeed, with the brightness (*epiphaneia,* "the shining forth, the manifestation, the outburst") "of his coming" *(parousia),* as Paul reveals later (2 Thess. 2:8). "Then shall the righteous shine forth as the sun in the kingdom of their Father" (Matt. 13:43). The Lord's feet will rest upon the Mount of Olives, which will instantly split asunder (Zech. 14:4).

Unfulfilled prophecy still awaits the rapture of the church, which will be a catalyst to set its fulfillment in motion. Panton says, "Nothing stands between us and the summons of God; no premonitions, no warnings, no signals, no prophecies. Again and again our Lord likens His coming to that of a thief, with the consequent need of our unceasing alertness . . . no thief gives warning of his coming. . . ."[2]

The *parousia,* then, includes the ordeal of the judgment seat of Christ. Paul never lost sight of that fact. It was his spur here (3:13) to the Thessalonians to urge them on to stability and holiness of life.

A preacher friend of mine was driving through Louisiana, past vast cotton fields, some years ago. He drove past the weighing station and the cotton wagons. It was very hot, although the sun had just gone down and the day was already dying in the west. He could see a small family of black people, a father and his family, coming in from the field. They had picked cotton to the end of the row and were now coming into the weighing station, bringing in their stuffed cotton bags to be weighed. The father was a massive man, well over six feet tall. He wore no shirt, just a pair of khaki pants. His black skin glistened with sweat. He had slung over his shoulder a cotton sack that must have weighed a hundred pounds or more. As he looked back along the row, the preacher could see the others straggling along behind. Besides this man and his family were all kinds of other cotton pickers—short ones, big ones, little ones, young ones, and old ones.

The preacher began to think of the great men of the past—the apostle Paul, Martin Luther, D. L. Moody, Spurgeon, Finney, men who had preached to thousands. At the time, my preacher friend was still a young man, new to the ministry. He compared himself unfavorably with the great preachers of the past.

He looked down the long cotton rows again. The cotton pickers seemed to

2. See D. M. Panton, "Rapture," no. 10 of *Present Day Pamphlets,* 2d ed. (London: Chas. J. Thynne, 1922), 6–10. Panton was one of the leading prophetic teachers of his day. His *Dawn* magazine was always packed with fascinating articles. However, his views on a partial rapture of the church took him further on the *parousia* issue than many are prepared to go.

him to represent the great soul winners of the past, men who had harvested the field for God. As he looked, he saw, way down at the end of the row, some twenty or thirty yards behind the others, a little black boy. He couldn't have been more than three feet tall. He had a little cotton bag made from an old flour sack in which he had about five pounds of cotton. The preacher could see him bobbing along back there. He, too, had been out in the hot sun all day. He, too, had been working hard, just as hard as had the big man out in front.

The young preacher bowed his head. He said, "Oh, Lord, I may never be a Jonathan Edwards or a Billy Sunday. I'm only a young preacher, but I want to be like that little boy. I want to keep hard at it. I want to have done all I could and have something in my sack for Jesus when I get to the weighing station in the sky."

When the sun goes down and we arrive at the judgment seat, we shall all be there. We shall all be in at the finish. The important thing is to be faithful, through the burden and heat of the day, and to have something in our sack to put at Jesus' feet.

PART 5

The Lord's Coming: A Strengthening Truth

1 Thessalonians 4:1–18

A. Our mighty potential (4:1–2)

Paul's thoughts of the *parousia* resulted in some practical teaching. He sets before us our *mighty potential* (4:1–2), our *moral purity* (4:3–8), our *measured progress* (4:9–10), our *manifest purpose* (4:11–12), and, as a grand, new revelation, our *magnificent prospect* (4:13–18).

Paul reminds us of our mighty potential as Christians. He reminded the Thessalonians, for example, of *what had been committed to them:* "Furthermore then we beseech you, brethren, and exhort you by the Lord Jesus, that as ye have received of us how ye ought to walk and to please God, so ye would abound more and more" (4:1). Paul had remained in Thessalonica long enough to see many people saved and to teach his new converts the essentials of Christianity. He taught them *what they should believe* as Christians, and he taught them *how they should behave* as Christians. He even taught them eschatology—not a subject that we, perhaps, would consider vital to the daily maintenance of the Christian life. Paul evidently thought otherwise. Truth about the second coming of Christ is intended to be a spur to holy living (1 John 3:3), an essential and integral part of the development of Christian character and conviction. The hope of the Lord's near return and the prospect of our being rebuked or rewarded at the judgment seat should motivate us to live godly lives.

We can be sure, too, that he taught them the essentials of what we have in his other epistles. Probably he would begin with what we now have in Romans—*salvation truth*—setting before them the principles, problems, and practice of the gospel.

He would teach them the essentials of what is recorded in Corinthians—*sanctifying truth*—warning them about the divisions, disorders, difficulties, and even the disbelief that can plague a local church. Both their personal walk in relation to marriage and meats and their public worship in relation to the table and tongues would pass in review.

He would set before them the great principles now recorded in Galatians—*separation truth*—warning them against legalism on the one hand and license on the other.

He would review with them the truth that we have in Ephesians—*soaring truth* concerning the church as a body, a building, and a bride.

He would teach them the truth of Philippians—*stimulating truth* about joy in suffering, sacrifice, service, and sickness.

He would set before them the truth of what we now have in Colossians—*sobering truth,* the truth about the Christ, the cult, and the Christian.

He would teach them the truth enshrined in Hebrews—*sanctuary truth,* how Judaism is obsolete and has been replaced by better things because we have a better Savior, a better sacrifice, a better sanctuary, a better security, a better spokesman, and a better society.

Now he could write to remind them of what they had received from him and Silas. We can be sure that he had taught them how to study the Old Testament Scriptures in the light of Calvary and two advents of Christ. He had taught them how to "rightly [divide] the word of truth" (2 Tim. 2:15). He might not have had time to give them a thorough theological education, but he had taught the essentials so that they could walk such as to please God. They were responsible for what had been committed to them. So Paul could write, "We beseech you, brethren, and exhort you by the Lord Jesus." The word for "beseech" is *parakaleō,* used of a beggar asking for alms. The word for "exhort" is *erōtaō,* which means literally to call someone aside to appeal to them. "We beg and urge you," Paul says as he underlines the supreme importance of living the Christian life.

He reminds the Thessalonians, moreover, of *what had been commanded of them:* "For ye know what commandments we gave you by the Lord Jesus" (4:2). Some Christians seem to be content with the bare fact of salvation. It does not seem to have dawned on them that commandments accompany Christianity. They seem to think that as long as they are saved that is all that matters, that all of the rest is optional. They think that they can please themselves as to whether they submit to Christian baptism and participate in the Lord's Supper; that it is up to them whether they read and study God's Word diligently. They think that it is optional whether they set aside a percentage of their income to support the Lord's work, that it is purely a matter of personal choice whether to attend the gatherings of the local church, maintain a life of Christian devotion and discipline, seek to win others to the Lord, love their own wives as Christ loved the church, and raise their families in the fear and nurture of Christ. These things are not optional at all; they are specifically commanded throughout the various New Testament epistles. They are obligations that attend a true profession of faith in Christ, God-given aids to holy living. Doing these things is our duty. We do them, however, not because we are under law but because we are under grace, not because we have to but because we want to.

B. Our moral purity (4:3–8)
 1. Immorality is a sin against God the Father (4:3–5)
  a. The need for sanctification (4:3)

Upon his return from Thessalonica, Timothy likely reported to Paul privately that a degree of immorality was still evident among the Thessalonian Christians. The Greek culture gave wide approval to all forms of sexual misbehavior. The idea that any kind of extramarital sex was wrong was quite foreign to the Greek mind. A blatant double standard existed. Wives were expected to be chaste, mothers of children, and keepers at home. Married men, however, could do as they pleased. They could keep mistresses and concubines and frequent prostitutes with the full approval of society. Conventional morality saw nothing wrong in having affairs, committing sodomy, or indulging in premarital and extramarital sex. Prostitution was legalized, and the state brothels' profits were often used to build temples. Our own social norms, indeed, are fast degenerating into those of ancient Greece. Paul's warnings against immorality are as needful today as they were in his day, and they sound just as strange to our contemporaries as they did to his early Greek converts. Sexual sins now surface frequently in the church, as evidently they did in the church of the Thessalonians.

Hence the need for teaching on sanctification: "For this is the will of God, even your sanctification, that ye should abstain from fornication." Sexual purity is not all that sanctification entails, but it certainly is a vital part of it.

We all enjoy *positional* sanctification by virtue of our position in Christ (1 Cor. 1:2). In the New Testament, all believers are called *saints*—"sanctified (holy) ones." We do not have to develop holiness by our own self-effort and self-denial. We are born into it by means of the new birth. Paul says that Jesus Christ is made unto us both righteousness and sanctification (1 Cor. 1:30). Sanctification simply means that we are set apart for God.

The other side of the coin is *practical* sanctification, God's demand upon us that we, as His children, separate ourselves from evil things and ways. This is something that we must cultivate and pursue diligently. It is learned behavior. It is made possible by the power of the indwelling Holy Spirit (2 Thess. 2:13).

"Abstain from fornication," Paul says. The Christian is to abstain totally from all forms of sexual impurity. The word *porneia* refers to all kinds of illicit sexual intercourse. It includes traffic with harlots, adultery, and premarital sex. The New Testament ethic calls for a total ban on sexual indulgence outside the marriage relationship. No sin is more destructive of the family, more dangerous to health, or more debilitating to spiritual life. The Holy Spirit warns, "Marriage is honourable in all, and the bed undefiled: but whoremongers [fornicators] and adulterers God will judge" (Heb. 13:4). The norms of our permissive society are pushed to the hilt by television programming, modern advertising, and widespread tolerance of pornography and perversion. There is a general acceptance of couples living together without regard to marriage vows. The norms of the world are now becoming the norms of the church. Once it was a scandal to be convicted of sexual sin, and the church openly disciplined the offenders. That is now rare. It is time to return to the standard set by the Holy Spirit.

b. The need for subjugation (4:4)

Paul follows the command with a comment: "That every one of you should know how to possess his vessel in sanctification and honour." In other words, the believer should learn to control his body. It is to be kept clean. Some scholars think that the word *vessel* here refers to a man's wife. In any case, each believer is to exercise self-control and not indulge in sexual misbehavior.

God takes a serious view of sexual sin. The supreme Old Testament example is that of David. His sin with Bathsheba exposed him to the displeasure of God. Murder and adultery broke out again and again in his immediate family circle. His son Absalom publicly shamed him on the advice of Ahiphothel (Bathsheba's grandfather). Some of David's penitential, tear-drenched psalms reveal the mental, moral, and spiritual toll that his sin extracted from him.

The Lord expects us to exercise firm control over this area of life. When the Lord frankly and freely forgave the woman taken in adultery, He did not for one moment condone her sin. His gracious "Neither do I condemn thee" was followed by His sobering "Go, and sin no more" (John 8:11).

c. The need for separation (4:5)

Paul elaborates: "Not in the lust of concupiscence, even as the Gentiles which know not God." We are not to regard the body as an instrument of self-gratification. This, Paul says, is what the pagans, who have no knowledge of God, do. Knowing God—or, to put it another way, knowing the Lord Jesus—is what makes the difference. To know Him is to love Him; to love Him is to want to please Him. To please Him, we must keep our body clean.

Elsewhere, Paul says, "I beseech you therefore, brethren, by the mercies of God, that ye present your bodies a living sacrifice, holy, acceptable unto God, which is your reasonable service" (Rom. 12:1). We are tripartite beings. Each of us has a body designed to be the vehicle of the senses. Because we live in a body, we can see, hear, smell, taste, and feel. Each of us has a soul. We can think, feel, and decide. We are aware of ourselves as individuals. We also have a conscience, a sense of right and wrong. We can be controlled by our senses, our intellects, our emotions, our wills, or our conscience. Or we can be controlled by a combination of these things.

God created us to be much more than intelligent animals. We were created with a spirit, the faculty that enables us to know, love, and obey God. Animals are controlled by instinct; we are to be controlled by God. We were created to be inhabited by God. The human spirit was to be inhabited by the Holy Spirit and cooperate completely with the Holy Spirit.

The Fall changed all of that. When Adam sinned, the Holy Spirit vacated the human spirit, leaving man without the divine direction and drive needed to live according to God's plan. Our empty and yearning spirits can never find rest apart from God. People seek to fill that internal void with religion, education, pleasure, sex, ambition, power, and human love and affection. The "Gentiles which know not God" are lost. They are spiritually dead (1 Cor. 2:14).

When we accept Christ, however, we are "born again," "born of the Spirit," "born from above" (John 3:6–7). The Holy Spirit once more takes up His abode within (1 Cor. 3:16–17) so that we can once again be indwelt by the Holy Spirit. It is the indwelling Holy Spirit who makes it possible for the regenerated believer to keep his body as a sacred vessel and not to defile it by sexual sin. Because we know God, a clear-cut line of separation must exist between our behavioral standards and those of the Gentiles.

Paul challenged the Romans to present their bodies to God. He added, "And be not conformed to this world: but be ye transformed by the renewing of your mind, that ye may prove what is that good, and acceptable, and perfect, will of God" (Rom. 12:2). The world around us wants to force on us its standards. Instead, we must let God fashion our minds from within.

2. Immorality is a sin against God the Son (4:6)

This sin is avenged: "That no man go beyond and defraud his brother in any matter: because that the Lord is the avenger of all such, as we also have forewarned you and testified." God draws the line beyond which we are not to go. The line is simple: no sex outside of marriage. To go beyond that is to defraud somebody. The word for "go beyond" is *huperbainō,* which means literally "to step over." God has written "No trespassing" over every man or woman who is not one's own wife or husband. He has done more. He has posted the warning "Trespassers will be prosecuted." The word for "defraud" is *pleonekteō.* It means to "wrong" or "overreach." The idea is that of crossing over a forbidden frontier, trespassing on territory that is clearly posted "Out of bounds."

The word for "avenger" is *ekidikos.* It is used of one who exacts a penalty from a person. The only other place where the word is used is in connection with a civilian magistrate, described by Paul as "a revenger to execute wrath upon him that doeth evil" (Rom. 13:4). The Lord Jesus is the One who deals out judgment to those who transgress God's moral laws. Both sternness and severity are in God's dealings with His people as well as goodness and grace (Rom. 11:22).

Punishment for sexual sin is severe. It might take the form of unbearable feelings of guilt that haunt the transgressor and spoil all of his or her legitimate relationships. It might take the form of exposure and shame. It might take the form of venereal disease, herpes, or AIDS. It might take the form of one's own wicked behavior being reproduced by one's own children. The defrauded person, the one whose wife or husband has been seduced, might take vengeance into his or her own hands. The Lord, however, gives the solemn warning that sexual sins *will* be punished. God has no lack of means—physical, psychological, or spiritual—to punish the transgressor.

"We also have forewarned you and testified," Paul reminds the Thessalonians. The word for "testified" is *diamarturomai,* an intensified form of the usual word. It can be rendered "we earnestly testified." The rich man in the flames of hades used the word first. He pleaded with Abraham to send Lazarus to preach to his five brothers: "I pray thee . . . send him to my father's house: for I have five brethren; that he may testify [*diamarturomai,* 'earnestly testify'] unto them, lest they also come into this place of torment" (Luke 16:27–28). The same word is used to describe Peter's efforts on the Day of Pentecost to persuade the Jews to repent and accept Christ. "And with many other words," says Luke, "did he testify [*diamarturomai*] and exhort, saying, Save yourselves from this untoward [crooked] generation" (Acts 2:40). Sexual sin, and its consequent punishment, is nothing to take lightly.

3. Immorality is a sin against God the Holy Spirit (4:7–8)

Paul takes immorality so seriously that he seems almost unable to stop warning against it. He calls all three members of the Trinity to witness against it.

He underlines here *the rule involved:* "For God hath not called us unto uncleanness, but unto holiness" (4:7). God sees all men as being either "in Adam" or "in Christ" (Rom 5:7). In Adam, we are controlled by *the Fall;* in Christ, we are controlled by *the Call.* Controlled by the dynamics of the Fall, we obey the dictates of a *ruined* nature; controlled by the dynamics of the Call, we obey the dictates of a *redeemed* nature. The characteristic of our ruined nature is *sin;* the characteristic of our redeemed nature is *sanctification,* holiness, because God has not called us unto uncleanness. Uncleanness is what we inherit by reason of our *natural* birth, but God has called us unto *holiness.* That is what we inherit by reason of our *new* birth. The natural man delights in *vileness;* the new man delights in *virtue.*

In our daily lives and in our character, conduct, and conversation, we exhibit either the results of the Fall or the results of the Call; it is impossible for our Adamic nature to be holy; it is impossible for the Christ nature to be unclean. Whether the Fall of man or the Call of God controls us hinges on which nature we obey (Rom. 6:16–18). The decision is always ours.

Paul next underlines *the rebellion involved:* "He therefore that despiseth, despiseth not man, but God . . ." (4:8a). The word for "despiseth" is *atheteō.* It means to displace, to set aside, and to reject. As used in Hebrews 10:28, it means "to set at nought": "He that despised [*atheteō*] Moses' law died without mercy . . ." The Lord used the word to convey the thought of rejecting: "He that heareth you heareth me; and he that despiseth [rejecteth, *atheteō*] you despiseth [rejecteth] me; and he that despiseth [rejecteth] me despiseth [rejecteth] him that sent me" (Luke 10:16). It is no light thing to reject Paul's teaching on sexual purity. All who engage in sex outside the bonds of marriage show, by their behavior, that they reject God's requirement of sexual purity. They "set at naught" His instruction and warnings. "It is not me," Paul declares, "it is not the other apostles, and it is not man that they set at naught. It is God."

Our own society—including even, to some considerable extent, the Christian community—has set at naught the moral standards of God. As a result, pornography, perversion, decadence, and depravity are destroying our homes, blasting our lives, and undermining our nation. Every form of sexual misbehavior is running wild and out of control. Children are born out of wedlock. We have child abuse, wholesale divorce, sodomy, rape, prostitution, and moral anarchy. The courts make little or no attempt to control it. The church looks the other way. But these sins bring their own punishment. The media, with its humanistic leanings that gives free rein even to sodomy, does not intimidate God. God detests liberal laws that condone so-called alternative lifestyles. Congress, the courts, and even the church itself set at naught God's laws. But God upholds His Word. Rebellion will bring its own retribution.

Some years ago, I was seeking to explain the gospel to a couple of well-educated Hindus. One of them sneered, "Your God seems to have done a very poor job of creating this world. Look at all of the wars and disease and poverty." I refrained from commenting on the vileness of Hinduism. The man added, contemptuously, "I could make a better job of creating and running the world myself than your God seems to have done."

"My friend," I said to him, "suppose that you were to buy an expensive and complicated appliance or piece of equipment for your home or office. It comes with a book of instructions. A large red label is displayed prominently on the item. It says, 'WARNING! Always press button A *before* you press button B; severe damage will result if you ignore this warning. NOTE. The manufacturer is not responsible for resulting damage, and your warranty will be canceled.' These are the manufacturer's instructions. He made the item. He knows its features. He gives instructions for its operation and maintenance so that peak performance can be enjoyed at all times. He gives fair warning of damage that will result if you ignore his instructions. Very well, you buy this thing and ignore the warning. You press button B before pressing button A, and the equipment reacts violently. Smoke and the smell of burning fills the room; the machine is damaged, almost beyond repair. Whose fault would it be—yours or the manufacturer's?" He saw the point at once, although he hedged and started a different argument.

Man is far more complex a creation than a mere machine. Adam and Paradise came complete with a warning: "Do *NOT* eat of the tree of knowledge of good and evil. Death and ruin will result if you do." The terrible damage done to the human race, resulting from the breaking of this rule, is evident everywhere. When we accept the Lord Jesus Christ, the worst of the damage is instantly repaired. The redemption of the body is still in the future. Repaired and restored, we can now be what God intends us to be. The warning still applies. Among other things, God warns, "Don't indulge in illicit sexual activity. Things will go wrong if you do." We had better pay good heed to the warning.

Then, too, Paul underlines *the rejection involved:* "but God, who hath also given unto us his holy Spirit" (4:8b). The indwelling Holy Spirit makes it possible for a believer to live a chaste life. In our ignorance and inexperience, we might grieve Him at times—He will warn us. We might skate on some thin ice at times—He will warn us. But let us beware of persisting. We might go too far.

The classic biblical example is Samson. He was Israel's strongman, a Nazarite from birth, consecrated to God and anointed with the Holy Spirit. In fact, the Holy Spirit is mentioned more in connection with Samson than with all of the other judges combined. There was nothing that Samson could not do in the power of the Spirit of God. The Philistines were terrified of him.

But Samson had one fatal weakness—women. He played the fool with women. He broke God's laws with women. The Holy Spirit was patient, but Samson persisted. In the end, the Philistines caught on to his weakness. They knew that no man could overthrow him—so they used a woman. Samson—blind, bound, bending to the millstone, and mocked and derided by the Philistines—is God's warning. The Holy Spirit is *holy.* God has called *us* to holiness. The Holy Spirit is outraged when we defile our body, His temple, by sexual misbehavior (1 Cor. 6:15–20). He is not to be trifled with in this matter.

C. Our measured progress (4:9–10)

When it comes to the Christian life, the "bottom line," as businessmen say, referring to the most important item on the profit-and-loss statement and on the balance sheet, is love. Paul sets *love* here in stark, staring contrast to *lust.* Lust has no part in Christian life; love is everything. So, here we have *love taught:* "But as touching brotherly love ye need not that I write unto you: for ye yourselves are taught of God to love one another" (4:9). Paul carefully uses here the word *philadelphia* ("brotherly love") to underline the kind of love that believers are to demonstrate toward each other.

Love is expressed in deeds, not just words (James 2:14–16). Love reaches out to the weak, the friendless, the unfortunate, and those who are ill or in need. Love delights in hospitality (Heb. 13:1–3). It is the evidence of genuine faith.

Nobody had to teach the Thessalonians to love one another. God Himself taught them that behavior. The obligation to love one's "neighbor" is revealed in the Old Testament (Lev. 19:18). God is love, an expression of His character. Love for one's fellow Christians is proof of the new birth and possession of the divine nature. The Holy Spirit develops this kind of love in His own.

Years ago, when I was a soldier in the British army, I was stationed on the Haifa docks. I found a fellowship of believers meeting in a small building on the lower slopes of Mount Carmel. What struck me most about that fellowship was the love that the believers showed toward one another and especially to me. In that small group of believers were Armenians, Russians, Jews, Arabs, Germans,

Britons. In the world outside, these nationalities were at each other's throats. In that fellowship, however, was love. It included people of different races and nationalities, different levels of education, and different strata of society. Some of them were strong Christians, some of them had suffered the loss of all things for Christ; others were weak Christians. That small local fellowship of believers was a microcosm of the universal church. Within that fellowship, I found love, hospitality, generosity, acceptance, encouragement, and lasting friendship. That's the way it ought to be. We, like the Thessalonians, surely do not need to have someone to tell us that we should have warm, brotherly love toward our fellow Christians. We might not always be able to agree with them, but surely we can love them. God Himself teaches us that fact.

Then we have *love wrought:* "And indeed ye do it toward all the brethren which are in all Macedonia: but we beseech you, brethren, that ye increase more and more" (4:10). While abiding in love, we must also be abounding in love because that, too, is the nature of love. It can never be content with what it has given; it has to give more. Love does not set quotas. Love does not quit. Love, like Niagara Falls, never ceases to pour itself out.

D. L. Moody was led to Christ by an indefatigable Christian worker, who hunted him down in the back room of a shoe store and pinned him down. "Now then, Dwight, you've heard it long enough; it's time you accepted Christ." Not long afterward, Moody was approached by a Sunday school teacher who was dying of cancer and did not have long to live. He had a class of young people, none of whom he had won to Christ. He wanted Mr. Moody to go with him to each home and to help him lead those young people to Christ. They went to home after home, and, one by one, they led every one of them to the Lord.

Moody went home and prayed, "God, if You spare me, I'll spend the rest of my life the way that Sunday school teacher spent the last ten days of his life, driven by the compulsive power of love to lead people to Jesus."

He heard someone say, "The world has yet to see what God can do through a man wholly yielded to Him." Moody said, "By the grace of God, I'll be that man."

He conducted campaigns all over the world. He led countless thousands of people to Christ. He stood on an empty plot of ground in Chicago, where the Moody Bible Institute now stands, and claimed it for God. "Lord," he said, "when I'm gone, I want to leave behind me a whole host of young men and women who will serve You and win people to You."

He went to Chicago and had a citywide gospel campaign. The Chicago's World's

Fair was in progress, but it had to close down on Sundays because Moody had the crowds. From the pulpit, he chatted to massed audiences of thousands of people at a time just as if he were chatting to five or six individuals. In his early days, he led large numbers of boys and girls from the Chicago slums to Jesus. All of his life he was driven by the love of Christ. He had an insatiable hunger, born of love, to see people saved.

Then his great heart gave out. The doctor told him to slow down. Moody decided to take the doctor's advice and went on a voyage to Europe. He thought things over. The doctor was right, he decided. He would have to slow down. That very night the ship was wrecked in a storm. Moody stood by the rail of the stricken ship and prayed, "O God, I'm sorry You had to remind me. Give me another chance. Spare the lives of those on this ship. I promise You, I'll spend the rest of my life the way that Sunday school teacher spent the last ten days of his." And so he did. That is love in action, love abounding more and more, love for lost people and for the Lord's people, love as the true driving force of new life in Christ.

D. Our manifest purpose (4:11–12)

Paul continues his practical teaching. He directs our attention toward *temperamental things:* "And that ye study to be quiet" (4:11a). Nothing compares with a quiet spirit. We all know people who are what we call "temperamental"—with the emphasis on—*temper!* They are difficult to get along with and hard to live with. They are touchy, stubborn, rude, opinionated, pushy, or get angry easily. The Lord was never like that.

The word for "study" is *philotimeomai.* Paul used it to describe his efforts to plant the gospel in fields that were not evangelized: "So have I strived [*philotimeomai*] to preach the gospel . . ." (Rom. 15:20). It carries the idea of earnestly endeavoring to accomplish a goal. It means "to be ambitious," "to love, honor, esteem," or "to make it a point of honor."

Our ambition, then, is to be quiet. The word is *hēsuchazō.* It is used to describe the cessation of activity by the women who were busy about the burial of Christ: "And they returned, and prepared spices and ointments: and rested [*hēsuchazō*] the sabbath day according to the commandment" (Luke 23:56). It is sometimes translated "held their peace" (Luke 14:4; Acts 11:18).

The Holy Spirit calls for something that is the very opposite of the spirit of the age. In the world, people are ambitious to make money, achieve business success, and ascend the social ladder. We urge our children to "succeed." In the Bible, the only reference to "success" has to do with the kind of life that results from meditation on the Scriptures (Josh. 1:8). The danger is that a worldly spirit might invade the church. Preachers can become ambitious and eye big pulpits, bishoprics, prestigious seats in seminaries, and the control of whole denominations. "Study to be quiet," says Paul. "Make it your ambition to stay out of the limelight." One suggested rendering of this statement is "Make it your ambition to have no ambition."

Then Paul directs our attention to *temporal things:* "Do your own business, and to work with your own hands, as we commanded you; that ye may walk honestly toward them that are without, and that ye may have lack of nothing" (4:11b–12). Paul calls attention to our work, our walk, and our wealth.

He has something to say about *our work:* "Do your own business," he says. "Work with your own hands." The gospel does not encourage people to be idle. Paul and Silas had set a good example when they were among them. Paul was always willing to engage in hard work to support not only himself but also others in the missionary party when necessary (2:9).

A heightened expectancy of the second coming of Christ seems to have encouraged some Christians to idleness and disinclined them to attend to their business affairs. Such has happened frequently over the centuries. It is often associated with the pernicious and unscriptural practice of setting dates for the Lord's return.

Lactantius set the date for the Lord's coming as A.D. 500. Half a century later, another date was set, inspired by the belief that a new millennium was about to begin. Multitudes of people sold their possessions and went to Palestine to await our Lord in A.D. 1000. Among those who were confident of that date were some prominent leaders in the church.

The Irvingites set the years 1835, 1838, and 1866 as dates for the Rapture. The great New Testament scholar John Albert Bengel, a German Lutheran theologian, worked out an elaborate scheme to prove that the Millennium would begin in 1836. William Miller, the most famous of all American date setters, preached to great crowds (with large charts to show how his hypotheses were determined) that Christ would return in 1843 (and, later, 1844). Michael Baxter, in his widely read volumes, variously set the years 1866, 1874, and 1881 as the time of the end, when Christ would return. Michael Baxter also taught that 144,000 watchful believers would be taken to heaven, without dying, on March 5, 1896, at about 3 P.M. When this event did not take place, he substituted two other dates for the event—February 26, 1924, or Tuesday, February 2, 1926.

Mother Shipton, a self-proclaimed psychic, chose 1881 as the date. Warren G. Harding's brother, a leading Adventist, chose 1923 as the magic date. The Adventists later changed the year to 1996. The Seventh-day Reformed Adventists, a splinter group, led by their prophet, Robert Rerdt, lined up on Long Island on February 6, 1925, in anticipation of the Rapture.

Many devout Christians attended a great gathering in the Royal Albert Hall (London) on March 1, 1927, and were told that the Battle of Armageddon would be fought on May 28, 1928.

On May 2, 1933, A. E. Ware, an earnest Christian with a well-worn Bible in his hand, announced to a group of people that "this present year, 1933, being seven years from 1940, is going to witness the opening of the end of the Age with all that means. . . ."

Dr. Grattan Guinness, a well-known believer, declared, "The termination of the 'times of the Gentiles' meets in 1934. No chronological prophecy of scripture indicates any date beyond this year."

Thousands of sincere Christians in the United States were disturbed by the prognostications of Edgar C. Whisenant, a retired NASA engineer, who published a booklet titled *88 Reasons Why the Lord Will Come in '88.*[1] According to Whisenant, the Rapture would take place on Sunday, September 11, 1988 (failing that, on either Monday, September 12, or Tuesday, September 13). He went further. He declared that the Antichrist would sign his treaty with Israel on September 21, 1988. The 144,000 witnesses would be divinely sealed on September 26, 1988. World War III would start on October 4, 1988, and would last for three-and-a-half weeks.

Even more recently, prophets of doom were foretelling the collapse of civilization as the year 2000 drew near. The year (Y2K) was to feature massive global computer breakdowns, banking and billing crises, and airplane crashes. Books were written encouraging people to stockpile food and other essentials and to prepare for anarchy. The end of the world was at hand. None of these calamities occurred.

The second coming of Christ was high-priority news at Thessalonica. Paul had more to say about it in his second epistle to them (3:6–12).

Paul has something to say, too, about *our walk:* "That ye may walk honestly toward them that are without . . ." (4:12a). The call is for Christians to ensure that they have a reputation for honesty in the outside world. The word *honestly* is *euschēmonōs* and it comes from a word with the original meaning of being "elegant

1. Edgar C. Whisenant, *88 Reasons Why the Lord Will Come in '88* (Nashville: World Bible Society, 1988).

in person, mien, and bearing." That summons a picture of a person who is graceful, poised, and well balanced. Such a person does not stumble and blunder and have to apologize all of the time. The word came to refer to one's outward deportment. It is translated "honestly" in Romans 13:13. This behavior is in contrast to the riotous living of the lost. Similarly, in 1 Corinthians 14:40, Paul concludes his correction of the flagrant errors and abuses of the gift of tongues by saying, "Let all things be done decently [*euschēmonōs*] and in order." When Paul told his readers to "walk honestly toward them that are without," he was demanding that Christians so behave that lost people might never have grounds to challenge a believer's testimony. Our beliefs and behavior should be beyond reproach. We should never have to apologize for things we have said and done. One thinks of the jibes and sarcasm leveled against the evangelical church in America by the media as a result of Whisenant's immoderate, erroneous, and widely publicized views.

The classical biblical example of a lapse in behavior before an unbelieving world is seen in, of all people, Abraham. He had responded nobly to the heavenly vision. He had become a believer and a pilgrim and had arrived in the Promised Land. There, he discovered the enemy in possession of the land and famine conditions prevailing everywhere. His faith faltered. He went down to Egypt (an Old Testament type of this present evil world), and there he lost his testimony. He and Sarah agreed to lie about their relationship because she was so good-looking that Abraham feared Pharaoh would have him assassinated to take possession of her. On the strength of Abraham and Sarah's word that Sarah was Abraham's sister, Pharaoh had Sarah put in his harem and proceeded to shower Abraham with costly presents.

Abraham, helpless and horrified, was hopelessly compromised. God stepped in and frightened Pharaoh out of his wits. Pharaoh indignantly protested that he did not know that Sarah was Abraham's wife. The next morning, Pharaoh summoned Abraham and demanded an explanation. When given, it was lame enough (Gen. 12:10–20). Pharaoh dismissed Abraham and Sarah, scornfully enough we might well imagine. We can imagine, too, what Pharaoh said to his court as an embarrassed and apologizing Abraham led his wife away. "Well! If that's an example of a believer, I hope I never meet another one." Thus, Abraham, who was called to be a blessing to all mankind (Gen. 12:3), in this, his first contact with a world superpower, was a curse instead (Gen. 12:17). Thankfully, Jacob was the opposite (Gen. 47:7, 10) and, in his blessing of Pharaoh, a much greater man than Abraham.

Finally, Paul has something to say about *our wealth:* "and that ye may have lack of nothing" (4:12b). Nowhere does Christianity endorse laziness.

Along with the good news, Timothy seems to have brought back some bad news from Thessalonica. True, they had a keen interest in prophecy. However, some believers had taken the imminence of the Lord's return so literally that they had stopped going to work and were idling around waiting for the Second Coming. Some of them, carried away by enthusiasm, might have even sold their property and become destitute. Now they had become a burden to their brethren and a mockery to the unsaved.

Paul wrote sharply to redress such behavior. A believer is to be a profitable and productive member of society, not a drone, always sponging and taking advantage of other people's charity. Paul offers a timely word for those who would prefer to live on welfare and charity than get a job and pay their own way. God wants us to "lack nothing." But He also expects us to do an honest day's work for an honest day's pay.

E. Our magnificent prospect (4:13–18)
   1. Those who are asleep (4:13–15)

Paul has now arrived at the central truth of this great epistle, a thrilling and comprehensive revelation of the pretribulation rapture of the church.

The inspired writers regarded the second coming of Christ as an important truth. It is mentioned some 318 times in the 260 chapters of the New Testament, an average of one reference in every twenty-five verses. In the Old Testament, the majority of prophecies relating to the Messiah have to do with His second coming.

Charles E. Fuller used to say of this great passage that it is Paul's exposition of John 14:1–3. The Lord's words "I will come again" are matched by Paul's explanation "The Lord himself shall descend from heaven." The Lord's promise "I will receive you unto myself" is matched by Paul's explanation "Then we . . . shall be caught up together . . . to meet the Lord in the air." The Lord's statement "That where I am, there ye may be also" is matched by Paul's statement "so shall we ever be with the Lord." And the Lord's announcement "Let not your heart be troubled" is matched by Paul's "Wherefore comfort ye one another with these words."

This remarkable passage (4:13–5:10) reveals five facts about the Rapture. Underlining key words in this Bible passage can emphasize these facts.

1. The second coming of Christ is a *positive* truth. Underline the repeated use of the words *shall* (4:15–17; 5:3) and *shall not* (4:15; 5:3).
2. It is a *personal* truth. Underline (preferably in a different color) the words *we, ye, us, I,* and *you* (4:13–15, 17; 5:1, 4–6, 8–10).
3. It is a *pivotal* truth. Underline the word *but* four times (4:13; 5:1, 4, 8).
4. It is a *progressive* truth. Underline the word *for* (4:14–16; 5:2–3, 7).
5. It is a *practical* truth. Also, underline the words *wherefore* and *therefore* (4:18; 5:6, 11).

The Thessalonians had welcomed Paul's teaching on the second coming of Christ. They had been intrigued by it. They wished that Paul had been able to stay longer and teach them more about it. With the passing of time, however, doubts and questions had begun to arise in their minds—especially about those who had died since Paul had left. Had these loved ones missed the Rapture? They probably deluged young Timothy with questions; doubtless, too, he did his best to answer them. What they needed was a more definitive word from Paul.

We have here an incidental sidelight on the wisdom of God in allowing Paul to be chased out of Macedonia so soon. If Paul had stayed in Macedonia as long as he would have liked, he undoubtedly would have answered all of these kinds of questions as they arose. And we should have been infinitely poorer by our lack of the two Thessalonian epistles. As it turned out, instead of answering their questions verbally, he answered them by mail. His divinely inspired letters were carefully preserved and ultimately incorporated into the New Testament. Thus, we have available to us the apostolic answers to these basic questions in exactly the same way they were available to the Thessalonians.

What, then, does happen to those who put their faith in Christ but who die before the Lord returns? Paul reviews three things in answer to that question. First, *our feelings are reviewed:* "But I would not have you to be ignorant, brethren, concerning them which are asleep, that ye sorrow not, even as others which have no hope" (4:13). Death is indeed a hopeless tragedy for those who were outside of Christ, regarding both those who die and those who are left behind to mourn.

We have all attended funerals. As we stand before the casket and gaze into the cold, calm face of the corpse, we confront the terrible finality of death. We are confronted, too, with the utter insolvency of the human race.

The philosopher comes. He expounds his thoughts and theories concerning death. He quotes from the sages of the past, none of whom could speak with authority as to the reason for death or say with authority what lies beyond. Here reason ends and revelation begins. Nor has any of the philosophers been able to come back from the grave to tell us whether their fine arguments were born out by the actual article of death itself.

The scientist comes. He says, "I'm sorry, my friend. I did my best. I trained your doctor and equipped your hospital. I provided you with the best of medicines. But I have failed. Nor can any scientist tell me how to bring you back to life, despite all that we know about cells, genes, chromosomes, and DNA. We have removed your name from our list of patients. We have failed you at the last."

The family comes. There stands the weeping mother and the brokenhearted father. He cries like David, "Oh, my son, my son! Would God that I had died for you, my son, my son!"

For those who are outside of Christ, death is final, cold, cruel, callous, and utterly uncaring. It is ugly, menacing, and inescapable. Paul calls it "the last enemy." When he arrives, it's all over.

The only consolation we have is in the Word of God. We have God's Word for it, that for the believer all is well. "Ye sorrow not," Paul says, "even as others which have no hope." Indeed, he deliberately describes death as sleep. We actually court sleep.

We sorrow! But we have God's Word for it, that our loved ones are only asleep—a reference to the state of the body. The soul does not sleep; the body does. The soul is made of the same stuff as eternity. It never gets tired, never gets old, never gets ill, and never sleeps. The body of the departed believer is asleep. Jesus said the same thing of Lazarus and declared His intention of going to Bethany to awaken him (John 11:1–15).

Outside of divine revelation, we have no word to comfort us when death strikes. Years ago, Henry Ward Beecher was invited to visit an atheist club presided over by the brilliant and blasphemous Robert Ingersoll. He went and listened to Ingersoll as he made a witty speech in which he unmercifully attacked Christianity and then sat down to thunderous applause. Ingersoll then turned to Beecher and invited the famous preacher to say a few words.

Beecher rose slowly to his feet. "Gentlemen," he said, "you will forgive me if I appear somewhat preoccupied. But this evening I witnessed something shocking. Let me tell you about it. I saw a blind man groping at the curbside. I saw a young fellow offer to help him across the street. But, just as he took the blind man's arm, a great hulk of a fellow came along. He boxed the young man's ears and chased him off down the road. Then he came back and seized the blind man's stick and beat him with it. Then he pushed him headlong in the mud and went on his way laughing."

A silence followed the telling of this tale. Then Ingersoll jumped to his feet. "The bully!" he exclaimed. "The bully! Do you know who he was, Beecher? The unspeakable bully!"

"Yes," said Beecher quietly, "as a matter of fact, I do know who he was."

"Who was it?" demanded Ingersoll

"It was you!" responded Beecher. "You are the man! Listen to me. Man is poor and blind and wretched. He has little enough to lean on as he gropes his way through life. Few will help him. So what do you do, Ingersoll? You come along and pull all of his props from under him. You rob him of his faith. You push him in the mud. You bully those who would help him. And then you go laughing on your way. Oh yes! I know who the man is. It is you."

Well, we can take Ingersoll's word for it—that there is no God, no heaven, no hell, no truth to Christianity. Or we can take Paul's word for it, the word of an anointed apostle of God. Indeed, Paul was speaking under direct revelation and inspiration of the Holy Spirit. Christianity is not a crutch. It is something real and solid upon which to lean when death comes in and when all around our soul gives way. "We sorrow," says Paul. He would not rob the Thessalonians of their tears. We do not pretend that death does not bring loss and tears. We sorrow, yes indeed, "but not as those who have no hope."

Next, *our faith is reviewed:* "For if we believe that Jesus died and rose again, even so them also which sleep in Jesus will God bring with him" (4:14). The *if* here is not the *if* of doubt. It actually means "since." The hypothesis is assumed to be an actual fact. There are four conditional (if) structures in the Greek New Testament. The first-class *if* is used here, and it means "since" because it assumes the certainty, not the contingency. The second-class *if* means "if it were so, but it is not so." It assumes contrary to the fact. The third-class *if* means "more likely," and the assumption is that it is most likely. The fourth-class *if* means "more remote and least likely."[2] Here, Paul does not mean to cast doubt upon their belief in the resurrection of Christ. He takes that for granted.

Then comes that grand and glorious certainty, the bedrock of all of our hope: "Jesus died and rose again." Indeed, no fact in all of history is greater. More evidence exists for the resurrection of Christ than for the conquest of Britain by Julius Caesar! "This thing was not done in a corner," Paul declared to Festus and King Agrippa (Acts 26:26). The facts concerning Jesus were public knowledge. It

2. E. W. Bullinger, *Companion Bible* (Grand Rapids: Kregel, 1990), app. 118.

is the one apologetic of the faith that no unbeliever has ever been able to assail. Paul himself had seen the risen Christ.

"Jesus died and rose again." When I was a boy in Britain, I once heard a refugee pastor from Nazi Germany give his testimony. He had been a well-known figure in Germany and was personally known to many of the Nazi leaders. He told how once he attended a giant rally at which the speaker launched into the usual tirade against the Jews. Then he spotted this pastor in the audience. He picked him out for special mention. "Pastor Schutez," he said, "you are a fool! Imagine anyone believing in a crucified, dead Jew!"

The pastor jumped to his feet. "I should indeed be a fool," he cried in ringing tones, "if I believed in a crucified, dead Jew. But I believe in the risen, living Son of God!"

Yes, indeed! There is all the difference in the world between the two. "Jesus died and rose again!" It is the central truth of the gospel.

"Even so!" That, ignoring all of the technicalities of the expression, suggests an exact parallel. For instance, "As Moses lifted up the serpent in the wilderness," Jesus said, "*even so* must the Son of man be lifted up" (John 3:14).

Having indicated the parallel between Christ's resurrection, now past, and our resurrection, still pending, Paul now points us to "them also which sleep in Jesus." Some authorities render that phrase "Them that are put to sleep by Jesus will God bring with Him." Everyone knows what that means! As the shadows lengthen and bedtime comes, we gather our little ones around us. We give them a bath and a cookie, tell them a goodnight story, and listen to their childish prayers—then we tuck them into bed and turn out the light. Nothing is strange or scary about that. Here is another parallel: for the Christian, dying is not to be feared any more than is sleeping.

No believer ever dies alone. Why? God attends even the funeral of a sparrow; Jesus said so (Matt. 10:29). When the time comes to die, we shall be safe in the arms of Jesus. He will tuck us in until the morning comes. Then, when He comes, He will bring us with Him.

Now *our future is reviewed:* "For this we say unto you by the word of the Lord, that we which are alive and remain unto the coming of the Lord shall not prevent [*phthanō,* 'precede'] them which are asleep" (4:15). The teaching now to be given is new. Paul received it by direct, personal revelation of the Lord Himself. He calls it "the word of the Lord." It is absolutely reliable.

It is remarkable how much faith we put in words. We begin when we are very young. The physicist tells us that $E = MC^2$. We take that as true. Most of us have no way of proving it, and most of us have but the haziest conception of what it means—energy equals mass multiplied by the speed of light squared! We do know that Einstein's equation gave birth to the nuclear age, so we simply accept the equation as true.

We are told that a large dose of arsenic is fatal. We believe it—we'd better believe it—although not many people want to put it to the test. Most of the things that we say we "know" we have accepted by faith. We have taken someone's word for it.

John says, "If we receive the witness of men, the witness of God is greater" (1 John 5:9). The Spirit says, "It [is] impossible for God to lie" (Heb. 6:18). Paul says, "God, that cannot lie" (Titus 1:2). We accept human guarantees, although they often turn out to be worthless. Here we have a guarantee backed by God's own Word—"the dead in Christ shall rise." The resurrection of the Christ unconditionally guarantees the resurrection of the Christian. The truth of the Rapture is confirmed to us by the resurrection of Christ. His resurrection demonstrates that our resurrection is not only entirely possible, an absolute certainty, but also is confirmed to us by the reliability of God. There is not the slightest shadow of doubt about it. God's integrity is beyond all question. His Word is His bond. As David Livingstone used to say about his own favorite promise of the Lord Jesus, "It is the word of a Gentleman of the strictest and most sacred honor, and that's an end of it!"

2. Those who will arise (4:16)

Now *the revelation is expanded:* "For the Lord himself shall descend from heaven with a shout, with the voice of the archangel, and with the trump of God" (4:16a–c). The shout means the *rapture for the church.* It summons the saints to glory.

One of the great mysteries of the past two thousand years has been the total and lasting silence of God. The world has been wracked by terrible wars, and God has remained silent. Fearful injustices plague society, and God is silent. Domestic tragedies occur, and God is silent. Famines wipe out whole populations. Pestilence, plagues, earthquakes, tornadoes, and volcanic eruptions occur, and God is silent. Persecutions, holocausts, crimes, and atrocities are committed, and God is silent. Wicked men grow rich on the misery of others, trading in alcohol, drugs, and sex, and empires are built and sustained on syndicated crime, and God is silent. Regimes have flourished on the systematic enslavement and exploitation of millions, and God is silent. False religions hold other millions in soul-damning spiritual darkness, and God is silent.

The great cry of humanity is, "Why? Why is God silent? Why does He not act? Why doesn't He speak?"

The answer is simple. He has! He has spoken. He has displayed might and miracle on an unprecedented scale on this planet. He has intervened. He did so two thousand years ago. What the world is witnessing, in this mysterious silence, is the infinite patience of God.

When God breaks this silence, it will be with a shout! He has spoke once in grace by sending His Son to this planet. And they murdered Him. He sent His Spirit, and the world ignores Him. The next time, He will speak in wrath. The whole creation today is holding its breath, waiting for that shout (Rom. 8:19–22). Jesus is waiting for the moment when He can descend the stellar spaces, burst through the clouds of the sky, and give that shout.

Perhaps He will use the wondrous words found in Solomon's song: "Rise up, my love, my fair one, and come away. For, lo, the winter is past, the rain is over and gone. The flowers appear on the earth; the time of the singing of birds is come . . . the fig tree putteth forth her green figs. . . . Arise, my love, my fair one, and come away" (Song 2:10–13).

What a mighty shout that will be! His is the voice that wakes the dead. We hear this shout three times in Scripture—and, each time, the gates of death are breached. The first time was at the tomb of Lazarus: "When he thus had spoken," John says, "he cried with a loud voice, Lazarus, come forth. And he that was dead came forth . . ." (John 11:43–44).

The second time the shout was heard was from the cross. Matthew tells what happened: "Jesus, when he had cried again with a loud voice, yielded up the ghost. And, behold, . . . the graves were opened; and many bodies of the saints which slept arose, and came out of the graves after his resurrection, and went into the holy city, and appeared unto many" (Matt. 27:50–53). The first time one man was raised; the second time many were raised.

Paul recorded in this letter to the Thessalonians the third time that the shout occurs. There will follow a wholesale exodus from the tomb. This mighty shout will ring out across the five continents and the seven seas. Its vibrant echoes will comb the mountain peaks, the arctic poles, the desert wastes, the ocean caves, the pampas and the prairies, the crowded urban graveyards, and the world's great battlefields. And the dead in Christ will rise!

Forth from their tombs, they will come! Martyrs of the faith will rise. Missionary pioneers will rise. Apostles and prophets, evangelists, pastors and teachers, the rank and file of the church will rise. Both those who were victorious in their lives and those who were weak in their faith will rise. There will be those who prevailed in prayer and those who hardly ever prayed. The ascending host will include both eloquent men, mighty in the Scriptures, and those who were biblically illiterate. There will be those who are laden down with sheaves from the ripened harvest fields of earth and those who are going home with empty hands. There will be those still bearing in their bodies the stigmata, the slave brands of Jesus Christ, and those who are being carried to the skies on flowery beds of ease.

Forth they will come, a countless host, ten thousand times ten thousand and thousands of thousands. There they are: men and women, boys and girls, all washed in the blood of the Lamb! For the first time in history, the whole church—universal, militant, and triumphant—will be seen. Every member will be present. As Moses said to Pharaoh when he was defining who should participate in the Exodus, "there shall not an hoof be left behind" (Exod. 10:26). The same principle applies in the Rapture. It is to be a *raptured* church, not a *ruptured* church, with some of its members left behind to face the horrors of the Great Tribulation.

The church will be seen to be perfect! Our meeting with the Lord in the clouds will take care of all spots and blemishes; the judgment seat of Christ will ensure that. All imperfections will be removed.

When, at the marriage supper of the Lamb, the angel hosts proclaim, "Here comes the Bride," we can be sure of this: she will not come in on a crutch or blind in one eye and with a leg and an arm missing! Nonsense! The church will be complete, the most beautiful, eye-catching sight in the universe.

The voice of the archangel means *ruin for the world.* That voice sends the angels forth to war. The Rapture means that the amnesty is over, that God has broken off diplomatic relations with the world that murdered His Son. For long centuries now, the warrior angels have been straining over the battlements of heaven, so to speak, eager to avenge the terrible wrongs that the wicked children of Adam's race inflicted on their Beloved on planet Earth. But the angels have been held back by sovereign grace.

Now, however, the archangel comes to the fore. So do the angels. During this age, ministering spirits (Heb. 1:14) are here to serve the Lord's people. Now come the martial angels, led by Michael, the high archangel of glory. We are told of at least one of his activities in the post-Rapture age: "And there was war in heaven: Michael and his angels fought against the dragon; and the dragon fought and his angels, and prevailed not; neither was their place found any more in heaven. And the great dragon was cast out, that old serpent, called the Devil, and

Satan, which deceiveth the whole world: he was cast out into the earth, and his angels were cast out with him" (Rev. 12:7–9).

Throughout the Apocalypse, angels are prominent. They sound the trumpets, pour out the vials, and issue warnings and proclamations. This sudden outbreak of angelic activity is heralded by the voice of the archangel. The removal of the church has cleared the way; now the angels can go to war.

The trump of God means *repatriation for Israel.* It sounds the alarm for the Jews. Once the church age is complete, the focus of God's dealings reverts to the nation of Israel. The church age is a parenthesis in God's dealings with mankind. The church was injected supernaturally into history on the Day of Pentecost and is to be supernaturally ejected back out of history at the Rapture. At that point, God will resume His Old Testament dealings with the nation of Israel and will fulfill the many prophecies concerning Israel, which is still awaiting their time.

The nation of Israel has been reborn in our own day, a sure sign that we are approaching the end times. Only a trickle of Jews has so far returned; the flood tide has not yet begun. The trumpet will summon them back. Trumpets were used throughout Israel's Old Testament history. When the law was given at Sinai, it was accompanied by the sound of a supernatural trumpet. Two silver trumpets were used to direct Israel's activities in the wilderness. They were used in connection with warning, worship, war, and Israel's walk. The fall of Jericho was in response to the sounding of trumpets. The Jews kept an annual Feast of Trumpets. It followed Pentecost after the lapse of a period of time. It was preceded by the fast of atonement and the millennium-picturing Feast of Tabernacles.

Trumpets are primarily connected with the nation of Israel; they are secondarily connected with the rapture of the church. Paul shows here that the rapture of the church is the catalyst to precipitate other end-times events. Paul now reaffirms that *the resurrection is expected:* "the dead in Christ shall rise first," he says (4:16). That should be sufficient answer to the concern of the Christians at Thessalonica about their deceased loved ones. They had not missed the Rapture! On the contrary, they would have priority; they would actually rise first!

Note here especially that reassuring word *shall,* which predominates in the theology of the Rapture. We do not know how God reassembles the scattered dust of the dead. We only know that He does. It is not hard for Him. After all, He is omniscient, omnipotent, and omnipresent. Indeed, to a God who lives in the eternal present tense, the future is already the past. We humans are locked into a space-matter-time dimension. We have to wait until a prophesied event happens, but God transcends all time.

My wife used to have a music box. Every time the lid was opened, it played a little tune: "Raindrops Keep Falling on My Head!" When someone opened the box, a small brass cylinder was exposed to view. It had a lot of little spikes sticking up all over it. Also, prongs produced the different notes when the revolving spikes hit them.

Now, in a sense, when someone opened that music box, they saw the whole tune. It was all pegged out. However, to *experience* the tune, they had to wait for the cylinder to complete its full cycle in its appointed time. As the cylinder turned, each spike hit the appropriate prong and was released, producing each successive note—ping! ping! ping-a-ping-a-ping!

It is rather like that with God. He sees the whole story. The whole of future time is all pegged out in glory. But we creatures of time must wait for the slow process, whereby the timeless, eternal purpose of God is worked out by us, in us, and through us in terms of human experience. But it is all pegged out in heaven by an omniscient God who—"calleth those things which be not as though they were" (Rom. 4:17).

So throughout this paragraph, Paul says, "Shall! Shall! Shall!" There is no doubt about it. One of these days, the graves all over the world will burst open, and "the dead in Christ shall rise first." That is God's compensation for those who are like Abraham, Isaac, and Jacob, of whom the Holy Spirit says, "These all died in faith, not having received the promises, but having seen them afar off, and were persuaded of them, and embraced them, and confessed that they were strangers and pilgrims on the earth. For they that say such things declare plainly that they seek a country. . . . a better country, that is, an heavenly: wherefore God is not ashamed to be called their God: for he hath prepared for them a city" (Heb. 11:13–16).

3. Those who are alive (4:17–18)

Finally, Paul has a word for all of those who are alive on the earth when the Rapture takes place: "Then we which are alive and remain shall be caught up together with them in the clouds, to meet the Lord in the air: and so shall we ever be with the Lord" (4:17). Paul always puts himself in this class (note the word *we*). Not until much later did he learn that he was going to die (2 Tim. 4:6–8). He lived in eager expectation of being caught up at any moment. The Rapture is always presented to us thus, as being imminent, something that could happen at any time.

People take many positions regarding this event. We have amillennialists, postmillennialists, and premillennialists. We have those who believe in a midtribulation Rapture, those who preach a post-tribulation Rapture, and those who herald a pretribulation Rapture. Some people have even embraced "a prewrath Rapture," which seems to be a loudly heralded version of the midtribulation Rapture.

Those who espouse the tribulation Rapture generally think it necessary to attack John Nelson Darby. Darby was a prominent leader among the so-called Plymouth Brethren. He did much to rescue the truth of the Lord's coming from the rubbish heap on which the professing church at large had dumped it. Darby was a scholar, a theologian, an intellectual, and a spiritual giant who was thoroughly at home in Hebrew and Greek as well as a number of European languages. His enemies say that he obtained his views on the Rapture from a hysterical, vision-prone woman. The statement is slanderous. It betrays an ignorance of the man, his mission, and his message that is inexcusable. About the last place Darby would have gone for his theology was to a woman. He had quite other ideas about the place of women in the church. He certainly did not advocate a woman's preaching, teaching, or usurping a man's role of authority in the church. Why should Darby need female instruction regarding Bible truth when he himself produced several translations of the Bible in English and other languages? He had a mind for the universe that was not to be narrowed by a hysterical, unstable "prophetess."

Many able expositors (e.g., Dwight Pentecost, John Walvoord, and Charles Ryrie) have taken in hand the defense of the pretribulation Rapture. Any position on the second coming of Christ that takes the edge off our expectancy and intrudes all kinds of prior events between the believer and the Rapture is a wrong position. The element of surprise is a key element in all New Testament teaching regarding the Rapture; hence, the repeated exhortations that we be watchful.

"Therefore be ye also ready: for in such an *hour* as ye think not the Son of man cometh" (Matt. 24:44). "But of that *day* and hour knoweth no man, no, not the angels of heaven, but my Father only" (Matt. 24:36). "Ye know not when the time [*season*] is" (Mark 13:33). "If [he] had known in what *watch* the thief would come, he would have watched, and would not have suffered his house to be broken up" (Matt. 24:43). "Watch ye therefore: for ye know not when the master of the house cometh, at even, or at midnight, or at the cockcrowing, or in the morning" (Mark 13:35). "Watch ye therefore, and pray *always* [at all seasons], that ye may be accounted worthy to escape all these things that shall come to pass" (Luke 21:36).

So then, in contrast with the actual return of the Lord to set up His kingdom on earth, which *is* a dated event (seven years after the signing of the Antichrist's treaty with Israel and 1,260 days after the breaking of the treaty, (Dan 9:26–27; Rev. 12:6–12), the rapture of the church is a secret event. We do not know its– "hour," its "day," its "year," its "season," or its "watch."

The Lord elaborated on our ignorance of the actual watch that would witness His return: "And if he shall come in the second watch, or come in the third watch, and find them so [i.e., watching], blessed are those servants" (Luke 12:38). The first watch has some of the preceding day's alertness about it, and the fourth watch has the approaching day's expectancy about it. The second and third watches, however, are when wakefulness and watchfulness are at their lowest ebb. It was, indeed, in the Middle Ages that the church fell sound asleep. It was in the midnight watch that Peter slept and at the "cockcrowing" that he so sadly denied his Lord. It was "in the fourth watch of the night," the morning watch, indeed, that Jesus came to the disciples to save them from the storm (Matt. 14:25). John significantly adds that "immediately the boat was at the land whither they were going" (John 6:21). It was in the morning watch that the Lord looked out from the pillar of fire upon the advancing Egyptian host and when their judgment fell (Exod. 24). We can see now that there is something special about that morning watch.

The Lord could have come at any moment in all of this long time since His ascension. He could have come in any of the night watches. It would seem that we are now in the last watch, the morning watch, and a new alertness and awareness of the church to Advent teaching is evident. We can thank the much-maligned J. N. Darby for that! The Lord could have come at any moment in the past two thousand years. He could come at any moment now.

"We which are alive and remain," says Paul, "shall be caught up together with them in the clouds, to meet the Lord in the air: and so shall we ever be with the Lord." He draws our attention to *our promised rapture* (4:17).

Caught up! The word is *harpazō*. It means literally "to snatch away." The word is used to describe Philip's sudden disappearance after he baptized the Ethiopian eunuch (Acts 8:39). It is used to describe Paul's rapturous experience of things untranslatable (2 Cor. 12:2, 4). The meaning of the word includes the idea of the event's being accomplished suddenly and by force.

A friend of mine who is very much at home in his Greek New Testament says that the word can convey the idea of "a loving, reaching out," of "taking hold," and of "lifting up." The word is used of the soul winner's "pulling" *(harpazō)* lost people out of the fire (Jude 23). In a completely contrasting setting, it is used to describe the activity of the Wicked One, who "snatcheth away" the good seed sown in the heart of those who hear the Word of God but who are careless about its truth (Matt. 13:19). It is used to describe the way the soldiers rescued Paul from the mob in the temple. Their commander told them to "take him by force [*harpazō*] from among them, and to bring him into the castle" (Acts 23:10). In like manner, we are going to be snatched away before the end-times judgments fall upon this planet.

We shall be "caught up together" with the resurrected saints. In a later revelation, Paul elaborates on the changes that will take place to our natural bodies. We shall receive a body that is engineered for eternity and capable of virtually annihilating the restrictions of time and space. It will be incorruptible, a body of power, triumphant over all of its current weaknesses and limitations. It will be a heavenly body, immortal and spiritual (1 Cor. 15:35–54). Paul adds that it will be like Christ's resurrection body (Phil. 3:21). John agrees: "We shall be like him," he says (1 John 3:2).

Suddenly, the pull of glory will exert its power, and the church will be gone. We shall assemble in the Lord's presence in the clouds of the air, and the *parousia* will have begun.

Nature provides us with two illustrations. Think, for instance, of the lowly caterpillar. It lives out its life on earth as a grub, earthbound and rooted to the dust. It lifts its little head and stares at the vast expanse of the sky. It thinks, *I wish I could fly! If only I had wings! I would catch the rising air currents and wing my way from tree to tree! But I' m only a wretched grub with a lot of legs crawling up and down the trunks of trees.*

Then comes a change. The caterpillar knows that the change is coming and prepares for it. It makes itself a little coffin, a chrysalis, attaches it to a twig, and crawls inside. Then it dies to the only life it has ever known. Time comes and goes, and still that silken coffin holds its contents. Then comes a call that we can't hear. Suddenly, that caterpillar bursts out of its tomb. And, wonder of wonders, it has been changed! It entered that silken coffin as a caterpillar; it emerges as a butterfly. It is the *same creature* that comes *out* of that chrysalis that goes *into* it, but it is so radically changed that we hardly recognize the two as being one. The transformed creature spreads its wings and soars upward to the sky in a blaze of beauty. It was "sown in dishonor," to borrow Paul's words, and it has been "raised in glory." The same kind of thing is going to happen to us. The God who keeps faith with the caterpillar will keep faith with us.

The other illustration is just as remarkable. Suppose that we were to take a mixture of metals and scatter them, burying some of them and strewing others over the ground here and there. We disperse gold and silver, copper and zinc, iron and tin. Then we take a powerful electromagnet and pass it over the area where the mixture of metals is scattered. Immediately, the magnet draws to itself just one kind of metal. It attracts only the iron, be it buried or still on the surface of the soil. It leaves behind all of the rest; the gold is left, the copper is left, and the silver is left. The question is, "Why does the magnet draw to itself just the iron?" The answer is simple high school physics. It draws the iron because the iron has the same nature as the magnet itself.

Just so at the Rapture! The Lord will draw to Himself only those who have the same nature as Himself. It matters not whether we are rich or poor, clever or ignorant, wise or foolish, black or white, prince or pauper, alive or dead. All that matters is that we have become "partakers of the divine nature" (2 Peter 1:4). That is why Jesus said to the cultured, successful, religious Nicodemus, "Ye must be born again" (John 3:7). For it is by means of the new birth that we are regenerated, that we are "born from above," that we receive the Holy Spirit and the very nature of Christ.

"So shall we ever be with the Lord," Paul says. And so we shall! It will take all eternity to enter into the joy and wonder of that fact.

Now Paul draws our attention to *our present rest:* "Wherefore comfort one another with these words" (4:18).

What comforting words they are! We read them at every funeral. None of the world's religions has their like. None of their founders came back from the dead. Only Jesus can give the comfort and assurance that we have in this our "blessed hope" of thus being forever with both our departed loved ones and the Lord.

The word for "comfort" here has a variety of meanings. It is akin to John's favorite word for the Holy Spirit—the Comforter (John 14:16). That suggests an interesting thought. One of the symbols of the Holy Spirit in the New Testament is a dove. When I was a boy, for the magnificent sum of one English penny, one could purchase a platform ticket and go onto the platform of the local railway station. Those were the days of steam engines, and because our town was on the main line from the city of London to the country of Wales, it was a very busy station. It was a favorite pastime to purchase a platform ticket and spend an enjoyable morning, in the summer holidays, watching the trains. They would come roaring in to the accompaniment of clouds of steam, blowing of whistles, banging of doors, and the rush of passengers. Then, off it went again with loud huffs and puffs of the mighty engine up front.

One day, I was idling away such a morning when I found myself down the far end of the main platform. There I came across some wicker baskets filled with doves and pigeons. A friendly porter saw me eyeing them.

"Those are homing doves and pigeons, son," he said. "We are loading them on trains going to different parts of the country. Sometime next week, they will all have arrived at their different destinations. At precisely the same time, they will all be released, and no matter where they are, they will head straight for home. It's a kind of race, you see. The one that gets home first will be the winner."

That's it, of course! The Holy Spirit is the dove of God. He has a strong homing instinct. When He is received into a human heart, He brings that homing instinct with Him. He heads us toward Home! At the time of the Rapture, He will simply pick us all up, living or dead, and take us there to the accompanying shout, trump, and voice.

PART 6

The Lord's Coming: A Sanctifying Truth

1 Thessalonians 5:1–22

A. A word of explanation (5:1–11)
  1. Some significant contrasts (5:1–8)
    a. Regarding beliefs (5:1–6)
      (1) Saints are directed by Scripture (5:1–2)

There is, of course, no chapter break here in the original text. The opening word of chapter five is *but,* which links us directly to what has gone before. The following discussion climaxes in the statement that those who participate in the Rapture will be delivered from the coming wrath. The key to understanding this passage is to consider carefully the personal pronouns involved in the discussion. Mark them carefully. Note the two classes. There are those addressed as *I, ye, you, yourselves, we,* and *us*. These pronouns embrace believers, those who are candidates for the Rapture. Paul continues, using these pronouns from the preceding paragraph, which describe the Rapture itself (4:13–18).

In contrast with this group, Paul referred to another group by using the personal pronouns *they* and *them.* By simply coloring them in your Bible using two different colors, you can highlight the contrast quickly. Saints and sinners will thus stand out in evident contrast—saints destined to be caught away from the coming wrath and sinners destined to be caught up in the maelstrom of coming wrath.

Paul begins with three things about the Lord's people. First, they are *directed by Scripture.* Paul refers first to *a prior revelation:* "But of the times and seasons, brethren, ye have no need that I write unto you" (5:1; Heb. 1:1–2). This undoubtedly refers to both the vast body of eschatological truth contained in the Old Testament and the Lord's own prophetic teaching, now enshrined in the Gospels. In the course of his instruction of his Thessalonian converts, Paul had seemingly gone over all of that ground, giving them, too, the benefit of his own insights. He had taught them about those "times and seasons" that will eventually culminate in the coming of the day of wrath.

Times refers to the various time periods involved in God's dealings with the human race. God has spoken "at sundry times" as well as "in diverse manners" (Heb. 1:1). Paul had doubtless taught his converts to distinguish between these various times (what we now call dispensations). Daniel referred to some of the specific time periods involved (9:24–27; 12:1–13).

"Seasons" refers to the special characteristics, features, highlights, and signs that mark the end times. Many of these are becoming clearer to us now that we are approaching the end of time—the rebirth of the state of Israel, the rise of Russia, the impending revival of the Roman Empire, the dawn of the nuclear age, the persistence of malignant anti-Semitism, global catastrophes, the emergence of a pornographic and sodomite society, the apostasy of the professing church, the spread of terrorism, persecution, famine, and earthquakes are all features of the end times. These are "the seasons" that herald His coming. The word used is *kairos.* It refers to the characteristics of a period, as of harvest, for instance (Matt. 13:20; Acts 14:17; Gal. 6:9). It is used of the fulfillment of prophecy (Luke 1:20; Acts 3:19; 1 Peter 1:11).

Paul felt no need to go over such ground again. He refers his converts back to a prior revelation. He refers them, also, to *a perfect revelation:* "For yourselves know perfectly that the day of the Lord so cometh as a thief in the night" (5:2). The Lord's coming for His church is likened to the coming of a thief. A thief comes unexpectedly, when people are asleep, or when they are busy and occupied with other things.

The "day of the Lord," to which Paul refers here, is the subject of extensive Old Testament revelation. There are seventeen references to it in the Old Testament (Isa. 2:12; 13:6, 9; Ezek. 13:5; 30:3; Joel 1:15; 2:1, 11, 31; 3:14; Amos 5:18, 20; Obad. 15; Zeph. 1:7, 14; Zech. 14:1; Mal. 4:5). The "day of the Lord" is sometimes found combined with such words as *wrath* and *vengeance.* It is referred to four times in the New Testament (here and in 2 Thess. 2:2; 2 Peter 3:10; Rev. 1:10).

We are now living in "man's day" (1 Cor. 4:3). Right now, man exalts himself and tries to rule God out of His own world. In "the day of the Lord," the Lord reasserts His claim over this planet. It is primarily a day of wrath and judgment. It does, however, extend on into the millennial age and to the dramatic climax and end of that magnificent era.

The focal point of "the day of the Lord" is the Apocalypse (the book of Revelation) and the judgments that follow the Rapture, especially the terrible vial judgments when God will pour out His undiluted wrath upon this world that murdered His Son.

The Thessalonians knew "perfectly" about these things. The word that Paul used means literally "accurately." Luke used the word to describe his own personal investigations into and knowledge of the story of the Lord Jesus (Luke 1:3). Matthew used the word to describe the instructions that Herod gave to the wise men. He inquired of them "diligently" as to exactly when the guiding star first appeared and urged them to search "diligently" for the young child and then bring him the coveted information (Matt. 2:7–8). Paul had taught his Thessalonian converts with painstaking care. As a result, they had accurate knowledge of the salient features of the Day of the Lord. Not all of the period, however, even that leading up to the outpouring of God's wrath, is filled with strife and turmoil. Paul reminds them of this next.

(2) Sinners are deluded by Satan (5:3)

The judgment era that opens with the removal of the church is not, entirely, without its years of promise. But they will be deceptive. Addressing himself now to the unsaved, Paul says, "For when they shall say, Peace and safety; then sudden destruction cometh upon them, as travail upon a woman with child; and they shall not escape."

A brief survey of the period covered by the Apocalypse underlines this fact. First, the seals will be poured out, resulting in *a world ruined by man.* There will be false Christs, wars, famines, pestilences, and persecutions dwarfing all of those of history. Men's hearts will be full of horror and alive with terror.

Then the trumpets are to be blown, resulting in a world *ruled by Satan.* The Antichrist will be revealed. He will bring order out of chaos. He will unite the European continent, strengthen the Atlantic alliance, and impose a Roman peace upon the Western world. The world will hail his power, policies, and very person. They will look upon him as a political and economic genius. Peace will seem to have come to the world at last. Economic prosperity and world trade will flourish. People will cry "peace and safety" and will congratulate themselves on the new order that has come. But they will be deceived.

The Antichrist, however, will not be content. He will be determined to rule the whole world from Rome. As a move toward that end, the Antichrist will sign a treaty with Israel. It will be a seven-year pact that unconditionally guarantees the security of the state of Israel and authorizes the Jews to rebuild their temple in Jerusalem. The Moslem nations will be warned, on peril of invasion and punishment, to leave Israel alone. The stage is set for a combined Russo-Islamic invasion of Israel. That invasion will take place "when my people of Israel dwelleth safely" (Ezek. 38:14). This condition will be true of Israel at no other time before the final coming of Christ. The earth basks in the new age. Israel is at peace. Serious troubles will be brewing.

We can well imagine Moslem reaction when the Jews seize the temple site and start work on their temple. Intimidated at first by the Antichrist's power, the

Moslem world will seethe with mounting rage. They will appeal to Russia. In a desperate bid to regain world dominance, Russia and its client states will launch a massive invasion of Israel—only to meet the disaster described by the Old Testament prophet (Ezek. 38–39).

The Antichrist, now all-powerful, will call on all nations to submit to his rule. The world will lie in his lap. By one masterstroke, he will have eliminated his two chief rivals, Russia and Islam. Even China will be cowed. Now, indeed, the world can say, "Peace and safety." Men will heave a sigh of relief. At last, a central world government exists that is strong enough to enforce peace and ensure worldwide prosperity.

But they will be deceived again because what the Antichrist really wants will be global worship and world rule. He will seize the rebuilt Jewish temple in Jerusalem. He will put his image in the Holy Place and demand that everyone have his mark, the famous "mark of the Beast." The Jewish remnant and the converts of the two witnesses and the 144,000 witnesses will refuse to comply. Determined now to rid the world of every last lingering vestige of Judeo-Christian influence and teaching, the Antichrist will launch a massive, global holocaust. His aim will be to exterminate the Jews and crush all resistance once and for all. Doubtless, too, the holocaust will include the extermination of all other possible political and religious rivals to the Antichrist's power and plans.

"Then sudden destruction cometh upon them, as travail upon a woman with child; and they shall not escape," says Paul. This will be the Great Tribulation, also called "the time of Jacob's trouble" that is referred to so pointedly elsewhere in Scripture (Matt. 24:15–22; Dan. 12:11; Jer. 30:7). It will be a bloodbath of persecution, the like of which the world, in all its long and violent history, has never seen.

Note that Paul's reference does not include the *we* and the *us*. It refers to the *they* and the *them*.

The Antichrist, however, will have reckoned without God. The vials of God's wrath will be poured out, resulting in *a world rescued by God.* The outpouring of the first four vials will undermine the Antichrist's power structure. He will lose his grip. The eastern half of his empire will break away, mobilize against him, cross the Euphrates, and march to Megiddo. The Antichrist will mobilize the West. The stage will be set for the return of the Lord in power and great glory.[1] Paul develops the story of the Antichrist in his second letter to the Thessalonians.

---

1. For a full treatment of this sequence of events, see John Phillips, *Exploring Revelation* (Grand Rapids: Kregel, 2001); Phillips, *Exploring the Book of Daniel* (Grand Rapids: Kregel, 2004); and Phillips, *Exploring the Future* (Grand Rapids: Kregel, 2003).

(3) Saints are different in spirit (5:4–6)

Paul now contrasts the essential differences between saints and sinners, between children "of the day" and those "of the night."

Their *condition* is different: "But ye, brethren, are not in darkness, that that day should overtake you as a thief" (5:4). Twice in the original text the personal pronoun is emphatic. The Holy Spirit thus draws emphatic attention to the marked difference between the nature and destiny of Christians and the nature and doom of unbelievers. Paul is now talking to "brethren," to the Lord's people.

Darkness is used in Scripture in various ways. It can be physical (Matt. 27:45), intellectual (Rom. 2:19; Eph. 4:18), moral (Matt. 6:23; Rom. 13:12), or spiritual (Luke 1:79; Acts 26:18). As it is used here, the word refers primarily to the world's abysmal ignorance of the purposes of God. The word is also used to describe Satan and his aides as the unseen rulers of the affairs of this world (Eph. 6:12). It is also used to describe the horrors of a lost eternity (Matt. 8:12; 2 Peter 2:17). The word is nearly always used in a bad sense.

The Lord's coming for His own is likened here to the coming of a thief. Terrible disasters will fall upon the human race, once the Lord has "stolen away" His own people. These disasters will likewise come as a thief. They will be wholly unexpected. People will be listening to the siren voices of the humanists, the New Agers, the evolutionists, and, supremely, the Antichrist and his False Prophet. The immediate post-Rapture horrors depicted under the seals will take the world unawares. A new optimism will be abroad, but the euphoria is ill-advised. Just so, when the Antichrist imposes his own drastic solutions to global problems, a new wave of optimism will sweep the globe. This, too, will be equally misplaced.

We are not in the dark about these things. We will not be overtaken by them. We see clearly what is coming. That day will not overtake *us* as a thief in the night! On the contrary, the Rapture is going to overtake us first.

Their *character* is different: "Ye are all children of the light, and the children of the day: we are not of the night, nor of darkness." Night and day are opposites; light and darkness are opposites. The Light of the world is Jesus; He said so Himself (John 8:12; 9:5). Darkness is simply the absence of light. The Lord warned His enemies, "Yet a little while is the light with you. Walk while ye have the light, lest darkness come upon you: for he that walketh in darkness knoweth not whither he goeth. While ye have the light, believe in the light, that ye may be the children of light." John added, "These things spake Jesus, and departed, and did hide himself from them. But though he had done so many miracles before them, yet they believed not on him" (John 12:35–37). We become "children of the light and the children of the day" when we believe in the Lord Jesus and His nature is imparted to us by the Holy Spirit.

God has sharp words for unbelievers: "He that believeth not is condemned already, because he hath not believed in the name of the only begotten Son of God. And this is the condemnation, that light is come into the world, and men loved darkness rather than light, because their deeds were evil" (John 3:18–19).

The destiny of the children of light is quite different. Jesus said, "He that followeth me shall not walk in darkness, but shall have the light of life" (John 8:12). And Solomon wrote, "The path of the just is as the shining light, that shineth more and more unto the perfect day. The way of the wicked is as darkness" (Prov. 4:18–19). Our hope and destiny is quite different from that of the unbeliever.

Then, too, their *conduct* is different: "Therefore let us not sleep, as do others; but let us watch and be sober" (5:6). We have met that word *others* before. Paul reminded the Thessalonians, "Ye sorrow not, even as *others* which have no hope" (4:13), referring to those outside of Christ. The word is not *allos* (those who are of the same kind), nor is it *heteros* (those who are of a different kind). It is *loipos* ("the remaining one," or, in the plural, "those who are left behind"). It refers to "the rest of mankind," who stand in contrast with the saved. It can be translated "them that are without" here in 4:13 and in Ephesians 2:3, where Paul writes, "Among whom also we all had our conversation [lifestyle] in times past in the lusts of our flesh, fulfilling the desires of the flesh and of the mind; and were by nature the children of wrath, even as *others* [them that are without]." All that has now been changed for the believer (Eph. 2:4–7).

"Let us not sleep," says Paul. When a person is asleep, he looks like one dead. From a few feet away, a sleeping person cannot be distinguished from a dead person. We are not to be like those who are dead in trespasses and sins. We are to be very much alive. We are not to sleep as Jonah did when the storm was raging and the mariners were in peril of their lives. We must be sober, in contrast with Lot, who was both drunk and dishonored even when the very world about him was a smoking ruin (Jonah 1:5–6; Gen. 19:30–38).

b. Regarding behavior (5:7–8)

First, Paul looks at the *lost people:* "For they that sleep sleep in the night; and they that be drunken are drunken in the night" (5:7). The word for "sleep" is *katheudō*. It occurs twenty-two times in Scripture and is rarely used of death. The word suggests composing oneself to sleep. The act involves a measure of deliberateness. The word is occasionally used metaphorically to illustrate carnal indifference to spiritual things on the part of believers. In Mark's account of the Lord's Olivet discourse, he concludes with this challenge of the Lord: "Watch ye therefore: for ye know not when the master of the house cometh, at even, or at midnight, or at the cockcrowing, or in the morning: lest coming suddenly he find you sleeping [*katheudō*]. And what I say unto you I say unto all, Watch" (Mark 13:35–37). This is a clear call for pre-Rapture alertness. Now is no time to be careless and lethargic about spiritual things. The truth of the Lord's coming is intended to keep us alert and watchful.

The Lord also warns against drunkenness, another sin of the indifferent. A man who is asleep is quite unaware of what is going on. A man who is drunk has lost his capacity to react properly to what is going on. Many are the warnings in Scripture against drunkenness. Far from becoming drunk, Christians are to be filled with the Spirit (Eph. 5:18–19). People get drunk for a variety of reasons, often looking for the courage supposed to be found at the bottom of the bottle, sometimes looking for a way to drown their sorrows, and frequently seeking the fellowship and approval of their peers. Paul warns that drunkards shall not inherit the kingdom of God (Gal. 5:21).

Then Paul looks at *the Lord's people:* "But let us, who are of the day, be sober, putting on the breastplate of faith and love; and for an helmet, the hope of salvation" (5:8). In contrast with lost people, who are asleep to spiritual realities and drunkenly incapable of properly responding to them, incapacitated by their own wicked lifestyle, the Lord's people are to be sober. They are to have all of their faculties about them and all of their spiritual nature alert.

Paul borrows a piece or two of a Roman soldier's armor to illustrate the fact that a war is on—light against darkness, day against night. The three cardinal Christian virtues of faith, love, and hope are to be in evidence. The breastplate protects the *heart;* the helmet protects the *head.* Our affections and our thoughts are to be kept protected from the enemy. We are not to love the things that this world has to offer. We are not to allow ourselves to be seduced by its philosophies, attitudes, and attractions. This world is not our home.

2. Some significant conclusions (5:9–11)
   a. Our great escape from woe (5:9–10)

Paul now arrives at the second great climax in this tremendous revelation regarding the Lord's second coming. The first great climax is in connection with *the truth* of the Rapture, when the dead and living saints will be caught up to meet the Lord in the air. The second great climax is in connection with *the time* of the Rapture. It will be in time to save us from wrath. Noah went into the ark before the Flood came; Enoch was caught away in the rapture before antediluvian wickedness came to a head; Lot was removed from Sodom before the fire fell; and the church will be removed from earth before the end-times troubles begin.

Paul tells us first *what we shall escape:* "For God hath not appointed *us* to wrath, but to obtain salvation by our Lord Jesus Christ" (5:9). Note the use of the personal pronoun again. There are people appointed to experience that wrath (the *they* and the *them* of the passage); but those he describes by the pronouns *ye, we,* and *us* (going right back to the actual revelation of the Rapture itself in 4:13–18) are to escape the wrath.

The "wrath" here is not the eternal wrath referred to by Paul in his letter to the Romans—"For the wrath of God is revealed from heaven against all ungodliness and unrighteousness of men, who hold the truth in unrighteousness" (Rom. 1:18). That is God's *eternal wrath* against sin. The Lord Jesus has already saved us from that wrath: "He that believeth on the Son hath everlasting life: and he that believeth not the Son shall not see life; but the wrath of God abideth on him" (John 3:36).

The wrath here is that wrath mentioned at the end of the seal judgments and described so graphically under the vial judgments of the book of Revelation—*end-times wrath.* That this is so is determined by the context here in 1 Thessalonians, which is concerned with the second coming of Christ, not the eternal state of the lost. Wrath is a feature of the end-times judgments, and it is a feature of a lost eternity. We must always allow the context to determine which aspect of the Lord's wrath is in view.

We have already noted the two words used for wrath in the Apocalypse (1:10). Here it might be appropriate to depict the kind of world it will be from which we are to be snatched away.

Consequent upon the Rapture, the breaking of the seals will witness all divine restraint removed from the world. Wickedness will be allowed to come to a head. No longer will there be any conscience. Pornography and perversion will walk abroad, cheered on by a godless world. Wickedness and war will encircle the world. Earthquakes and epidemics, persecution and panic, famine and fear will be epidemic. The lost themselves will see in these things tokens of the wrath of God. Jesus Himself foretold the need for such days to be shortened if anyone was to remain alive (Matt. 24:22).

A brief respite will come with the unveiling of Satan's man, but it will not last.

He is called "the Man of Sin," and he will be the very incarnation of wickedness. Once he has sufficient power, he will throw off his benevolent mask. He will have goals that brook no delay—to rule the world and unite mankind in the worship of Satan. To this end, he will wage war, sign deceptive treaties, and kill off his rivals. The Roman Catholic Church will be wiped out, the Russians will be annihilated, and Islam will be crushed. The Jews and post-Rapture Gentile believers will be targeted for extermination. The shadows of Armageddon will lengthen every day.

The world will be caught up in the throes of repeated judgments from on high, all culminating in the outpoured wrath of the Lamb. The mounting din and noise will be that of a world gone mad, given free rein to work out its own ruin. The terror, the horror, the hatred, and the despair will be totally unrelieved. Then, to climax it all, the Lord Himself will return in person, in flaming fire, to make war on His own account and to tread out "the winepress of the fierceness and wrath of Almighty God" (Rev. 19:15).

Blessed be God! He has promised to save His church from all of that. "For God hath not appointed *us* to wrath," Paul says. The word *not* is emphatic. It indicates a full and direct negation, absolute and independent of all conditions. We are not appointed to go through the Tribulation or any part of it. Believers throughout this age of grace have had to keep an appointment with death (Heb. 9:27). The Rapture will save them even from that! No Christian has an appointment with either God's eternal wrath or His dispensational wrath.

Years ago, Dr. Ralph Keiper, speaking at the Moody Bible Institute's Founder's Week Conference, parodied an old hymn. The new words illustrate how those who would teach that the church will be in the Tribulation rob us of our "blessed hope." His version went something like this:

> Sad day, sad day, Jesus won't come today
> So gloomy and worried and fretful be
> The beast and false prophet we soon shall see;
> Sad day, sad day, Jesus won't come today!

There is a very good reason why God's wrath will never touch a child of God regardless of whether that wrath is temporal or eternal. The law of the burnt offering suggested the reason:

> And the LORD spake unto Moses, saying, Command Aaron and his sons, saying, This is the law of the burnt offering: It is the burnt offering,

> because of the burning upon the altar all night unto the morning, and the fire of the altar shall be burning in it. And the priest shall put on his linen garment, and his linen breeches shall he put upon his flesh, and take up the ashes which the fire hath consumed with the burnt offering on the altar, and he shall put them beside the altar. And he shall put off his garments, and put on other garments, and carry forth the ashes without the camp unto a clean place. And the fire upon the altar shall be burning in it; it shall not be put out: and the priest shall burn wood on it every morning, and lay the burnt offering in order upon it; and he shall burn thereon the fat of the peace offerings. The fire shall ever be burning upon the altar; it shall never go out. (Leviticus 6:8–13)

The "law of the burnt offering" was concerned with two things—the ashes and the fire. *The fire* was never to go out. God's wrath against sin is as hot and fierce today as when it fell in all of its fury on the Savior, when He bore our sins in His own body on the tree. We shall never know what Jesus suffered during those three dark and dreadful hours, when He who knew no sin was made sin for us.

Millions of people reject the sacrifice of Calvary. That aggravates their doom. Of them, God says, "Of how much sorer punishment, suppose ye, shall he be thought worthy, who hath trodden under foot the Son of God, and hath counted the blood of the covenant, wherewith he was sanctified, an unholy thing, and hath done despite unto the Spirit of grace? It is a fearful thing to fall into the hands of the living God" (Heb. 10:29, 31). The fire of God's wrath burns hot indeed for them. And that fire never goes out. That is one lesson of the law of the burnt offering. God's wrath has been kindled, and it never goes out.

But, by contrast, reference is made to *the ashes* of the burnt offering. The ashes were infinitely precious to God. Indeed, everything about the burnt offering was precious to God because everything about it spoke of the Lord Jesus as being "obedient unto death, even the death of the cross." Because it was precious to God, it had to be precious to the priest and should be precious to us.

The priest, arrayed in linen, was to gather the ashes carefully when the fire had done its work. Then he changed his clothes, took those ashes outside the camp, and carefully put them to rest in a clean place.

What was the significance of all of this care and concern for the ashes? Well, we can stir a fire and get sparks and bring a fire back to a white-hot heat. But we can stir ashes forever, and we will get nothing. *It is impossible to stir God's wrath against one of His own.* God's wrath, so far as His own are concerned, has been completely burned out at Calvary. Nothing is left but ashes. This holds true whether one is referring to His end-times wrath, as here, or to His eternal wrath, as elsewhere.

This point leads Paul to add a further word: *We have not been appointed to wrath.* On the contrary, we have been appointed "to obtain salvation by our Lord Jesus Christ." The word for "salvation" is *sōtēria,* which means literally "deliverance." Sometimes the word is used to depict national deliverance (Luke 1:69–71; Acts 7:25). Sometimes it is used to denote personal deliverance (Acts 27:34; Phil. 1:29; Heb. 11:7). It is, of course, frequently used to depict our spiritual and eternal salvation from sin. Here it is clearly used to declare the deliverance of believers at the *parousia,* at the coming of Christ, from all of the horrors of the end times.

Paul concludes this part of his teaching by telling *why we shall escape.* It is because Jesus "died for us, that, whether we wake [watch] or sleep, we should live together with him" (5:10). The fact is that Calvary covers it all. Our participation in the Rapture, and the deliverance that it brings from the terrors of the ensuing judgment age, does not, in the final analysis, depend on whether we are watchful. That will determine our position in the kingdom but not our participation in the rapture. Our deliverance from end-times wrath by means of this rapture is secured for us by the Lord Jesus, "who died for us." It is the law of the burnt offering. That is what secures our great escape from wrath and woe.

b. Our great escape from worry (5:11)

Paul has one more word to say: "Wherefore comfort yourselves together, and edify one another, even as also ye do." It is hard to see how we can comfort one another with the assurance that we are all going to go through the Great Tribulation, whether in whole or in part. The word for "edify" is *oikodomeō,* which means "to build a house." It is used to depict the development of spiritual growth and the building of Christian character. It implies that spiritual progress results from patient and diligent labor. All believers are to help develop Christian character in others in view of the Lord's return. Paul now turns his full attention to that point.

B. A word of exhortation (5:12–22)

1. As to our values (5:12–13)

The teaching of Paul concerning the Rapture has to do with the universal church. The actual life and growth of the believer during this age, however, is expressed through the local church. Paul develops truth concerning the universal church in Ephesians and truth concerning the local church in Corinthians. The teaching here now concentrates on the local church. Each local church is to be a microcosm of the universal church.

Paul concentrates first on church leaders and *what they do:* "And we beseech you, brethren, to know them which labour among you, and are over you in the Lord, and admonish you" (5:12).

The properly appointed leaders of the local church are vested with authority. The church is not a dictatorship, and it is not a democracy; it is a theocracy. The Holy Spirit qualifies and calls people to roles of leadership (Acts 20:28).

They are to be known—the word is *oida,* which carries the ideas of recognizing, acknowledging, appreciating, and valuing. Spiritual people will quickly recognize those whom God has raised up to evangelize, teach, and pastor the flock. Those who refuse to acknowledge such leadership label themselves as carnal (1 Cor. 2:14).

The scope and sphere of the labors and authority of church leaders is spiritual. They have no authority to encroach on the authority and sphere of secular powers operating within the bounds of their office.

The characteristic of a true spiritual leader is that he labors.

The word used carries the idea of toil that results in weariness. Those who have accepted a role of leadership in the local church are expected to work hard. There is no room for laziness in the Lord's work. Moses so wore himself out that, when he was finally persuaded to delegate some of his responsibilities, it took no less than seventy men to pick up the duties that he laid down (Exod. 18:13–26). Paul himself often worked at his tent making all day and then evangelized and preached at night.

Paul continues with church leaders and *what they deserve:* "And to esteem them very highly in love for their work's sake" (5:13a). One lexicon suggests the phrase "regard them as being so-and-so" as an appropriate rendering of the word for "esteem" *(hēgeomai).* "Hold them in highest honor" is another way to put it.

The early church held Peter and John in high esteem. The Sanhedrin scorned them as "unlearned and ignorant men" (Acts 4:13). When William Carey was aboard ship on his way to India, he was surrounded by peers of the realm and diplomats, the high British officials who ruled the Indian subcontinent. He was looked upon as a nobody. One snobbish individual sneered at the missionary, "Just a shoemaker, aren't you, Carey?" he said disdainfully.

"No, sir," replied William Carey. "I am not a shoemaker. I am only a cobbler."

Nobody knows now the name of that civil servant, but the whole church honors William Carey.

One of the finest preachers I ever heard was a Yorkshire chimney sweep. His hands and nails were grimed with soot that no soap could remove, and his accent was so thick that it could be cut with a knife. But when he stood up to speak, he reigned as a prince in the pulpit and ruled over the affections of God's people. He left an indelible impression on my mind although I heard him only once. Many years later, I was trying to prepare a message on the lost ax head. I recalled this man, his oratory in the pulpit, and his sermon on this very subject, and I blessed his memory. I found the long-forgotten key to his miracle that he had placed in my hand in that service so many years ago.

After this warm commendation of the elders, Paul adds a brief note calling for peace to reign in the church. Eldership frequently calls for attention to be paid to dissention among the believers (5:13b).

2. As to our virtue (5:14–15)

Paul now begins a series of short, staccato statements in which he fires off a number of brief but pregnant and memorable statements regarding Christian conduct. The whole theme of the epistle being the second coming of Christ, we can surely take for granted that these admonitions are given to prepare us for that anticipated event. We can almost hear him preface each unerringly thrown dart with the words "The Lord is coming!"

There are, first of all, *people to be helped.* Paul suggests four kinds of people who often present problems to the local church. There are those who are *disorderly:* "Now we exhort you, brethren, warn them that are unruly" (5:14a). The Lord is coming! He is coming to summon the saints to the judgment seat. He is coming to impose law and order on human life and society and to rule the nations with a rod of iron. Lawlessness has no part in Christian life.

The context here has to do with the rule and respect of those whom the Holy Spirit has placed in positions of authority in the local church. The authority of elders is not political. In the New Testament, the Holy Spirit raises them up. The idea that they are nominated for and elected to office by popular vote is quite foreign to the Pauline Epistles and to the illustrations found in the book of Acts.

Nor is the authority of elders moral in the sense that a man with a dominant and forceful personality is allowed to impose his will.

Nor is that authority social. Just because a man moves in aristocratic circles, is far better educated than the average man, or is wealthy does not qualify him for office.

The authority of elders in the local church is spiritual. The power that they exercise comes from their Christian character, their Christlikeness, their knowledge of the Word of God, their care and compassion for other people, and their ability to rule well in their own homes.

The Holy Spirit now tells these men to exercise their God-given authority by warning the disorderly. There is a solemn process of binding and loosing (Matt. 18:15–20). The Lord introduces this sobering function of the local church in a chapter that clearly has to do with the function and government of the church (still in prospect when He spoke) in its local aspect. Indeed, the church is specifically mentioned.

The church is mentioned by name twice in Matthew's gospel and is referred to prophetically elsewhere in that gospel (e.g., the parable of the pearl). The first mention of the church in Matthew is a reference to the *universal* church (Matt. 16:17–19), and the authority to bind and loose was vested in Peter (Matt. 16:19).

The second mention of the church in Matthew introduces the *local* church (Matt. 18:1–35). Three functions of the local church are mentioned in that chapter, which deals with the *reception* of the believer (Matt. 18:1–10), the *restoration* of the backslider (Matt. 18:11–14), and the *reconciliation* of brethren (Matt. 18:15–35).

It is in connection with the excommunication of an unruly brother that the Lord again mentions binding and loosing and, this time, vests that authority in the local church. The average local church today is weak and divided because it has abandoned sound doctrine, uses unscriptural practices to select its officers, and has lost the will and the power to carry out effective spiritual discipline.

There are those, too, who are *despondent:* "Comfort the feebleminded," Paul says (5:14b). The word used means literally "those of little soul." It refers to those who are dispirited or fainthearted. It really has nothing to do with mental deficiency, although doubtless the feebleminded do have a claim upon the care and compassion of the church. The Lord is coming! Reach out to the despondent. They are the opposite of the unruly. The unruly are too sure of themselves, and the despondent lack confidence in themselves. They cannot take criticism. Off they go in a huff the moment someone disagrees with them or hurts their feelings. They are afraid of persecution. They worry about the future.

The word used here for "comfort" means "to speak with someone," that is, to speak kindly or soothingly. It suggests pacifying someone, speaking persuasively and tenderly. The fainthearted need constant encouragement. Often, we tend to be impatient with such people. They call for so much of our time and attention. We regard them somewhat as a burden; not so with the Lord.

When the children of Israel came out of Egypt, the rate of march was not set by the strongest but by the weakest. Something beautiful is said about Ittai and his noble six hundred men. When they came in a body to take sides with David at the time of the Absalom rebellion, these Philistine warriors, converts of David, were quite prepared to fight to the very last man and die for David. Ittai told David so. David passed them in a parade before him. The Holy Spirit says, "And Ittai the Gittite passed over, and all his men, *and all the little ones* that were with him" (2 Sam. 15:22). Ittai was as much concerned about the little ones as he was about his grim-faced swordsmen. It is a poor excuse for Christianity that has little or no concern for the feeble ones among the flock of God.

Then, too, there are those who are *dependent:* "Support the weak," Paul says (5:14c). The word refers to those "without strength." The Lord is coming! Reach out to the weak. The philosophy of the world takes little enough account of the weak. The devilish doctrine of Darwin is what the public schools teach and what the media promote. Darwin's doctrine is summarized by a single phrase: "the survival of the fittest." More than once in our generation, we have seen that doctrine applied with ruthless thoroughness to human life and society. It is the underlying concept of both Nazism and communism. Hitler used it to support his concept of the master race. All who were not of Aryan blood were considered inferior. Some people were to be reduced to perpetual slavery. Others were to be exterminated. Christianity was scorned. Its doctrine of grace and compassion and care for the weak, the infirm, the handicapped, the disenfranchised, the poor, the aged, the sick, and the feebleminded was treated with contempt. Only the fit should be allowed to live. Hitler wanted to breed a race of blonde giants, supermen who were worthy citizens of his thousand-year reich.

In Paul's day, Rome and Greece had much the same attitude. Not until Christ came did the world at large see exhibited a care and a concern—regardless of religion, race, or response—for the failures and misfits of society. Christianity taught the world the value of a human life. Christianity built hospitals, asylums, and orphanages. Christianity broke the back of slavery, emancipated women, campaigned against prostitution, and fought for the repeal of unjust laws. Our modernistic society has forgotten the debt it owes to the Judeo-Christian ethic.

"Support the weak," Paul said. The word used for "support" means "cleave to," "faithfully care for," or "keep close by." We must not march on heedlessly, rejoicing in our strength. That's not the way the Christian army goes to war. It never abandons the weak. After all, the passing of time robs most of us of our strength and leaves us numbered among the weak. The Lord was always willing to stay close by the weak. Much of His ministry was concerned with healing the sick, feeding the hungry, and defending those who were unable to fend off their foes. Jesus is coming! Let us be found doing what He did when He comes—helping those who need to be helped.

Then there are those who are *different:* "Be patient toward all men" (5:14d). The word for "patient" means to be long-tempered, in contrast to being short-tempered. The idea of long-suffering implies some form of provocation or outright persecution. The Thessalonians had tasted that. The kind of patience, or long-suffering, that Paul demands is one of the fruits of the Spirit (Gal. 5:22). He says that it is one of the characteristics of *agapē* love (1 Cor. 13:4). It is not of mushroom growth. James likened the person who had developed it to the farmer who has long patience to wait for the rains to bring his crops to harvest (James 5:7). "The coming of the Lord draweth nigh," is James's immediate comment (James 5:8). God exercises this kind of long-suffering toward sinners (Rom. 2:4), a long-suffering that the unsaved often misinterpret, Paul warns.

Within the fellowship of the local church, we find all kinds of people. Many of them are, by nature, quite incompatible. They would never be found grouped together anywhere else. In the fellowship of the church, doctors, lawyers, and professionals rub shoulders with plumbers, clerks, and shop hands. Cultured socialites sit down with farmers and fishermen. People of opposite temperaments seek to work together for the cause of Christ. Converted thieves, harlots, and drug addicts fellowship with saved housewives, policemen, and athletes. Rich and poor make common cause. Young and old, wise and foolish, and gifted and retarded are all thrown together and united by the mystical bonds of Christ. Nor is this just a casual association of people brought together temporarily by some fortuitous chain of circumstances. We are bound together by a common faith, the blood of Christ, and the baptizing work of the Holy Spirit; we are members of Christ's body and members one of another (1 Cor. 12:12–27). With so many and varied natural differences, and with each person at a different stage of spiritual development, no wonder Paul calls for "long-suffering toward all men."

But there are not only people to be helped but also *principles to be held* (5:15). Paul says, "See that none render evil for evil unto any man; but ever follow that which is good, both among yourselves, and to all men." Jesus is coming! We must learn to be like Him because that is what He was like. He loved Judas just as much as He loved John. He loved Annas just as much as He loved Andrew. He loved Pilate just as much as He loved Peter. He loved the man who spat in His face just as much as He loved the woman who washed His feet with tears. He loved the dying thief who went to paradise, and He loved the other thief who died still cursing Him. He would have saved him, too, only he wouldn't let Him. He rendered evil to no man. He ever followed what was good toward both His own disciples and all men.

In affirming all of these injunctions for holy living, Paul is reminding us of a spiritual principle. Only Jesus can live the Christian life. He lived it for thirty-three and a half years. "He went about doing good" was Peter's pregnant summary of the life of Christ (Acts 10:38).

Nor did He live His extraordinary life on different terms than those required of us. He was always absolutely and completely God. However, the Lord Jesus made Himself wholly available to His Father in all situations. He did not draw upon His own deity. He recognized that every demand upon Him was a demand upon His Father. The Father, correspondingly, made Himself wholly available to Jesus. The Holy Spirit was the Mediator between all that Jesus was *as Man* and all that the Father was *as God.*

We, too, as regenerated believers, must make ourselves wholly available to the Lord Jesus. Every demand upon us is a demand upon the Lord Jesus. The Lord Jesus makes Himself wholly available to us, and the Holy Spirit is the Mediator between all of our human needs and all of the Lord's divine enabling.

It is a simple fact of Scripture, common sense, and daily experience that, apart from Christ, it is utterly impossible for even the sincerest born again believer to live the kind of life that God demands (John 15:4–5) in his own strength.

3. As to our victory (5:16–22)

Paul's pointed demands are now shorter and sharper than ever. He has a word to say about *praise:* "Rejoice evermore" (5:16). The Lord is coming! That should be cause enough for rejoicing. There is no point in looking at the long time that has now elapsed since the promise was given. He could have come at any time in all of that lengthy period, but He didn' t. So now the promise is nearer than it has ever been. We are to rejoice.

Those to whom this admonition was first addressed were suffering persecution. No matter! Let them rejoice. Paul could have reminded them of the words of Jesus: "Blessed are ye, when men shall revile you, and persecute you, and shall say all manner of evil against you falsely, for my sake. Rejoice, and be exceeding glad: for great is your reward in heaven" (Matt. 5:11–12).

When Paul wrote to Philippi, one of Thessalonica's sister cities in Macedonia, he urged them to display joy and also to rejoice. When they read the words *rejoice evermore* in this letter, the Thessalonian believers might have been tempted to say, "Well, it's all very well for him. He's safe there in Corinth. Here we are in the midst of persecution in Thyatira."

Paul could have said, "Do you want to see my back?" Maybe some of them had seen it. When Paul wrote his epistle, full to overflowing with rejoicing, to the Philippians, he was in prison in Rome, awaiting trial before Nero. He was facing the real possibility of a death sentence, for Nero had changed, for the worse, since the day Paul appealed to his Roman citizenship. "Rejoice evermore!" he said.

After all, the praising person is the prevailing person. What can the enemy do to the man who is so full of joy, the second fruit of the Spirit, that no matter what happens, his soul overflows with song?

Paul has a word, also, about *prayer* (5:17–18). He tells us two things. First, we have *access at all times:* "Pray without ceasing," he says (5:17). The door to the throne room of the universe has been thrown wide open. Imagine being an American to whom the door of the White House and the door to the president's office is always open, or imagine being a Britisher able to walk into No. 10 Downing Street in London at will. We have something better than that—open access at all times to the immediate presence of God. Well, the veil *has* been rent. We *can* obtain instant audience day or night. We can have boldness to enter into the holiest by the blood of Jesus (Heb. 10:19–20).

God says, "Come on in! I'm so glad to see you! Stay as long as you like. Talk to Me about anything you like! Tell Me about your family and friends. Tell Me about where you work. Tell Me about your church. Tell Me about where you live and all about your neighbors. Tell Me your troubles, your joys and sorrows, your hopes and fears, your sins and shortcomings, and your goals and ambitions."

Indeed, God urges us to "pray without ceasing." We can pray with the upward glancing of the eye. We can pray when waiting for a bus or when driving the car. We can pray as we meet someone or say good-bye. Prayer does not have to be sermonic or even structured. When Nehemiah was given his golden opportunity to ask the Persian emperor for permission to go to the Promised Land to rebuild the walls of Jerusalem, Scripture says, "Then the king said unto me, For what dost thou make request? So I prayed to the God of heaven. And I said unto the king, . . . send me . . . unto the city . . . that I may build it" (Neh. 2:4–5). We can be sure that Nehemiah, when he prayed, did not pray like Solomon when he was dedicating the temple or like Daniel when he was confessing Israel's sins. No, indeed! Nehemiah's prayer was what Guy King once called "a sky telegram." It did not even need words. God can read the unformed words of a praying heart.

Paul wants us to know, too, that when it comes to prayer, we not only have access at all times but also must have *acceptance in all things.* It's no use for us to pray, "Not my will but thine be done," and then to rebel against what God sends by way of answer. "In every thing give thanks: for this is the will of God in Christ Jesus concerning you" (5:18).

Years ago, I heard Alan Redpath tell an amusing story at the Moody Bible Institute spiritual emphasis conference. A friend of his seems to have read this very verse in his morning devotions. He decided to put it into practice. Starting that very morning, he would give thanks in everything.

He was leaving Mobile, Alabama, by Greyhound bus that morning for an all-day trip. It was one of those hot and humid summer days, and it was back before air-conditioning was common in buses and cars. The man arrived at the bus station in good time and secured himself a seat by the window. "Thank You for this window seat, Lord," he said. "It's going to be a hot trip, but at least I can get some breeze." The bus began to fill up. However, the seat next to him remained vacant. He said, "Thank You, Lord. It's going to be a hot trip, but at least I will have some room to spread out." The driver took his place, started the bus, and closed the door. "Thank You, Lord," the man said. "You've kept this seat beside me empty."

Just as the bus was about to pull away from the terminal, however, someone banged on the door. It was a late-arriving passenger, a very large woman towing behind her a very small boy. She clambered aboard, pouring with perspiration and glowing with heat like a furnace. She came down the aisle of the bus, passed a number of empty seats, and flopped heavily down into the seat beside this man. She was quite unable to limit her bulk to the allotted space. The overflow pressed hot and heavy against the dismayed and disappointed man. Waves of heat and the strong odor of perspiration engulfed him. The woman hauled her little boy upon her lap, and he began to howl and kick his feet. The man received his share of the flying feet on his legs. The woman slapped the little boy, but that only made him worse. By way of consolation, the woman pulled out a pack of cigarettes, lit one, and blew out volumes of smoke that added immeasurably to the man's discomfort. The boy settled down. The cigarette smoldered. The woman fell asleep. As she relaxed, her bulk sagged heavily in the direction of the unfortunate man, who was now pressed so hard against the side of the bus he could hardly breathe. Tentative shoves proved that he was hopelessly trapped. He sat there in growing misery, his temperature rising, his limbs cramped, and his senses assailed with smoke and body odor.

Then he thought of his morning's text: "In every thing give thanks; for this is the will of God in Christ Jesus concerning you." He said, "Lord, what is there in *this* situation for which I can be thankful?" He waited. It flashed into his mind: "You can be thankful that you are not married to her!"

The point is that God expects that we shall rise triumphant over our circumstances. There is always something for which to be thankful.

We notice, too, that the apostle says, "*In* every thing give thanks." He does not say, *"For* everything give thanks."

The preposition here is *en.* "It denotes being or remaining *within,* with the primary idea of rest and continuance. It has regard to place and space." For instance, Jesus told His disciples, "I send you forth as sheep *in* the midst of wolves" (Matt. 10:16). When Jesus found Himself being pressured by the thronging crowds, "He withdrew himself *into* [*en*] the wilderness, and prayed" (Luke 5:16). It also refers to a sphere of action. We read of Herod that he had "laid hold of John, and bound him, and put him *in* [*en*] prison" (Matt. 14:3). Paul congratulated the Roman Christians and thanked God for them. He said, "I thank my God through Jesus Christ for you all, that your faith is spoken of *throughout* [*en*] the whole world" (Rom. 1:8). He told them later in his letter that, by virtue of their having been buried with Christ by baptism unto death, therefore "as Christ was raised up from the dead by the glory of the Father, even so we also should walk *in* [*en*] newness of life" (Rom. 6:4).

We find ourselves in indigent circumstances, facing persecution or bereavement, or pressured by events beyond our control. We can complain, worry, or rebel, or we can thank God that He is still on the throne and that He is too wise to make any mistakes, too loving to be unkind, and too powerful to be thwarted in this sublime purpose (Rom. 8:28). He has some wonderful lesson to teach, some glorious purpose to fulfill; and as the catchy little chorus puts it, "We'll understand it better by and by."

We have the supreme example of the Lord Jesus, who took that loaf into His hands in the Upper Room; declared that this loaf represented His body; deliberately broke it, signifying what was soon to be done to Him; and *gave thanks* (1 Cor. 11:23–24).

Paul has something to say, also, about *presumption:* "Quench not the Spirit" (5:19). The Holy Spirit is a person. He can be resisted, grieved, and quenched.

The *unsaved* can resist the Holy Spirit. Stephen, in his terrible indictment of the Sanhedrin, said, "Ye stiffnecked and uncircumcised in heart and ears, ye do always resist the Holy Ghost: as your fathers did, so do ye" (Acts 7:51).

An individual *believer* can grieve the Holy Spirit. Paul warned the Ephesians to let no corrupt communication come out of their mouths. "And grieve not the holy Spirit of God, whereby ye are sealed unto the day of redemption" (Eph. 4:30). He goes on to warn against other sins. The word *grieve* is a love word. You cannot grieve someone who does not love you. You may annoy him, infuriate him, or disgust him, but you cannot grieve him.

A *church* can quench the Holy Spirit. The ascended Lord warned the Ephesian church that their loss of love for Him was so serious that unless they repented, unless they experienced a Holy Spirit revival, He would remove their lamp stand (Rev. 2:5). Where are all of those great churches today that once flourished in Asia Minor? Islam holds empire now in many a place where once revival fires burned.

The word *quench (sbennumi)* is used literally and figuratively of extinguishing a fire. The word here is in the present continuous tense. In other words, Paul urges the church at Thessalonica to "desist from quenching" the Holy Spirit. The corresponding adjective is interesting. It is *asbestos,* the name we have given to a fire-resisting substance commonly used, until recently, in places where we wanted to make it difficult or impossible for a fire to get started or spread.

We all know churches that were once on fire for God. Souls were being saved; lives were being blessed. Then false doctrine took root, squabbles broke out, jealousy reared its head, or immorality was countenanced—and the Spirit was quenched. He simply left the church. For a while, the usual machinery kept things going, but—"Ichabod" had been written across its doors—"the glory is departed" (1 Sam. 4:21).

Paul has something to say, too, about *prophecy* (5:20–21). In the first place, we are not to be *disparaging* of it (5:20). We do need to remember, however, that the gift of prophecy in the New Testament church was a temporary phenomenon. Paul says so himself (1 Cor. 13:8). Like the gift of tongues and the other sign gifts, direct utterance of truth by means of Holy Spirit inspiration and illumination has served its purpose. Now that the New Testament canon is complete, direct prophetic utterance and the gift of the prophet have ceased. The prophets of the New Testament, like the apostles, were necessary to make truth available to scattered congregations before the New Testament was committed to writing and in general circulation. Apostles and prophets are both associated with the foundation of the church (Eph. 2:20; 3:5) and both have now been removed. The gifts of the evangelist, the pastor, and the teacher, however, endure (Eph. 4:11).

A Mormon once asked me if we had apostles and prophets in our church. I said, "No!"

He replied, "How can your church be a New Testament church then?"

I explained the role of a New Testament prophet and its temporary nature.

He said, "Suppose that I were to tell you that God has raised up a new prophet for this age?"

I replied, "What does he prophesy? If it's in the Bible, I don't need it, and if it isn't in the Bible, I don't want it. Besides, if you are talking about Joseph Smith, I have to tell you that he was a false prophet." He consigned me to hell and left me to my doom.

It was the presence of false prophets in the early church that made the exercise of this gift suspect. Its place has been taken now by preaching. The New Testament prophet received his message by direct illumination of the Holy Spirit. Thus, he was able to make New Testament truth available to those who had no other access to it. The preacher also makes New Testament truth available, but his message is based on the completed revelation contained in the Bible.

Paul, then, has to warn his friends *not* to be disparaging of prophecy, for prophecy was still a valid gift in those early days of the church. On the other hand, he has to warn them not to be *deceived* by it: "Prove all things; hold fast that which is good" (5:21). Excellent advice! The Lord is coming! We would not want to find ourselves gathered with those who pay no heed to the Scriptures. Nor would we want to find ourselves associated with those who have gullibly swallowed the deceptions of false teachers. Paul calls for a proper balance. Teachers are to be tested by Scripture.

Years ago, I lived in a town in northern Canada. Among other things, I was engaged in planting a church. A number of people were won to Christ and added to the fellowship, including one young man who had suffered from a chronic illness. He claimed to have been healed by a doctor who specialized in curing ailments by means of diet. The diet was an odd one. According to the doctor, one should never mix proteins and carbohydrates at the same meal.

Our new convert was as enthusiastic about his diet as he was about his newfound faith. He wanted us to add his diet to our doctrine! "Well," he exclaimed, "the Lord surely wants what's best for us. Surely He wants us to be healthy. This diet works. It has worked wonders for me. It will help people to keep well so that they can serve the Lord better. We should teach it along with the Bible."

While I was digesting this relatively harmless heresy and wondering how to refuse him without offending him, another of our new Christians spoke up.

"Ron," he said, "do you believe that the Lord created us?"

"Of course I do."

"Do you believe that, since the Lord made us, He would know what was best for us? That He knows what was good for us to eat and what was not good for us to eat?"

"Well, yes."

"Then how come, if your diet is right, the Lord fed proteins and carbohydrates at the same meal to the five thousand when He gave them loaves and fishes to eat?"

Needless to say, one verse of Scripture put an end to the proposed new doctrine! Paul said, "Prove all things; hold fast that which is good." The Lord is coming!

He has a final word. It is about *propriety:* "Abstain from all appearance of evil" (5:22). In the early days of my life as a traveling preacher, I occasionally found myself in some odd and awkward situations. Nowadays, I invariably stay in motels, but years ago it was far more common to billet the visiting preacher with one of the church families. Some of these experiences were pleasant enough. Some of them were not so pleasant.

On one occasion, I was directed to the home of a man and his wife. They had one small child. I arrived midafternoon on Saturday and had a pleasant enough time. After the Sunday evening service, we all arrived back at the house, and the wife was soon busy preparing a meal. The man disappeared. Shortly afterward he reappeared, dressed in what were obviously work clothes. I thought that perhaps he had something to repair around the house. We sat down at the table, and the man ate a hearty meal. When the meal was over, he disappeared again. Shortly afterward, he reappeared wearing his hat and coat. I thought that his repair work must concern the outside of the house. "Well, good night, brother," he said. "I'm off to work now. I'm on the night shift." And off he went, leaving me alone in the house for the night with his wife and small child.

It was an awkward and embarrassing situation for everyone concerned, except for the man himself, who went blithely to work, apparently oblivious to the awkward situation he left behind.

Paul says that we are to "abstain from all appearance of evil." The word for "abstain" is *apechō.* The immediate context suggests holding oneself back from false teaching, but evidently the word itself is more comprehensive and includes any kind of wrong behavior. Paul has already used the word in this letter to warn the Thessalonians to "abstain from fornication" (4:3). Peter uses the word in a similar way (1 Peter 2:11). The word for *appearance* means "from every form of" or "from every sort or kind" of evil. The word for "evil" is *ponēros.* It is used of Satan (Matt. 5:37) and of demons (Luke 7:21). The Lord taught us to pray, "deliver us from evil" (Luke 11:4). The Lord is coming! We must not allow ourselves even to be placed in a situation where our testimony might be compromised even inadvertently. Steer clear of evil! That's Paul's rule.

PART 7

Conclusion

1 Thessalonians 5:23–28

The apostle now concludes his letter with half a dozen final remarks. We have, first, *a parting intercession:* "And the very God of peace sanctify you wholly; and I pray God your whole spirit and soul and body be preserved blameless unto the coming [*parousia*] of our Lord Jesus Christ" (5:23). Jesus is coming! We need to keep ourselves in "spotless integrity" in view of our meeting with Him in the air. Who would want to meet the Lord, caught in the act of some shameful sin or involved in some mean squabble?

The reference here to our whole spirit, soul, and body is arresting. The soul and the spirit, which comprise the immaterial part of our being, are actually separate entities. However, we, as human beings, sometimes have trouble dividing between them, although the distinction is clear to God (Heb. 4:12). Man is of a higher order of creation than the animals, just as the animals are a higher order of creation than the plants and plants than minerals. Angels are higher still in the order of things (Heb. 2:7).

The higher animals, like men, have bodies and souls. In an animal, the governing principle of behavior is instinct; an animal does what it does because it is what it is. Each kind is locked into its own particular behavior pattern. In man, the soul embraces the intellect, the emotions, and the will. Since the Fall, conscience—the inner knowledge of right and wrong—has been added.

God, however, has given to people something that He gave to no animal—a spirit. "The spirit of man is the candle of the LORD" (Prov. 20:27). In the case of human beings, the spirit makes us God conscious. Before the Fall, the human spirit seems to have been inhabited by the Holy Spirit. Thus, in the case of people, the governing principle was not instinct but an intelligent, emotional, and volitional cooperation of soul and spirit with the indwelling Holy Spirit. The body was the vehicle for expressing human life in terms of our physical environment and our nature.

The Fall of man ruined all of that. The Holy Spirit now applies the Word of God to man's conscience to awaken in him a conviction of his sin and utter lostness. The same inspired Word shows that the blood of Christ alone can cleanse from sin. When we accept Christ as Savior, the blood of Christ cleanses us (1 John 1:8–10), and the Holy Spirit quickens us, returns to take up His abode in us, and turns our bodies into God's temples.

The redemptive process has not yet been consummated by the redemption of our body, so we are under constant attack from our three cardinal foes—the world, the flesh, and the Devil. Hence, the need that Paul expressed here, that the very God of peace sanctify us wholly and that our whole spirit, soul, and body be preserved blameless until the day of the Lord's return. Although the world, the flesh, and the Devil are against us, the Father, Son, and Holy Spirit—the whole Trinity of the Godhead—are on our side. We can be thankful for that.

Now Paul gives *a parting proclamation:* "Faithful is he that calleth you, who also will do it" (5:24). There is no possibility of a truly saved and regenerated person's ever being lost again. God is faithful. He keeps His Word. He is still on the gold standard; all of His promises are backed by the pure gold of His own character.

When He called us, He knew all about us and took everything into account, including the fact of our personally trusting Christ as Savior and Lord. As Paul has said elsewhere, "For whom he did foreknow, he also did predestinate to be conformed to the image of his Son, that he might be the firstborn among many brethren. Moreover whom he did predestinate, them he also called: and whom he called, them he also justified: and whom he justified, them he also glorified" (Rom. 8:29–30). All of the verbs in this passage are in the past tense. It is already settled in heaven. We need have no doubt that He "will do it," as Paul says. Our eternal security is settled beyond all question.

Then comes *a parting supplication:* "Brethren, pray for us." Paul was a great believer in prayer. He had just prayed for them (5:23), now he asked them to pray for him. He wanted them to have a share in what was being accomplished at Corinth. He wanted them to pray for his continued anointing of the Holy Spirit. He wanted them to pray that souls would be saved, a great church established right there in the pornography capital of the Roman Empire. He wanted them to pray for his safety, for his converts, for his eventual return to Thessalonica, and for God's clear and unmistakable leading in his life. He wanted them to pray for Silas and for young Timothy. He wanted them to pray for him. If Paul were to have set out all of his prayer requests, probably the world itself could scarce have held all of the prayer books he could have written! He contents himself with a brief "Brethren, pray for us."

He follows with *a parting salutation:* "Greet all the brethren with an holy kiss" (5:26). "Give a hearty handshake all around the brotherhood" is one vivid way it has been put. How Paul wished that he could have been there to do it himself. We can imagine some presiding elder of the church at Thessalonica reading this letter to a packed house. The people have hung on every word. No sooner will the reading be finished than they'll want it read all over again. Then they'll each want a copy. Everyone with paper and pen to his name will sit down and write down the words while the letter is read at dictation speed. But at these words—"Greet all the brethren with an holy kiss"—we can see the elder hastily finish reading the last two verses, then step down and faithfully go around the entire company and personally greet each one as Paul's surrogate. The gospel makes all men equal. If Paul had been there, he would have left nobody out. He would have greeted each one personally, regardless of rank, in the appropriate and socially accepted way.

There was *a parting intimation:* "I charge you by the Lord that this epistle be read unto all the holy brethren" (5:27). For many centuries, the Roman Catholic Church did all in its power to keep the Scriptures from the common people. The only ones who were allowed to read them were her ordained priests—and even then only in accordance with a nonexistent—"unanimous consent of the Fathers." Rome's excuse was that the uninitiated would fall into error if they were allowed to read the Bible for themselves. Paul had no such fears. On the contrary, he considered biblically literate laity the best antidote for error. Paul put the church authorities at Thessalonica under a solemn charge to ensure that this letter was read to everyone.

Finally, we have *a parting benediction:* "The grace of our Lord Jesus Christ be with you. Amen" (5:28). The letter has come around full circle and ends where it begins—with grace. Grace takes us back to the beginning. It takes us on to the end. As John Newton put it in the song "Amazing Grace,"

> 'Twas grace that taught my heart to fear,
> And grace my fears relieved;
> How precious did that grace appear
> The hour I first believed!
>
> Thru many dangers, toils, and snares
> I have already come;
> 'Tis grace hath brought me safe thus far,
> And grace will lead me home.
>
> When we've been there ten thousand years,
> Bright shining as the sun,
> We've no less days to sing God's praise
> Than when we'd first begun.

So ends this first letter. From page to page, Paul has kept to the fore the coming of Christ for His own. He has now wound it all up with plea after plea for a belief that behaves. For Jesus is coming—soon!

Dr. Harry Ironside, for many years the beloved pastor of Moody Memorial Church in Chicago, was speaking to a group of students who were preparing for the ministry. One of them asked him, "Dr. Ironside, what would you do if you *knew* for *sure* that the Lord was coming back tonight?"

Said Dr. Ironside, "I'd have something warm to drink in about an hour or so, and then I'd go to bed."

The young man seemed shocked. So Dr. Ironside added, "Gentlemen, I try to live every day in the light and hope of His coming. I would see no reason to change my usual routine."

Exploring 2 THESSALONIANS

Complete Outline of 2 Thessalonians

PART 1: INTRODUCTION (1:1–2)

- A. Greeting (1:1)
  - 1. Who it was from (1:1a)
  - 2. Who it was for (1:1b)
- B. Grace (1:2)

PART 2: PAUL'S WORD OF ADMIRATION (1:3–12)

- A. A word of undiluted praise (1:3–4)
  - 1. What Paul was impelled to do (1:3a)
  - 2. What Paul was impressed to declare (1:3b–4)
    He praised God for:
    - a. Growth unstunted (1:3b)
    - b. Grace unstinted (1:3c)
    - c. Glory unsurpassed (1:4)
      - (1) Where Paul gloried (1:4a)
      - (2) Why Paul gloried (1:4b)
- B. A word of undisputed promise (1:5–10)
  - 1. As to the proof (1:5–6)
    - a. God is righteous in judging saints (1:5)
    - b. God is righteous in judging sinners (1:6)
  - 2. As to the present (1:7a)
  - 3. As to the prospect (1:7b–10)
    - a. A day of revelation is coming (1:7b–c)
      - (1) He is coming from His home (1:7b)
      - (2) He is coming with His hosts (1:7c)

- b. A day of revenge is coming (1:8–9)
  - (1) The essential nature of His wrath (1:8)
  - (2) The eternal nature of His wrath (1:9)
- c. A day of reward is coming (1:10)

C. A word of undefeated prayer (1:11–12)
1. When Paul prayed (1:11a)
2. What Paul prayed (1:11b–12)
   - a. About the nature of their calling (1:11b)
   - b. About the name of the Christ (1:12)

PART 3: PAUL'S WORD OF ADMONITION (2:1–3:15)

A. The greatness of the coming lie (2:1–12)
1. The local deception (2:1–2)
   - a. The plea of the apostle (2:1–2a)
   - b. The plot of the adversary (2:2b–e)
     - (1) Why the deception convinced (2:2b–d)
       - (a) A false spirit (2:2b)
       - (b) A forged letter (2:2c)
       - (c) A fabricated prophecy (2:2d)
     - (2) What the deception contended (2:2e)
2. The larger deception (2:3–12)
   - a. The Man of Sin (2:3–6)
     - (1) The coming apostasy (2:3a)
     - (2) The coming apocalypse (2:3b–6)
       - (a) Sovereignly determined (2:3b–4)
         - i. The names of the deceiver (2:3b)
         - ii. The nature of the deceiver (2:4)
           - *a.* His aim (2:4a)
           - *b.* His claim (2:4b)
       - (b) Sovereignly delayed (2:5–6)
         - i. What the Thessalonians had forgotten (2:5)
         - ii. Who the Thessalonians had forgotten (2:6)
   - b. The mystery of sin (2:7–12)
     - (1) The present conflict (2:7)
       - (a) The working of a diabolical activity (2:7a)
       - (b) The working of a divine adversary (2:7b)
     - (2) The prophetic climax (2:8–10)

(a) When (2:8)
(b) Who (2:9–10a)
i. The Antichrist's master (2:9a)
ii. The Antichrist's miracles (2:9b–10a)
(c) Why (2:10b)
(3) The practical conclusion (2:11–12)
(a) Delusion (2:11)
i. It will be sent (2:11a)
ii. It will be strong (2:11b)
(b) Damnation (2:12)
i. Declared (2:12a)
ii. Deserved (2:12b)

B. The greatness of the Christian life (2:13–3:15)
1. The believer is chosen (2:13–14)
a. The sovereignty of God (2:13a–b)
(1) Something for which to be thankful (2:13a)
(2) Something about which to be thoughtful (2:13b)
b. The salvation of God (2:13c–d)
(1) Receiving the Spirit (2:13c)
(2) Believing the Scripture (2:13d)
c. The splendor of God (2:14)
(1) The gospel declared by Paul (2:14a)
(2) The glory determined for all (2:14b)
2. The believer is challenged (2:15–3:5)
a. To trust (2:15–17)
(1) Our responsibility (2:15)
(2) Our resources (2:16–17)
(a) Whence they come (2:16a)
(b) What they convey (2:16b–17)
i. Divine love (2:16b)
ii. Divine life (2:17)
b. To travail (3:1–2)
(1) An exhortation (3:1a)
(2) An explanation (3:1b–2)
(a) Pray for the proclamation of the message (3:1b)
(b) Pray for the protection of the messengers (3:2)
c. To triumph (3:3–5)

- (1) Because of the Lord's reliability (3:3–4)
  - (a) The Lord and His purposes (3:3)
    - i. To ground them (3:3a)
    - ii. To guard them (3:3b)
  - (b) The Lord and His people (3:4)
- (2) Because of the Lord's return (3:5)
  - (a) A word about their position (3:5a)
  - (b) A word about their patience (3:5b)

3. The believer is charged (3:6–15)
   - a. The need for discipline (3:6–11)
     - (1) Paul's exhortation (3:6)
     - (2) Paul's example (3:7–10)
       - (a) His integrity (3:7)
       - (b) His industry (3:8)
       - (c) His intention (3:9)
       - (d) His intimation (3:10)
     - (3) Paul's exclamation (3:11)
   - b. The nature of discipline (3:12–15)
     - (1) Discipline avoided (3:12–13)
       - (a) A word of command (3:12)
       - (b) A word of caution (3:13)
     - (2) Discipline advocated (3:14–15)
       - (a) Excommunication (3:14)
       - (b) Expectation (3:15)

PART 4: CONCLUSION (3:16–18)

- A. Paul's last prayer (3:16)
- B. Paul's last precaution (3:17)
- C. Paul's last pronouncement (3:18)

PART 1

Introduction

2 Thessalonians 1:1–2

A. Greeting (1:1)

Paul's first letter to the Thessalonians had been sent on its way. Paul must have felt a certain satisfaction in having thus addressed his friends and converts at Thessalonica. He had encouraged them, enlightened them, and exhorted them to keep belief and behavior in balance. He had put in clearer perspective the great truth of the second coming of Christ. Expectation of the Lord's return was high. After all, it was only about twenty years since the Lord had left the world. He had promised to come back. No date had been set, but His coming was imminent; it could be expected at any time. That it was to be immediate was quite another question. Conditions in both the church and the world, however, might well have heightened expectancy.

Paul's letter had answered some of their questions, but now a different cause for concern had surfaced. In his letter, Paul had referred to "we which are alive and remain" (1 Thess. 4:17). Apparently, some people had seized upon the phrase and taken it to mean that Christ would return in Paul's lifetime, and the idea had taken root. Added to that misconception were certain spurious communications, supposedly from God, that added fuel to the fire. The Thessalonian church was agog with excitement. Some people were filled with fanatical expectation and even gave up their jobs in anticipation. Others were filled with fearful apprehension. After all, terrible things were to happen. In spite of the positive assurances in Paul's letter that the church would not go through the Great Tribulation, some people still were not convinced. Their false teaching had aggravated the situation.

So Paul had to write a second letter. We can be glad that he did because he tells us some fascinating details about end-times events that are mentioned nowhere else in the Bible. Besides giving us a vivid description of the Antichrist, he tells us that the Day of the Lord will not come until after two events take place: an *apostasy* in the church and an *apocalypse* (an unveiling) in the world. The Devil's messiah must come and be revealed in all of his glitter and glamour to a bemused, Christ-rejecting world. The Day of the Lord is not the same day as the day of Christ—an expression that refers to the Rapture.

Each of the dispensations had ended in apostasy, failure, and judgment. The current dispensation will be no exception. The previous dispensation ended with the crucifixion of Christ; the current dispensation will end, for the world, with the reign of the Antichrist. Events today are accelerating the pace. Both the church and the world are heading toward the climax of the age.

This second epistle corrects new errors in the Thessalonian church. It also deals with end-times events. It was probably written toward the end of Paul's stay in Corinth or sometime near the end of A.D. 53.

Paul begins with these words: "Paul, and Silvanus, and Timotheus, unto the church of the Thessalonians in God our Father and the Lord Jesus Christ"—virtually the same words with which he began his earlier letter.

Paul, Silas, and Timothy: the evangelist, the teacher, and the pastor. They were God's Big Three for invading the European continent for Christ and changing the course of history. Paul was commander in chief. He took the lead, made the decisions, set the pace, engaged the foe, and did the preaching.

Silas was second in command. He never sought the limelight, never broke rank, never tried to hurry the pace, never dragged his heels, and was never out of step. In the synagogues, he must have been invaluable to Paul. Silas might have spread the word quietly to those in charge, the Jews who had trusted Christ, that Paul was a trained rabbi, indeed, that he had been a disciple of the renowned Gamaliel, the heir and successor of the revered Hillel himself. He might have reminded the Gentiles that Paul was a citizen of Rome. Silas's command of the Greek language would open many doors. And in the heated debates that so often followed, Silas would be right there, answering questions, adding his testimony, pointing to key Scriptures, and supporting Paul all of the way.

Timothy was Paul's aide-de-camp, ever at the apostle's beck and call, ever ready, and ever willing. He would run here, there, and everywhere at a nod or a word from Paul. No task was too small or too great for Timothy. Paul loved him as though he were his own son.

No general, invading a new continent at the bidding of his king, would have wanted better staff officers or companions in arms than Paul had in these two men. No veterans could have wanted a better commander in chief.

Paul was a cosmopolitan, a citizen of the world. He enjoyed Roman citizenship, had been born and raised a Jew, and had been brought up in a Greek city. He was thoroughly conversant with the best and the worst of all three worlds. He planned with all of the strategy of a Roman, thought with all of the clarity of a Greek, and believed with all of the passion of a Jew. Paul never knew a stranger. He never met a man of whom he was afraid. He never met anyone to whom he could not talk about Jesus. He was at home preaching to the Jewish high priest or the Roman governor as he was talking to the Philippian jailor or Lydia and that handful of women at the riverside. He could talk more sense about the sea than could the captain of a ship. He was as willing to pick up sticks for a campfire as to make tents for a living. He was as unafraid of Nero as he was of Peter. He was as willing to tell a man to his face that he was a hypocrite, even though that man was Israel's high priest, as he was to breathe new life into a poor fellow who had fallen asleep at one of his meetings. He was an intellectual genius, blessed with sound common sense, a heart of gold, a will of iron, and a deathless vision of a lost and dying world desperately in need of Christ.

Silas was an urbanite. More than likely, he had been an eyewitness of Christ's ministry. He was a confidante of the apostles in Jerusalem, loved and trusted by men such as Peter and James. But he wasn' t impulsive like Peter or narrow-minded like the austere James. He tramped the long, dusty highways with Paul. He shared in both the blessings and the beatings. He never intruded himself. If not for the fact that Paul was forever mentioning him in his letters, we would never know that Silas was there.

Timothy was a provincial, half Gentile and half Jew, a sturdy hybrid, more Jew than Gentile through his association with his mother and grandmother and more Gentile than Jew through his association with his pagan father and Paul. Paul trusted him. That about says it all. Paul knew how to size up a man. He did not have a great deal of patience with fools, quitters, or cowards. Paul knew that if he gave Timothy a task, it would be done. Moreover, it would be done promptly and cheerfully. It would be done right.

Paul! Silvanus! Timotheus! The names spoke for themselves to "the church of the Thessalonians in God our Father and the Lord Jesus Christ." That, by the way, is *our* new address. What a magnificent address it is!

Some years ago, I had occasion to write a letter to a believer in Ireland. The letter directed him to a home where he had agreed to call upon a contact that had been made at the World's Fair in Montreal. The address was impressive—"Powers Court Castle"—an address, incidentally, that was connected years ago with the ministry of John Nelson Darby. Although my address down here is nothing so arresting as that, I have another address, held in common by all of the children of God; I have a heavenly address. If anyone wants to get in touch with me at that address, here it is: "The church . . . in God our Father and the Lord Jesus Christ." The postman will probably have trouble finding it, but it is well known to the angels; they hold it in awe. To have that address, one must be a member of the royal family of heaven.

It is a very real address. We have already noted, in Paul's earlier epistle, the significance of that little preposition *in,* but it might be as well to remind ourselves. It "denotes being or remaining *within,* with the primary idea of rest and continuance. It has regard to place and space or sphere of action. . . ." The believer lives "in Christ in God." The concept of being "in Christ" is common in the Pauline Epistles. That is where we "live and move and have our being." It was the Lord Jesus who introduced the concept in His teaching in the Upper Room when He told us to "abide in the vine" (John 15:1–8).

B. Grace (1:2)

Paul continues with his customary greeting: "Grace unto you, and peace, from God our Father and the Lord Jesus Christ." How easily and naturally Paul links the name of the Lord Jesus with the name of the Father. He took the deity of Christ for granted.

Never to his dying day would he forget his first encounter with Jesus on the Damascus road. All of his doubts were settled in one blinding flash of light and a few words addressed directly to him by the Lord from heaven. At the same time, he, the archpersecutor of the church, learned the meaning of grace. There he lay, prostrate on the ground—"the chief of sinners," as he later described himself—with the blood of the martyrs on his hands and a warrant in his pocket to extend his depredations to Damascus. What did he deserve but instant death and eternal damnation? But what did he receive? Grace! He was not only forgiven then and there but also called and commissioned to be an apostle of the Lamb, to take the news of a risen Christ to the great Gentile world on the fringes of which he had lived all of his life.

It was then, also, that he learned the meaning of peace. The turmoil that had raged in his soul ever since he had met Stephen and had a hand in his death was stilled at last. Stephen had said that he saw heaven opened and the Son of Man standing at the right hand of God (Acts 7:55–56). The testimony had filled young Saul of Tarsus with fury. Now, however, he knew that Stephen was a faithful witness because now, he, Saul, saw heaven opened and saw *Jesus!* Stephen had prayed for his forgiveness. Now he was forgiven indeed. Peace! The war was over!

No wonder Paul never tired of writing these two wonderful words into his letters. They simply summarized what the gospel was all about.

PART 2

Paul's Word of Admiration

2 Thessalonians 1:3–12

A. A word of undiluted praise (1:3–4)

1. What Paul was impelled to do (1:3a)

Paul could not say enough good about his beloved Thessalonians. His first thought, however, was to tell them how much he prayed for them: "We are bound to thank God always for you, brethren, as it is meet" (1:3a).

The word *bound* here means "to be under obligation." It is used of a man who is in debt and who has to pay what he owes. Paul used the idea behind the word when he told the Romans that he was "debtor both to the Greeks, and to the Barbarians; both to the wise, and to the unwise" to preach the gospel to them (Rom. 1:14). He felt a similar obligation to pray for his converts. It was not only right that he should do so but also required that he would do so. The work of the evangelist does not end when he closes his campaign, makes his final appeal, picks up his check, and leaves town. God lays on him an obligation to pray for his converts.

Who can tell what trials they will have to face at home now that they are saved and what testings they will have to face from those at work, organized religion, and hostile government officials? Who can tell what temptations will assail them from the combined forces of the world, the flesh, and the Devil? They now need to grow in grace and increase in the knowledge of God. They need to develop habits of prayer and Bible study. They need to be baptized, join a good local church, cultivate their spiritual life, learn sound doctrine, let Christ live out His life in them, witness to others, and become active in the ministry of the church. For all of this, someone has to pray. Who more so than the one who led them to the Lord?

Paul's prayers for his friends at Thessalonica took the form of continual thanksgiving. They were responding to the means of grace available to them. They were not perfect; some doctrinal and practical matters still had to be sorted out. But for all of that and for the most part, they were a joy to Paul's heart. He did not have to remind *them* of his apostleship and "pull rank" on them, as he had to do, for instance, with his Galatian converts. The Thessalonian believers would respond to teaching without that kind of warning. He lifted up his heart in thanksgiving to God. It was as much an obligation to give thanks as it was to make requests.

2. What Paul was impressed to declare (1:3b–4)

He elaborates. He thanked God for three things whenever he thought of his Thessalonians. First, he thanked God for *growth unstunted:* "We are bound to thank God always . . . because that your faith groweth exceedingly" (1:3b). Growth is evidence of life. Nobody expects a pebble to grow. Vigorous growth is evidence of vigorous life. The thing that struck the apostle about his Thessalonian converts was their growth in faith. Developing faith is a direct result of occupation with the Word of God, of specific answers to prayer, and of increasing personal knowledge of and confidence in the Lord Jesus. Evidently, the Thessalonians were putting the Lord to the test and growing accordingly.

He thanked God, also, for *grace unstinted:* "and the charity of every one of you all toward each other aboundeth" (1:3c). Not only was their faith growing but also their love. Love is what Christianity is really all about. Henry Drummond called it "the greatest thing in the world." Note Paul's expressions "of every one of you" (which takes in each individual) and "of you all" (which takes in the whole). There was plenty of love to go around—love for God, love for each other, and love for lost people. There was love for the church leaders, love for those who were at all of the meetings and love for those who weren't at the meetings, love for the old people and love for the young people, love for those who gave generously and love for those who were miserly, love for those who stood out boldly for the truth and love for those who were going astray, love for those with charisma and charm and love for those who had no personality at all, love for those who were kind to them and love for those who were cruel to them. No wonder Paul felt bound to give thanks.

Moreover, there was *glory unsurpassed:* "So that we ourselves glory in you in the churches of God for your patience and faith in all your persecutions and tribulations that ye endure" (1:4). The persecution of the believers at Thessalonica was first instigated by the Jews, who hired bullies and bravados to do their dirty work for them (Acts 17:5). They had some of the Christians hauled into court and accused of high treason. Not content with that, they followed the missionary trail to Berea and stirred up the mob there as well. Nor had their hatred and malice subsided. When Timothy went back to visit Thessalonica, the persecution was still going on. It was continuing even as Paul sat down to write his second letter.

Persecution has been the common lot of the church throughout its history. Before long, Nero would make it official. There would be ten terrible outbursts of persecution, lasting on and off for some three hundred years and climaxing in the fearful tribulations under Diocletian. Every age has contributed its martyrs. The roll call of the martyrs at the judgment seat of Christ will be long. The nobility of heaven will be the martyrs, the aristocracy of the church.

What a sight it will be to behold! All of the apostles will receive the martyr's crown if the traditional history of the church is true. Every land will yield its prizewinners. Every age has its quota because the malice of Satan has raged from age to age, if not here, then there; if not there, then somewhere else; if not expressed this way, then that way. The records will show them coming from Nero's garden, where they were used as living torches to shed lurid light on his bestial revels. They will come from the arena, where they were torn to shreds by wild beasts. They will come bearing the marks of crucifixion, the ax, the fagot, and the fire. They will come from the dungeons of the Inquisition, having endured fiendish tortures, and from modern concentration camps, where they experienced starvation, beatings, torture, and death.

And out front is Stephen, the first martyr of the church, followed closely by James, the first of the apostles to die for the faith. Marching in rank, willing to endure privation, heavy punishment, scorn, and contempt; harassed by the law; abused by their neighbors; assaulted, their goods despoiled; and with death itself awaiting them. Paul's beloved Thessalonians will be among their number. Paul gloried in them and told other churches about them. The word that Paul uses for "glorified" is in the superlative. The ordinary word means "to boast" or "to glory." The word here means "to exult."

Paul boasted to other churches about his Macedonian converts. He did so, for instance, to the Corinthian church when he described not so much their willingness to endure persecution as their magnificent method of giving. He wanted the Corinthian believers to know "of the grace of God bestowed on the churches of Macedonia; how that in a great trial of affliction the abundance of their joy and their deep poverty abounded unto the riches of their liberality. For to their power, I bear record," he says, "yea, and beyond their power they were willing of themselves; praying us with much entreaty that we would receive the gift, and take upon us the fellowship of the ministering to the saints. And this they did, not as we hoped, but first gave their own selves to the Lord, and unto us by the will of God" (2 Cor. 8:1–5). Evidently, Paul had been overwhelmed by not only their generosity, made all the more glorious because of their deep poverty, but also the spirit of personal commitment to the Lord and His servants, which accompanied it.

They had backed up this commitment. Their patience and faith, in the midst of continuing persecutions and tribulations, awed Paul. The word *persecutions* points to the malicious hostility of others. The word *afflictions* underlines the agony of body and anguish of mind endured by those being persecuted. The word for "endure" is in the present continuous tense, indicating that the suffering was still occurring.

B. A word of undisputed promise (1:5–10)
   1. As to the proof (1:5–6)

The next two verses deal with the time when God settles accounts, when He deals in judgment, first with His church and then, fearfully indeed, with the world. Behind both judgments is the unimpeachable righteousness of God.

God is righteous when it comes to the matter of *judging saints:* "Which is a manifest token of the righteous judgment of God, that ye may be counted worthy of the kingdom of God, for which ye also suffer" (1:5). Paul knew the persecutions and tribulations through which the believers at Thessalonica were passing. Let them "take heart!" he says. "The crowning day is coming by and by." Meanwhile, God used their tribulation to develop their character.

This world is our sphere of probation. The Lord uses all of the things that come into our lives to prepare us for high office in the kingdom. But what does it mean to be "worthy" of the kingdom of God? It has nothing to do with an entrance exam; rather, it has to do with a final exam, an exam to determine where we will fit in the kingdom. The word used has to do with fitness. We do not get into either the kingdom or the church by our own merit. We get into *the kingdom* by *birth,* by virtue of the regenerating work of the Holy Spirit. Jesus said to Nicodemus, "Except a man be born again, he cannot see the kingdom of God." We get into *the church* by baptism, by virtue of the baptizing work of the Holy Spirit. Paul said, "By one Spirit are we all baptized into one body, whether we be Jews or Gentiles, whether we be bond or free; and have been all made to drink into one Spirit" (1 Cor. 12:13). The church is not the kingdom, although it is related to the kingdom. We are put into both the church and the kingdom supernaturally at the moment we are saved. In view here is the judgment seat of Christ.

It has always been God's plan to establish a kingdom on earth When He created Adam, He said, "let [him] have dominion" (Gen. 1:26). Adam's calling was to rule the Garden. Later, he would rule the globe; later still, perhaps, if sin had not intervened, he might have ruled the galaxy. Everything has been spoiled and interrupted by the Fall.

The concept of the kingdom came closer when first David and then Solomon ascended the throne. When the Lord returns finally to establish the kingdom, He will reign first in His David character and subdue all of His foes; then He will reign like Solomon in glory and splendor as the Prince of Peace.

Solomon's sins spoiled all of that, however, and sowed the seeds of schism in the nation. Worse still, they paved the way for the terrible idolatries and immoralities that, in the end, called for the suspension of both the northern kingdom of Israel and later the southern kingdom of Judah. With the coming of Nebuchadnezzar, "the times of the Gentiles" began, and kingdom hopes were eclipsed.

After the Captivity, a remnant of Jews returned to the Promised Land, but the kingdom was now in abeyance. The repatriated Jews were subjects first of Persia, then of Greece, and ultimately of Rome. The throne of David was almost gone.

Then the King was born in Bethlehem, and there was a brief flurry of interest. Thirty years later, John the Baptist announced that the kingdom was at hand and sought to bring revival and moral reform to the nation. The King came, but they rejected Him. He was not the kind of Messiah they wanted. They wanted a ruler, not a redeemer. They crucified Him, and Pilate wrote this mocking title for His cross: "JESUS OF NAZARETH THE KING OF THE JEWS."

The kingdom was now postponed indefinitely. Its spiritual aspect flourished in the church, but its secular prospects dimmed. The mystery parables (Matt. 13) trace the hidden fortunes of the kingdom during this age. Once God's purposes with the church are complete, prospects will again brighten for the establishment of the earthly kingdom. The church age is a parenthesis in the time line of God's dealings with this world. The rapture of the church will clear the way for God to resume His dealings with the nation of Israel, dealings that He suspended soon after Pentecost (Rom. 11).

The nation of Israel has already been reborn. This is a sobering indication that the church is about to be removed. Once that has happened, "the gospel of the kingdom" will be preached to reap from an utterly godless world a final harvest of souls before the return of Christ to reign (Matt. 24:14). "The King is coming" will be the cry. However, the Antichrist will come first, and His terrible persecutions will purge the Christ-rejecting nation of Israel of its unbelieving majority, clearing the way for the Lord's return.

Meanwhile, the church will be reviewed at the judgment seat of Christ. It will be made ready for its role in the heavenlies in the coming millennial kingdom on earth.

When the Lord comes back to reign, He will depose "the high ones that are on high [Satan's angel rulers], and the kings of the earth upon the earth [the Gentile rulers]" (Isa. 24:21). The Jews will administer the earthly empire under Christ as He sits enthroned in Jerusalem "on the throne of his father David." We will reign with Christ on high from the heavenly Jerusalem. In view of this fact, Paul introduces here the thought of the kingdom of God and points to the judgment seat of Christ.

God is likewise righteous when it comes to the matter of *judging sinners:* "Seeing it is a righteous thing with God to recompense tribulation to them that trouble you" (1:6). This verse anticipates the Great White Throne judgment. The word used here for "recompense" means "to repay," "to requite," or "to pay back." It applies equally to things both good and bad. Jesus said that we should invite the poor, the maimed, the lame, and the blind to our suppers "for they cannot recompense thee: for thou shalt be recompensed at the resurrection of the just" (Luke 14:14). The word is also used to describe the judgment of apostates: "Vengeance belongeth unto me, I will recompense, saith the Lord. . . . It is a fearful thing to fall into the hands of the living God" (Heb. 10:30–31).

We feel instinctively that in spite of all of the terrible wrongs and evils about us, this *is* a moral universe. The wickedness, injustice, oppressions, and deceptions of men demand a day of judgment. Quite apart from atrocities, persecutions, and holocausts; quite apart from wars and the ruthless wickedness of international terror and organized crime; quite apart from murder, rape, arson, prostitution, sodomy, frauds, abortion, child abuse, drug trafficking, and the like, there are countless petty lusts, hatreds, spites, and lies that are a part of everyday life for millions of people. Lives are blasted, homes are divided, and people are cheated. A drunk driver causes an accident, people are killed or maimed, and the courts simply slap his wrists and excuse him. A young man seduces a young girl, abandons her to her shame, laughs, and seeks new conquests. Someone drops some dope into a friend's drink deliberately to hook him on drugs, the friend is ruined, and the law sleeps. A husband contracts some foul sexual disease and gives it to his wife. Little ones are bruised and bullied, and no one interferes. Children are taught God-denying, soul-destroying, and life-ruining philosophies in school while the government applauds. The list is endless. By far, the majority of wrongs are never righted in this life. Our sense of justice, quite apart from divine revelation, tells us that there *has* to be a Day of Judgment. What about the Alexanders, the Caesars, the Genghis Khans, the Napoleons, the Hitlers, and the Stalins who have plunged the world into war and caused miseries beyond all human ability to redress? What about the Mao Tse-tungs who have deliberately murdered, tortured, starved, and brainwashed millions of people? There has to be a Day of Judgment.

The other side of the coin is just as positive. Every day, deeds of care and compassion go unnoticed and unacknowledged. Still less are they rewarded down here. There has to be a judgment day.

God's Word assures us that there is. The subject, however, is not quite as simple as that. Actually, the following five major judgments are set before us in the Scriptures.

1. There is the judgment of sin. As far as the believer is concerned, this judgment has already passed. Our sins were judged at Calvary. When Jesus died, we died; when He was buried, we were buried; when He was raised, we were raised. God says to the believer, "There is therefore now no condemnation to them which are in Christ Jesus" (Rom. 8:1). The wrath of God was poured out against sin at Calvary, and now we stand, in Christ, where the fire has already been. "For God so loved the world, that he gave his only begotten Son, that whosoever believeth in him should not perish, but have everlasting life" (John 3:16). Our *state* might be as yet imperfect, pending the Rapture and the redemption of our bodies, but our *standing* is perfect.

The unbeliever, by contrast, walks through life under the brooding shadow of the wrath of God. "The wrath of God abideth on him" (John 3:36). God, in grace, stays His hand, but as long as the unbeliever continues to reject Christ, all that stands between him and a lost eternity is the beating of his heart.

2. There is the judgment of saints. God judges His own people in two ways. First, He judges them *as sons* in this life: "Whom the Lord loveth he chasteneth, and scourgeth every son whom he receiveth" (Heb. 12:6). We stumble and fall, we sin and grieve the Holy Spirit, and we need to be chastened. This is all part of our Adamic legacy. However, "if we confess our sins, he is faithful and just to forgive us our sins, and to cleanse us from all unrighteousness" (1 John 1:9).

We must distinguish between "sin" and "sins." *Sin* has to do with what we are. We are sinners. We are not sinners because we sin; we sin because we are sinners, just as an apple tree is not an apple tree because it bears apples, but it bears apples because it is an apple tree. Sin is the root; sins are the fruit. *Sin* has to do with what we *are; sins* have to do with what we *do*. God has already dealt with the root of sin. He expects us, in cooperation with His indwelling Holy Spirit, to deal with the fruit of sin. His chastisement is part of the process and part of the proof that we are indeed His children (Heb. 12:7–11). The principle that operates in

God's judgment of us as sons is one of self-judgment: "For if we would judge ourselves, we should not be judged" (1 Cor. 11:31).

God judges His saints not only as sons but also *as servants.* This judgment takes place during the *parousia,* as we have seen, at the judgment seat of Christ (Rom. 14:10; 1 Cor. 3:10–15; 2 Cor. 5:10). At that time, our lives and works as believers will come into review and our position in the impending kingdom will be determined. Unconfessed sins will be dealt with at the judgment seat of Christ. All of the loose ends of our lives, in all of their myriad contacts and responses, will be finally tied down. The judgment seat of Christ is just that—a *judgment* seat. Rebukes and rewards will be in evidence. Our standing will not be called into question, but our state certainly will be reviewed. God's salvation is free; His rewards have to be earned.

3. There is the judgment of states. God is sovereign lord of the universe. He has His own sublime and infinitely inerrant ways of maintaining moral control over His creatures. Although His hand is seldom seen in human affairs, He rules over the kingdoms of men. Nebuchadnezzar had to learn that "the most High ruleth in the kingdom of men, and giveth it to whomsoever he will" (Dan. 4:25). Daniel read the same lesson to wicked King Belshazzar just hours before the Babylonian Empire passed into oblivion and the Medo-Persian Empire took its place (Dan. 5:17–28). One basic moral principle in God's general judgment of the nations in the course of history is that their woe or weal is determined, to some extent, by their treatment of the Jewish people (Gen. 12:1–3).

Two prophetic focal points exist in God's judgment of states. One has to do with the *Great Tribulation,* when the nations will unite in their universal persecution of the Jewish people and their determination to get rid of the Jews once and for all. It will terminate when the Lord comes back in flaming fire at the time of Armageddon. God will use this time of terror to bring a remnant of the Jews to their senses and to a saving knowledge of Christ. The Lord's return will also effect the wholesale conversion of the Jewish remnant to Christ (Dan. 12:11; Matt. 24:15–31).

The other focal point has to do with the *Great Tribunal* that will be set up, subsequent to the Lord's return, in the Valley of Jehoshaphat (Joel 3:1–3, 12; Matt. 25:31–46). The criteria of judgment will be individual treatment of Jews during the time of the Antichrist's reign of terror. The purpose of the judgment will be to determine who, of the Gentiles, will go into the coming millennial kingdom and who will go directly to a lost eternity.

4. There is the judgment of sinners. God, of course, pursues His moral judgment of sinners throughout their lives. Often, His hand is not discerned. Occasionally, He gives signal demonstration of His government, as when Haman was hanged on the very gallows that he had prepared for Mordecai (Esther 6:10) and when Jezebel was slain and later devoured by dogs in Jezreel where she had murdered Naboth (1 Kings 21–24; 2 Kings 9:30–37). Generally, however, God's dealings with sinners are beyond our ability to trace. Those who seem to escape all retribution for their misdeeds often pay for them in ways that we do not discern. The time is coming, however, when all sinners will face their sin and guilt, especially their crowning guilt of rejecting Christ, at the Great White Throne (Rev. 20:11–15). That is when the books will be opened and even men's idle words brought to account (Matt. 12:36). There will be degrees of punishment commensurate with privilege, opportunity, and relative guilt (Matt. 10:15; 11:22–24).

5. There is the judgment of Satan. One of the great mysteries of the universe is why God has permitted fallen Lucifer so much power, time, and scope to work his dreadful ills upon this planet. He would have had no power at all over us if Adam had never sinned. The Fall, however, delivered this planet and its people into his hands. Nonetheless, restraints, of which we know little or nothing, are placed upon him (Job 1:6–10). His doom is sure. Just before the beginning of the millennial reign of Christ on this earth, Satan will be incarcerated in the Abyss (Rev. 20:1). After his final wickedness on earth, a thousand years later, Satan will be cast into the lake of fire (Rev 20:7–10).

Such are the judgments referred to in Scripture. We must not mix them up. One of the basic rules of Bible interpretation is that we must always make a difference where God makes a difference in our handling of the Word of God. But we must come back to our text.

2. As to the present (1:7a)

Judgment is coming for saint and sinner alike, but what about now? Paul has a wise word for his converts: "And to you who are troubled rest with us," he says. The word for "rest" is *anesis.* It has to do with "loosening" or "relaxing" as, for instance, of strings or chords that have stretched tightly. It is not simply rest from labor. It has to do with relaxation from endurance and from expectation. Felix, the procurator of Judea (himself a cruel and treacherous man), used the word when he was so convinced that Paul was the victim of a Jewish plot that "he commanded a centurion to keep Paul, and to let him have liberty [*anesis*], and that he should forbid none of his acquaintance to minister or come unto him" (Acts 24:23). In other words, Felix relaxed the terms of Paul's detention.

In describing his tension at one time in his ministry, Paul wrote, "When I came to Troas to preach Christ's gospel, and a door was opened unto me of the Lord, I had no rest [*anesis*] in my spirit, because I found not Titus my brother" (2 Cor. 2:12–13). He was unable to relax. He says the same thing about his experiences in Macedonia, where he was bitterly persecuted everywhere he went: "When we were come into Macedonia, our flesh had no rest [*anesis*], but we were troubled on every side; without were fightings, within were fears" (2 Cor. 7:5). This admission, incidentally, gives us an interesting glimpse into Paul's own heart. We see a very human person. Bold he was and as brave as a lion, but even while he was fearlessly facing the foe, fear gripped his soul. But that is what courage is all about. The coward shows his fear and responds to it; the brave man doesn't show his fear.

Paul was now at Corinth and, in that great, pagan city, he faced the same hostility that he faced elsewhere. But by then he had learned to rest, to relax, to "let go and let God." Paul did not pray that the troubles facing his converts might cease. He urged them to relax, but how? The word we find in his opening greeting, *grace*, tells them how.

Later, writing to his converts at Corinth, Paul described some of the persecutions and pressures that he had faced in the cause of Christ, and an impressive list it is (2 Cor. 11:23–33). He then told of a remarkable experience through which he had gone some fourteen years earlier. He had been caught up into the third heaven and had seen things that left him speechless. The heavenly vision was so glorious that God had subsequently given him "a thorn in the flesh, the messenger of Satan to buffet [him]" (2 Cor. 12:7). The word for "messenger" was the usual New Testament word for angel. It is possible that he was tormented by one of Satan's angel princes. Three times Paul prayed that he might be delivered from this affliction. Back came the answer: "My grace is sufficient for thee: for my strength is made perfect in weakness" (2 Cor. 12:9a). Paul's response was magnificent. He stopped praying for relief from this thorn. He said, "Most gladly therefore will I rather glory in my infirmities, that the power of Christ may rest upon me. . . . For when I am weak, then am I strong" (2 Cor. 12:9b–10).

That, then, was Paul's answer to the problem of persecution and suffering. Grace! God will give grace sufficient for the occasion. So relax. God is still on the throne.

3. As to the prospect (1:7b–10)
    a. A day of revelation is coming (1:7b–c)

The enemies of God and of His people are having their little day now. The hearts of many people are being revealed (Luke 2:34–35). But another day is coming, and it is already on the way: "The Lord Jesus shall be revealed from heaven [He is coming from His home] with his mighty angels [He is coming with His hosts]."

When the Lord Jesus opened the Scriptures in His hometown synagogue in Nazareth formally to proclaim Himself as Israel's Messiah, He read these words from the prophecy of Isaiah: "The Spirit of the Lord is upon me, because he hath anointed me to preach the gospel to the poor; he hath sent me to heal the brokenhearted, to preach deliverance to the captives, and recovering of sight to the blind, to set at liberty them that are bruised, to preach the acceptable year of the Lord" (Luke 4:18–19). Luke tells us that He then closed the book and sat down. Every eye was on Him. His fame had preceded Him from other parts of the country. Interest and expectation was high. They knew the quotation from Isaiah 61:1–2 by heart. They knew that He had stopped reading and closed the book in the middle of a sentence. "This day is this scripture fulfilled in your ears," He said (Luke 4:21). He had hardly said a dozen more sentences when they were filled with murderous rage and tried to kill Him.

Fortunately for them, He had closed the book where He did; fortunately for us and all of mankind as well. It meant that God had decreed a dispensation of grace, grace so vast that it could take Calvary in its stride and grace so strong in its flow that it would run on for more than two thousand years, even to this present day. For the next words in the passage proclaimed "the day of vengeance of our God." The Thessalonians were living in an age of grace. Grace holds back God's hand from wrath. Grace reaches out to the vilest and the most violent of men. Grace writes our names in life's eternal book. Grace gives us what we need to accept what God sends our way. Grace is the soil in which the fruit of the Spirit grows.

But the book is to be opened again. The last sentence of the prophecy is to be read: "And the day of vengeance of our God; to comfort all that mourn; . . . to give unto them beauty for ashes" (Isa. 61:2–3). The apostle's eye now sees the coming of that long-delayed "day of vengeance of our God." He sees the Lord Jesus revealed from heaven with His mighty angels. The word for "revealed" is *apokalupsis*, "an unveiling," the word that gives us our title for the book of Revelation. It is at the end of the judgment age—covered by the seals, the trumpets, and the vials—that the Lord will come from heaven with His holy angels (Rev. 19:11–18).

b. A day of revenge is coming (1:8–9)

Paul sets before us the *essential* nature of God's wrath: "In flaming fire taking vengeance on them that know not God, and that obey not the gospel of our Lord Jesus Christ" (1:8). Elsewhere, the Holy Spirit reminds us that "our God is a consuming fire" (Heb. 12:29). When Nadab and Abihu, the sons of Aaron, presumed to approach God, censers in hand but with "strange fire" (i.e., fire other than that which the Lord had commanded, required, and given from heaven, Lev. 1:7; 6:12; 9:24; Exod. 30:9), "there went out fire from the LORD, and devoured them, and they died there before the LORD" (Lev. 10:2). When Elijah demonstrated to apostate Israel the folly of Baal worship, he did so spectacularly on Mount Carmel. In response to his prayer, "The fire of the LORD fell, and consumed the burnt sacrifice, and the wood, and the stones, and the dust, and licked up the water that was in the trench" (1 Kings 18:38). The only thing that prevented its falling on the people was the sacrifice upon the altar. When wicked King Ahaziah sent soldiers to arrest Elijah the prophet, Elijah called down fire from heaven to consume them (2 Kings 1:9–15). Fire is one of the weapons in God's hand.

At His coming again, the Lord Jesus will be panoplied in the Shechinah cloud of fire (Exod. 14:24) and accompanied by the armies of heaven. Because one angel in one night could smite all of Sennacherib's army (2 Kings 19:35–36), the assembled armies of the earth will stand no chance against this avenging heavenly host, although, in very truth, the Lord will have no intention whatsoever of calling for their aid. He intends to handle His foes by Himself. The hosts of heaven will be present simply to demonstrate how utterly impotent wicked men have been to hurt and harm God's people apart from God's mysterious permissive will (2 Kings 6:15–17). In the time of His vengeance, He will be quite able to handle His enemies Himself. It is fitting that He should execute His own judgment upon a world that spat in His face, plowed His back, crowned Him with thorns, nailed Him to a cross, and has blasphemed Him ever since.

The word for "vengeance" means literally "that which issues out of justice." It has to do with the execution of justice, the maintenance of right. This is not mere revenge or vindictiveness. It is not personal rage striking back in passion. This is righteous retribution. Those who will face this terrible vengeance are those who are willfully ignorant of God (Rom. 11:30) and who have willfully rejected the gospel of Christ. That, in the last analysis, is the ultimately unpardonable sin, the essence of all sin (John 16:8–9).

Then, too, Paul sets before us the *eternal* nature of God's wrath: "Who shall be punished with everlasting destruction from the presence of the Lord, and from the glory of his power" (1:9). The day of His glory has come at last! The wicked will catch one glimpse of it and then be banished from it. It will haunt them forever.

The doom here described is terrible beyond all thought. The word *eternal* is *aiōnios.* It is used frequently in the New Testament. In sixty-seven occurrences of the word, it is used to signify something endless. For instance, it is used of God, who is eternal in His nature (Rom. 16:26). It is used to describe our redemption in Christ (Heb. 9:12) and to describe the resurrection body of the believer (1 Cor. 15:53; 2 Cor. 5:1). The use of the word here shows that the punishment in view is not temporary but forever. The purpose of such punishment is retribution with no thought of reclamation.

Similarly, the word *destruction* is *olethros.* It means literally "ruin." It is used of the man in the church at Corinth who was guilty of incest and was to be delivered over to Satan "for the destruction of the flesh, that the spirit may be saved in the day of the Lord Jesus" (1 Cor. 5:5). In warning against the deceptiveness of riches, Paul says, "They that will be rich fall into temptation and a snare, and into many foolish and hurtful lusts, which drown men in *destruction* and perdition" (1 Tim. 6:9). The wicked, then, at the Lord's return, will be handed over to eternal ruin. Who can imagine the horrors that will accompany the dissolution of their personality, the gnawings of conscience, the torments of memory, the anguish of guilt, and the terrible knowledge that their doom is deserved, hopeless, and unending?

The Lord's living foes will be assembled before Him when He comes. Many of them will be at Megiddo. More will be arraigned in the Valley of Jehoshaphat. As, at the Rapture, living saints are gloriously changed and caught up to be with Christ, so now living sinners will be grievously changed and hurled headlong from His presence. As the dead in Christ will rise to be bathed in the glory of the *parousia* and to participate in the splendor of the apocalypse, so the wicked dead, when their time comes, will be raised only to be convicted, sentenced, and hurled into eternal ruin in what the Bible calls "the lake of fire"—a horror that defies description in spite of the creative imaginations of Dante and Milton.

c. A day of reward is coming (1:10)

"When he shall come," Paul continues, "to be glorified in his saints, and to be admired in all them that believe (because our testimony among you was believed) in that day." It will be a day of "splendor unimaginable." Amazing! Unbelievable! Awesome! So, over against their present persecutions, privations, and pains, Paul sets that glorious day when we shall be paraded before the universe to hear the cheers and hosannas of the angels. As Paul told the Corinthians, "For our light affliction, which is but for a moment, worketh for us a far more exceeding and eternal weight of glory" (2 Cor. 4:17).

The angelic hosts have long wondered about the mystery of God's interest in, love for, and dealings with the human race generally and the church particularly. When He laid the earth's primeval foundations, they sang and shouted for joy (Job 38:4–7). They visited this planet on numerous occasions during the Old Testament age. They crowded around the cradle and awoke the echoes of the Judean hills when heaven's Beloved was born in Bethlehem (Luke 2:8–15). They dogged His earthly pathway from His cradle to His grave. They are now servants of those who are salvation's heirs (Heb. 1:14). They desire to look into these things (1 Peter 1:12). One day they will understand. The church will be God's object lesson to the universe of His grace, kindness, and wisdom (Eph. 1:7; 3:10). They have glimmerings of it now. They will see it fully then. The coming of Christ in glory will make it all clear. He will be gloried in His saints. An admiring universe will look at us and glorify Him.

C A word of undefeated prayer (1:11–12)
1. When Paul prayed (1:11a)

Paul himself seems to have been overwhelmed at the magnificence of this prospect. As usual, when Paul found himself overwhelmed, he prayed! "Wherefore also we pray always for you," he says. Paul did not pray just when he was in a tight corner; he also prayed when he was in a bright corner.

The daily habit of saintly George Müller of Bristol was to spend the first part of every day getting his own soul "happy in the Lord," as he put it. His procedure was simple. He would read a small portion of Scripture and meditate upon it until the truth that it revealed burned into his soul. He would then turn that truth into prayer. He would relate it to his own needs and the needs of others and carry the truth of it back to God in praise, worship, thanksgiving, petition, and intercession. That seems to be what Paul did here. The wondrous revelation concerning the coming day of glory needed to be returned to God at once in prayer for his beloved Thessalonians.

2. What Paul prayed (1:11b–12)

He prayed for two things. He prayed about *the nature of their calling:* "That our God would count you worthy of this calling, and fulfill all the good pleasure of his goodness, and the work of faith with power" (1:11b). What a calling they had! To be the vehicle through which the universe of created beings will give glory to God and admiration to Christ! Oh, that God would make them worthy of such a calling! How could He do that? By making them good, even as He is good. What a challenge to our faith!

That was the sum and substance of this prayer. Paul prayed that every desire of goodness would be fulfilled and that every work of faith would be achieved.

In our average modern prayer meetings, we pray that sister so-and-so might recover from her illness or that brother what's-his-name would be able to get a better job or that Dr. Sawbones would be able to find a suitable assistant. It's not that it's wrong to pray for things like that, but most of our prayer requests are for such things. Paul rarely records a prayer for physical or material things. If we individually and collectively adopted Paul's plan, or George Müller's plan, our prayers would soar. Probably, too, they would cease to be so boring.

Then, too, Paul prayed about *the name of the Christ:* "That the name of our Lord Jesus Christ may be glorified in you, and ye in him, according to the grace of God and the Lord Jesus Christ" (1:12). The Lord Jesus *is* going to be glorified in His saints; Paul has already assured us of that. We shall come with Him, straight from the *parousia,* with the judgment seat behind us and the apocalypse before us. Every spot, every wrinkle, and every such thing will be gone. We shall be His Bride, fit indeed to sit with Him in heavenly places, able to bask in the fierce light that beats upon His throne. He is to be glorified in His saints.

One way to hasten that glorious consummation is for His name to be glorified in us here and now. Twice in this part of his petition, Paul gives Him His full title—Lord Jesus Christ.

Lord! That is His *sovereign* name. The word is *kurios,* meaning "owner." It carries the idea of lordship arising out of ownership. Jesus said, "Ye call me Master and Lord: and ye say well; for so I am" (John 13:13). In the Gospels themselves, the name Jesus occurs many times, but He is rarely addressed as Jesus.

Demons addressed Him so (Matt. 8:29), and He invariably silenced them. It is irreverent to address Him as "Jesus" or as "dear Jesus" or with any such terms. He is Lord.

That means, of course, that we are to do what He says. He warned,

> Not every one that saith unto me, Lord, Lord, shall enter into the kingdom of heaven; but he that doeth the will of my Father which is in heaven. Many will say to me in that day, Lord, Lord, have we not prophesied in thy name? and in thy name have cast out devils? and in thy name done many wonderful works? And then will I profess unto them, I never knew you: depart from me, ye that work iniquity. (Matthew 7:21–23)

He is Lord. Thomas discovered it once all of his doubts were settled (John 20:24–29). Peter had to learn that he could not say, "Not so, Lord" (Acts 10:14). It is either one or the other. If He is Lord, we cannot say, "Not so"; if we say, "Not so," He is not Lord—at least in that situation.

Jesus! That is His *saving* name The name is derived from Jehoshua (Joshua) and means "Jehovah the Savior." It is the name we associate with His cradle because when He was born the angel instructed Joseph, "Thou shalt call his name JESUS: for he shall save his people from their sins" (Matt. 1:21).

We associate the name with His *character* because Paul tells us, "Whatsoever ye do in word or deed, do all in the name of the Lord Jesus" (Col. 3:17). It is a stainless name, above reproach. As Christians who share that name, we must do or say nothing to bring reproach upon it. The world fouls that name, uses it as a swear word, and joins it to the foulest words known to the tongue; Satan fears that name, and demons flee before it. Rather, we must further that name. The character it embodies must be our character, too.

We associate that name with His *cross.* When Christ was crucified, Pilate wrote an inscription in Latin, Hebrew, and Greek and nailed it above His head—"JESUS OF NAZARETH THE KING OF THE JEWS."

We associate that name with His *concern.* When He went back home to heaven, He took His place on the throne of God. Now He ministers there on behalf of His people. He is that "one mediator between God and men, the man Christ Jesus" (1 Tim. 2:5). He is there to be our "advocate with the Father, Jesus Christ the righteous" (1 John 2:1).

We associate that name with His *coming.* At the time of His ascension, while the awestruck disciples were still riveted to Olivet and still staring up into heaven, two angels appeared. "This same Jesus," they said, "which is taken up from you into heaven, shall so come in like manner as ye have seen him go into heaven" (Acts 1:11).

We associate that Name with His *coronation.* For "God also hath highly exalted him, and given him a name which is above every name: that at the name of Jesus every knee should bow . . . and . . . every tongue . . . confess that Jesus Christ is Lord, to the glory of God the Father" (Phil. 2:9–11).

Christ! That is the *sufficient* name. The name is simply the Greek translation of the Hebrew word *Mashiah* (Messiah). *Christos* has the same meaning, deriving from *chriō,* "to anoint." The name embraces all of our needs. In the Old Testament, three people were anointed for their office—the prophet, the priest, and the king. As the Christ, He is the Lord's Anointed One. As such, the Holy Spirit came upon Him and anointed Him at His baptism (Matt. 3:16). As such, too, He announced Himself in the Nazareth synagogue (Luke 4:18–19). The Holy Spirit not only filled Him from the beginning but also was given to Him without measure at His anointing so that He might be all-sufficient for every need or demand made upon Him (John 3:34). The three offices of the Old Testament era that were associated with anointing were climaxed in Him. He was a revealing prophet—"Never man spake like this man" (John 7:46). He was a righteous priest, a priest after the order of Melchizek (Heb. 7:1–8:6). And He is a returning prince (John 14:1–3; Rev. 1:7).

Lord Jesus Christ! Lord—that emphasizes His *power;* Jesus—that emphasizes His *person*; and Christ—that emphasizes His *position.* No wonder Paul saw in this name the guarantee that all of God's purposes concerning Him and us will be fulfilled. He is yet to be glorified in His saints publicly before an awestruck universe. His name is yet to be glorified in us. We are yet to be glorified in Him. The "grace of God and the Lord Jesus Christ has underwritten it all." This truth occupied Paul's mind and heart as he prayed.

PART 3

Paul's Word of Admonition

2 Thessalonians 2:1–3:15

A. The greatness of the coming lie (2:1–12)
   1. The local deception (2:1–2)
      a. The plea of the apostle (2:1–2a)

In the brief period between the writing of Paul's two Thessalonian epistles, some teachers had arisen in the church at Thessalonica who were advocating a false doctrine. Their teaching was that the Day of the Lord had come and that the church was already in the Great Tribulation. Doubtless, the persecution that the Christians were suffering had something to do with that fact. If so, these false teachers failed to distinguish between "tribulation," which the Lord foretold would be the common and universal lot of believers in this world (John 16:33)—ruled over by the enemy—and "the great tribulation" (Matt. 24:21), a special period when the Jews and believing Gentiles in particular will be persecuted by the Antichrist (Rev. 7).

Had the Thessalonians been post-tribulationists, they should have been very happy about it because it would have been a sure sign that the Rapture was about to take place. Instead, they were upset. Paul's first epistle had set before them a pretribulation Rapture; now other teachers were telling them that the Tribulation had already come.

Paul went to work right away to set the record straight: "Now we beseech you, brethren, by the coming of our Lord Jesus Christ, and by our gathering together unto him, that ye be not soon shaken in mind, or be troubled . . ." (2:1–2a).

The word *coming* here is *parousia,* about which Paul has already written to the Thessalonians. As we have seen, it refers to the period between the Rapture and the final return of Christ. It refers to the time when the church will be with the Lord in the air, appearing at the judgment seat of Christ and participating in the marriage supper of the Lamb. The root meaning of the word is "to be near." It refers to the Lord's physical presence. The word is used in a variety of ways in the New Testament, but its basic meaning is simply "presence." When it is translated "coming," it denotes the actual presence of the person who comes.

It occurs twenty-four times in the New Testament; twice (in the KJV) it is rendered "presence," the rest of the times it is rendered "coming." Six times it is used of individuals (Stephanus, Titus, and Paul) and always refers to their personal presence. It is used half a dozen times of Christ's presence in the air when He comes to meet His raptured bride before the Great Tribulation (1 Thess.

2:19; 3:13; 4:15; 5:23; 2 Thess. 2:1; 1 John 2:28). It is used eleven times in reference to Christ's presence on the earth when He comes to the earth with the church, in the Day of the Lord, immediately after the Great Tribulation (Matt. 24:3, 27, 37, 39; 1 Cor. 15:23; 2 Thess. 2:8; James 5:7–8; 2 Peter 1:16; 3:4, 12). Once it is used of the personal presence of the Antichrist, who is to be destroyed by Christ's own presence (2 Thess. 2:9).

The passage of Scripture now before us is of particular interest because *parousia* is used in it in three different contexts: for the presence of Christ in the air (2:1), for the presence of the Antichrist (2:9), and for the presence of Christ on earth (2:8).

The expression "by our *gathering together* unto him" occurs just twice in the New Testament, here and in Hebrews 10:25, where we are told not to forsake "the assembling of yourselves together" *(episunagōgē),* and so much more as we see the day of the Lord's return approaching. One major reason for our "gathering together" down here with those who love the Lord and are of like precious faith is that it is a foretaste of our gathering in the air. We are gathered together *unto* Him now (Matt. 18:20); we shall be gathered together *with* Him then. His presence in our midst is invisible now; it will be visible then.

Paul beseeches his Thessalonian brothers not to be so easily swayed by wrong teaching. The word *beseech* is *erōtaō.* It is used to denote our asking or requesting a person to *do* something, to ask specifically. When the Syro-Phoenician women came to Jesus, pleading, "O Lord, thou Son of David; my daughter is grievously vexed with a devil," the Lord answered her nothing. The disciples, however, had plenty to say: they "came and besought him," Matthew recalls, "saying, Send her away . . ." (Matt. 15:22–23).

When the woman at the well went home and told how she had met the Master, the city headed straight to the well. "When the Samaritans were come unto him, they *besought* him that he would tarry with them" (John 4:40). Similarly, the Capernaum nobleman "*besought* him that he would come down, and heal his son: for he was at the point of death" (John 4:47). So Paul pleads with the Thessalonians.

Paul beseeches his converts that they "be not soon shaken in mind, or be troubled. . . ." The word *soon* can be translated "quickly." The subversion of the Thessalonians had been done swiftly. Satan does not let any grass grow under his feet. No sooner is he checked by Paul's first epistle, in which the whole rapture question is spelled out, than he counters with another error.

The word *shaken* is *saleuō,* which means "to shake," "to move to and fro," "to agitate." The word was used to describe a ship's shifting from its moorings in a storm. A parallel use of the word is found in Peter's Pentecostal sermon: "I foresaw the Lord always before my face, for he is on my right hand, that I should not be moved" (Acts 2:25). That is what Satan always tries to do—move us away from sound doctrine and get us to drag our anchor. Everything else follows from that.

The word for "troubled" is *throeomai.* It means "to cry aloud" or "to wail." Here the thought seems to be that of being frightened so as to make a clamor. No wonder! If Paul was right that the Rapture preceded the Great Tribulation, and if they were already in the Great Tribulation, then they had missed the Rapture—and that was something about which to wail. If the false teachers were right and the Rapture followed the Great Tribulation, and if that dreaded event had already begun, doom and gloom, terrors and horrors unimaginable, lay ahead. That, too, was something about which to wail. Neither view offered any comfort (1 Thess. 4:18; 5:11). Paul pleads with his friends not to be so gullible, so swiftly moved from the truth.

b. The plot of the adversary (2:2b–e)

(1) Why the deception convinced (2:2b–d)

Paul pinpoints the source of their deception: "That ye be not . . . troubled, neither by spirit, nor by word, nor by letter as from us. . . ." The Thessalonians had been ensnared in a threefold cord of deception. They were the victims of wrong information, and wrong information is always dangerous. For a traveler to be told to turn left when he should turn right, for a doctor to prescribe medicine when he should prescribe surgery, and for a financial advisor to suggest buying when he should suggest selling is the giving of wrong information. In each case, it could be disastrous. For a preacher to teach one thing when he should be teaching the opposite is equally dangerous—more so, in some instances, because it imperils immortal souls.

The first strand in the error at Thessalonica derived from a spirit utterance. Someone had spoken a lying message in tongues, something that was not at all uncommon. Even when tongues was a valid gift, the apostle had to warn, "Beloved, believe not every spirit, but try the spirits whether they are of God: because many false prophets are gone out into the world" (1 John 4:1). John said that in his day the spirit of antichrist was already at work in the world. The test for a false spirit that he gave is still valid (1 John 4:1–3). Indeed, because the Holy Spirit has withdrawn the gift of tongues (1 Cor. 13:8), and because many people today claim to have that gift, it is all the more imperative that such spirit utterances be regarded with a lively suspicion and that the spirits producing the tongues phenomenon be exposed. The completion of the New Testament canon has rendered tongues-speaking unnecessary. God has told us all that we need to know in His written Word.

A lying spirit, then, had deceived the Thessalonians. They had also been deceived by a spoken pronouncement, by what Paul here calls a "word." The word is *logos,* which here refers to some teaching that claimed to be revealed truth but that was nothing of the kind. Here the teaching concerned the second coming of Christ. It was false teaching. The Thessalonians should have been more cautious, like the Bereans, about accepting teaching at its face value, no matter how respected the teacher (Acts 17:10–11).

Moreover, a forged letter ("by letter as from us") had deceived the Thessalonians. The apostle had indeed written them a letter in which he had differentiated between "the day of Christ" (a day of joy for the church) and "the day of the Lord" (a Day of Judgment for the world). Now they had seemingly received another letter. The words *as from us* can be rendered "as if" or "purporting to be from us." The word for "letter" is the usual word for an epistle.

We have examples of this kind of thing in our own day. The Mormons are deceived by a false book that is widely distributed, cleverly advertised, and utterly a lie.

Having thus disassociated himself from the forged letter and repudiated the other lying communications, Paul turned the whole wretched affair to good account. He used the local deception at Thessalonica as a springboard from which to launch a disclosure of a coming universal deception. Satan's most secret plans are hauled out into the open and exposed for everyone to see. Thus, Satan overreached himself at Thessalonica. His lie concerning the Day of the Lord becomes the basis for the unmasking of his most carefully guarded strategy for the end times.

(2) What the deception contended (2:2e)

The Thessalonians were being told that "the day of Christ [i.e., here, *the day of the Lord*] is at hand," that it was present or already had arrived. There is all the difference in the world between *the day of Christ* and *the Day of the Lord.* The day of Christ has nothing to do with the unveiling of the Man of Sin, except insomuch as the removal of the church makes the coming of the Antichrist possible. Phrases such as "the day of Christ" (Phil. 1:10; 2:16), "the day of our Lord Jesus Christ" (1 Cor. 1:8), and "the day of the Lord Jesus" (1 Cor. 5:5; 2 Cor. 1:14) refer to the *parousia,* the day when the Lord Jesus will come for His church at the time of the

Rapture (1 Thess. 4:16). Second Peter 1:19 speaks of this day as "the day." Peter says that Jesus is "the day star." As the morning star in the sky heralds the dawn of a new day, so Christ as the daystar, the light bearer, heralds the dawn of a new day for the church, a day that will never end, a day when all of the Scriptures regarding His second coming will be fulfilled.

Many translations correctly render this phrase as "the day of the Lord," not "the day of Christ."[1] What follows is clearly related to the Day of the Lord and to the terrible events connected with that day. The "day of the Lord" is first mentioned in Isaiah 2:11–12, where it is defined as being the day when God will be exalted and man abased. It occurs in connection with words such as *wrath* and *vengeance.* It refers to the time when God will overthrow Israel's foes. It will be a time of darkness and judgment. To Israel's foes, it will be "that great and terrible day." It will climax in the setting up of the millennial kingdom and end, a thousand years later, with the dissolution of the heavens themselves.

The Thessalonians were being told that this day had already come. But Paul told them that it had *not* come and will not come until certain other things have happened. The "day of Christ" is imminent; the "day of the Lord" can come only after numerous other things have prepared the way. The day of Christ is for the church; the day of the Lord is for the world. The day of Christ is primarily a day of joy; the day of the Lord is primarily a day of judgment. The day of Christ is the church's; the day of the Lord is the world's horror.

Everything that Paul is now about to reveal is true of the Day of the Lord; none of it is true of the day of Christ. The day of Christ is the subject of the previous verse: "We beseech you, brethren, by the coming [*parousia*] of our Lord Jesus Christ . . ." (2:1). The Day of the Lord is the subject of this verse (2:3) and the teaching that follows.

2. The larger deception (2:3–12)
    a. The Man of Sin (2:3–6)
        (1) The coming apostasy (2:3a)

"Let no man deceive you," Paul says, "by any means: for that day shall not come, except there come a falling away first . . ." There are seven words for "deceive" in the New Testament. This one is *exapataō.* It means "to deceive wholly,"

1. For instance, see F. F. Bruce, *1 and 2 Thessalonians,* Word Biblical Commentary (Waco: Word, 1982), 45:161. (F. F. Bruce is said to have memorized the entire New Testament in *Greek*—with all of the footnotes!)

or "to delude thoroughly." The Thessalonians were in danger of swallowing Satan's lie, hook, line, and sinker. Paul uses the word to describe the activity of the flesh in his life: "For sin, taking occasion by the commandment, *deceived* me, and by it slew me" (Rom. 7:11). He was thoroughly deceived, at one time, by the notion that he could live a life pleasing to God in the energy of the flesh. He used the same word to describe the deception of Eve: "The serpent *beguiled* Eve through his subtilty" (2 Cor. 11:3).

Here Paul warns, "Let no man deceive you by any means." The words contain a double negative. The same kind of thing occurs in Matthew 24:21–22, where the Great Tribulation is described: "For then shall be great tribulation, such as was *not* since the beginning of the world to this time, *no, nor* ever shall be." In Greek, two negatives do not make a positive as they do in English. "No! No! Not! Nor!" Paul writes. What that means is that we had better believe it! The Lord described it in such a way as to emphasize that there has never been anything like it and never will be afterward.

Similarly, the use of the negative here is for emphasis. It can be rendered, "Don't let anyone deceive you by any means whatsoever." The end-times deception will be so strong and so subtle that more than the ordinary degree of watchfulness will be needed.

First, there has to be "a falling away." The word used is *apostasia.* The Jerusalem church leaders used the word in persuading Paul to participate in a temple ceremony. They said to him, "Thou seest, brother, how many thousands of Jews there are which believe; and they are all zealous of the law: and they are informed of thee, that thou teachest all the Jews which are among the Gentiles to forsake [*apostasia*] Moses . . ." (Acts 21:20–21). Paul, in other words, was accused of causing Jews to apostatize from Moses and the law. It is the only other time the word is used.

Some scholars contend that the word should be translated "depart," that "there must be a *physical* departure first." They say we should take this literally, in the ordinary sense of a person's departing. If so, then this would be an express declaration that the departure, the rapture of the church, must take place first.

However, other people contend that there must be a *theological* departure from the faith first, that the word refers to a widespread apostasy that will take place before the coming of the Man of Sin. The verse foretells, in other words, a global and final rebellion against God.

If we take this to be the meaning, then Paul indicates that the last days will be marked by a falling away from the truth, a turning away from God, abandonment of the Christian faith and the Judeo-Christian ethic. With the rise of atheism, communism, and humanism and the spread of false, oriental religions, this seems to be a marked feature of the current age. The media are the tool and ally of all those subversive forces in our society favoring unbridled permissiveness. Pornography and perversion are championed. Bible reading and prayer have been banned from our schools, but every form of moral deviation can be espoused there. The soul-destroying dogma of evolution is accepted as a matter of course, and the Christian view of creation is refused a hearing. Many churches have become liberal, cold, and spiritually dead. Satanism is on the rise. The courts tolerate abortion and lifestyles abhorrent to New Testament Christianity. The stage is being set for the coming of the Man of Sin. Far from being pre-Rapture, Holy Spirit revival on the horizon, all we see is an encroaching apostasy. Such voices as concerned Christians can raise against these things are largely ignored.

(2) The coming apocalypse (2:3b–6)
(a) Sovereignly determined (2:3b–4)
i. The names of the deceiver (2:3b)

Paul says that the apostasy will climax in the revelation of a person called "the man of sin," or "the son of perdition." The word for "revealed" is *apokaluptō*. The word means "to uncover" or "unveil." It reminds us of the unveiling *(apokalupsis)* of Jesus Christ (Rev. 1:1). It reminds us, too, of the closing book of the Bible, which details the facts, circumstances, and judgments related to the second coming of Christ and gives further details of the coming of the Antichrist, the Devil's messiah. The use of the word *apokaluptō* underlines the fact that the Antichrist is to have his unveiling in imitation of Christ. Satan always tries to mimic God and His works and ways.

The Antichrist will be known as "the man of sin." The word for "sin" is *hamartia,* which means "to miss the mark," a very common word for sin in the New Testament. Some scholars think that the name should read "son of lawlessness" *(anomia).* Whichever reading is adopted, the idea is that this terrible human being will be the incarnation of all wickedness. Sin will be his meat and drink, the very breath of life to him. He will encourage sin. He will make full use of it. Pornography, perversion, sex, drugs, murders, lies, deceptions, gambling, and graft will all be grist for his mill. His personal charisma and charm will doubtless be very great. No wickedness is so insidious as that which is cloaked by a magnetic, attractive, and forceful personality. He will undoubtedly be a man of vast intellect with an easy command of languages, the arts, and the scientific disciplines. He will be a wily politician. He will be thoroughly bad, evil through and through, Satan's spawn, demon inspired, the seed of the serpent, a man of sin.

The world today is moving rapidly to meet him. Permissiveness is the prevailing spirit of the age. The world is riding a moral, political, and economic roller coaster and is preparing now for the dizzying and ever-accelerating descent into what the Bible calls "all sin." Since the beginning of the twentieth century, each generation has been worse than the one it replaced. What was outrageous sin to one generation is the norm of the next generation. The generation of the Antichrist is coming into focus and will soon be ready to rule the earth. Moreover, there is no hint of a Holy Spirit revival. The so-called charismatic "renewal" has its roots in utter deception. Rather, the Holy Spirit warns us to look for total and complete apostasy before the Rapture.

Our generation has been given a graphic and terrible indication of how far the rot has gone into the wood of American society. Hollywood, an old enemy of Christianity, saw fit to spit in the face of Jesus by releasing a movie titled *The Last Temptation of Christ.* Universal Pictures, a subsidiary of MCA, produced the film. The chairman of the board of MCA is, or was, a Jew, named Wasserman, who tried to defend the movie's blasphemies. The movie depicted our beloved Lord as a collaborator who built crosses to enable the Romans to execute Jews. He was shown as a weak and dithering, wild-eyed guru who was confused about his own message. In one place, "Jesus" calls himself a liar—"I am a hypocrite, I am afraid of everything, Lucifer is inside me." The movie shows him having sex with Mary Magdalene and later committing adultery. Judas is portrayed as a hero, the best of the apostles. Paul is depicted as a hypocrite. Worse still, Americans flocked to see the movie, and the critics acclaimed it. Christians were lampooned for protesting it. Had Hollywood produced such a movie about Martin Luther King, race riots would have occurred. Truly apostasy is well under way when such blasphemy can be spewed in the face of a country that was founded on the Bible by men who worshiped the Lord as the Creator of the universe, the Son of the living God, and their Redeemer and personal Friend.

Satan's coming man is not only titled "the man of sin" but also is called "the son of perdition." The word is *apōleia,* which means "destruction," or "ruin." The word is used of all those who reject Christ (2 Peter 3:7). The word is used also of those who are deceived by the love of money (1 Tim. 6:9–10). It is used, in one of those terrible warning passages in Hebrews, to describe the difference between a believer and an apostate: "But we are not of them who draw back unto perdition; but of them that believe to the saving of the soul" (Heb. 10:39). The word depicts the terrible loss that all of the unsaved will suffer. It suggests that all that they had, or might have had, is now gone forever. It refers to the destruction of body, soul, and spirit, to an utter and complete ruin that will not be reversed. This is the word now used to describe the Antichrist. He will be "the son of perdition." The expression itself embodies a Hebrew idiom as, for instance, "son of peace" (Luke 10:6), or "son of thunder" (Mark 3:17), and "son of consolation" (Acts 4:36). It is used to depict character. It unveils the son of perdition.

The description is applied to only one other individual—Judas Iscariot. Jesus called *him* "the son of perdition." Kenneth Wuest took this to be a positive identification linking the Man of Sin with Judas. He declared that, by all of the laws of grammar, the use of the definite article points to *one* son of perdition, whereas the indefinite article would leave room for two or more. He adds that the Greek text has the definite article in both John 17:12 and 2 Thessalonians 2:3.

G. Campbell Morgan went further. He believed that Judas was not an ordinary human being at all but an incarnate fiend. He based that position on the Lord's statement: "Have not I chosen you twelve, and one of you is a devil? He spake of Judas Iscariot the son of Simon: for he it was that should betray him, being one of the twelve" (John 6:70–71). Thus, when we are told that Judas went "to his own place" (Acts 1:25), the inference is that he went to a different place in the underworld than that to which other departed human beings go. Wuest maintained that Judas did not go to "sheol" or "hades" but to the Abyss (the "bottomless pit"), where certain dangerous spirit beings are incarcerated (Rev. 9:1–11; 20:1–3). Some scholars think that Judas is being tutored and prepared there for his reappearance as the Antichrist.

That the Antichrist, in his final form, is to be a resurrected man is clear from the Apocalypse. He is described as the wild beast that *was* (that is, he lived on the earth once before), that *is not* (he died), and that will *ascend out of the bottomless pit* (where his soul was imprisoned) and will go into perdition (Rev. 17:8). In the Apocalypse, the Antichrist has two comings; the Devil always mimics God. When he first appears, he will be an ordinary man, brilliant, persuasive, attractive, powerful, and possessed by Satan (as Judas was, John 13:27). He will be killed (he is called the first beast, whose "deadly wound was healed," Rev. 13:3, 12) and brought back to life again. Thus, Satan imitates both the resurrection of Christ and His second coming.

The Antichrist will come back as one of the seven kings referred to in Revelation 17:10–11. Whether, at this time, the soul of Judas enters into the corpse of the Antichrist we are not told. Certainly the effect of this "resurrection" will be startling. Before, he was simply "the beast . . . out of the sea" (Rev. 13:1), presumably a reference to his human origin in a Gentile nation bordering the Mediterranean; now he is "the beast . . . out of the bottomless pit" (Rev. 11:7), a supernatural being, and, as such, awes the people of this planet (Rev. 17:6). He will now feel powerful enough to demand that universal worship be given to himself and Satan. This is graphically described here and elsewhere (2 Thess. 2:4; Rev. 13:11–18).

At this point, we might well pause to tabulate the various comparisons and contrasts (that characterize Christ and the Antichrist) scattered throughout the prophetic Scriptures.

Comparisons with Christ

Christ	Antichrist
1. Is—was—is to come (Rev. 1:18)	Was—is not—shall ascend (Rev. 17:8)
2. 3-year ministry	3 1/2 year monarchy
3. The coming One (Matt. 25:13)	The coming one (2 Thess. 2:3)
4. The church's hope (Titus 2:13)	The world's hope (Rev. 13:3–4)
5. Prince of Princes (Dan. 8:25)	The coming prince (Dan. 9:26)
6. Many Diadems (Rev. 19:12)	Ten diadems (Rev. 13:1)
7. Has a bride—mystic New Jerusalem	Has a bride—mystery Babylon
8. Indwelt by God (John 3:34)	Indwelt by Satan (Rev. 13:2)
9. A slain Man, risen (Luke 24:34)	A slain man, risen (Rev. 13:3)
10. God manifest in flesh works many miracles	Satan manifest in flesh works many miracles

Contrasts with Christ

Christ	Antichrist
1. From above (John 6:38)	From below (Rev. 11:7)
2. Came in Father's name (John 5:43)	Comes in his own name (John 5:43)
3. Humbled Himself (Phil. 2:8)	Exalts himself (2 Thess. 2:4)
4. Despised (Isa. 53:3)	Admired (Rev. 13:3–4)
5. Did Father's will (John 6:38)	Does his own will (Dan. 11:36)
6. Exalted by God (Phil. 2:9)	Cast down by God (Rev. 19:20)
7. Came to save (Luke 19:10)	Comes to destroy (Dan. 8:24)
8. The Good Shepherd (John 10:4–15)	The false shepherd (Zech. 11:16–17)
9. The Truth (John 14:6)	The lie (2 Thess. 2:11)
10. The Holy One (Acts 3:14)	The lawless one (2 Thess. 2:11)
11. Man of Sorrows (Isa. 53:3)	Man of Sin (2 Thess. 2:3)
12. Son of God (Luke 1:35)	Son of perdition (2 Thess. 2:3)
13. Mystery of godliness (1 Tim. 3:16)	Mystery of iniquity (2 Thess. 2:7)
14. Seed of the woman (Gen. 3:15)	Seed of the serpent (Gen. 3:15)
15. The Lamb (John 1:36)	The Beast (Rev. 13:1)
16. Loves and saves His bride (Eph. 5:25)	Hates and destroys his bride (Rev. 17:16)
17. Refused power from Satan (Matt. 4:8–10)	Receives power from Satan (Rev. 13:2–7)
18. Jesus has a name above all names with a numeric value of 888	Antichrist will have a name with a numeric value of 666

ii. The nature of the deceiver (2:4)

The apostle underlines, first, *the aim* of the Antichrist: "who opposeth and exalteth himself above all that is called God, or that is worshipped" (2:4a). The word for "opposeth" here is *antikeimai.* It means literally "to lie opposite," "to be adverse," or "to be repugnant to." It signifies "an adversary." The word is used of Satan (1 Tim. 1:14–15). It is used to depict the opposition of the Holy Spirit and the flesh (Gal. 5:17). Here, Paul uses the word as a descriptive title. The Antichrist is the opponent. He is diametrically opposed to Christ and to all that He represents.

His aim is to undermine all divine authority in human life and society on this earth. The Judeo-Christian ethic is already being vilified by the anti-Christian, humanistic, and atheistic forces in our society. We can expect that the opposition will increase.

He also "exalteth himself." The word is *huperairō.* Here it is a superlative and means that the Antichrist will exalt himself exceedingly. The verse points us back to Daniel 11:36. Conceit and arrogance are behind the act, and the two thoughts are implied by the word.

When the conspirators were recruiting key people for the plot to murder Julius Caesar, Shakespeare has Cassius complain to Brutus, Caesar's close friend:

> Why man, he doth bestride the narrow world
> Like a Colossus, and we petty men
> Walk under his huge legs, and peep about
> To find ourselves dishonorable graves.

But Caesar, as ambitious as he was, was nothing compared with what the Antichrist will be. This same arrogance and pride marks all dictators. None of them, however, compare with this coming one whose pride and rebellion have been surpassed only by that of Satan himself. In a dim and distant past, Satan, known then as Lucifer, declared, "I will ascend into heaven, I will exalt my throne above the stars of God: I will sit also upon the mount of the congregation, in the sides of the north: I will ascend above the heights of the clouds; I will be like the most High" (Isa. 14:13–14). He tempted Eve with the same bait: "Ye shall be as gods . . ." (Gen. 3:5).

The aim of the Antichrist will be to reign supreme over all of the affairs of men and especially to subordinate all religion to himself. Satan knows the power and passion that religion can generate. He is the ultimate author of all false religion. Although people are sinful, and the inner shrine of their spirit is vacated by the Holy Spirit, yet they must worship something or someone. Satan sees to it that multitudes worship him, often ignorantly and sometimes openly. He uses false religion to further his own ends. His ultimate aim is to rid the world of all religions that will not yield to the Antichrist and to create a new world religion centered in himself. As God found a perfect vehicle of expression in the Lord Jesus, so Satan will find a perfect vehicle of expression in the Man of Sin, and he will present him to the world as the christ of all of the cults, as the messiah of the Jews, as the Mahdi of Islam, the reincarnate Buddha, the Krishna of the Hindus, the incarnate god of this world.

Now comes *the claim* of the Antichrist: "so that he as God sitteth in the temple of God, showing himself that he is God" (2:4b). This verse, along with Revelation 13:11–18, makes clear that the Jews are yet to rebuild their temple in Jerusalem. From time to time, stories surface of radical factions in Israel who are determined to do just that. The Six-Day War (1967) put the temple mount firmly in the hands of the Jews. Opposition to rebuilding the temple on its ancient site centers in the ranks of liberal and agnostic Jews, who resent and fear the power of the rabbis and the religious fanatics. Pragmatic Israelis fear the reaction from the Moslem world if any attempts were made to clear the site and begin work. The site is sacred to Islam, too. Still, the religious bloc in Israeli politics wields enormous power out of all proportion to its size.

As to what will happen, probably no serious attempt will be made until the Antichrist has secured his power base in a revived Roman Empire comprising Europe and the West. He will then be strong enough militarily, economically, politically, and industrially to enforce his will. His seven-year treaty with Israel will give the Jews the backing they need. Initially, the might of the Antichrist will overawe the Arabs. The presence of the Antichrist's troops in Israel will call for caution. Any attack on Israel will be an attack on a revived and revitalized West, now united, ably led, and determined to defend its interests and further its ambitions.

At this point, it seems likely that the Moslem world will appeal to Russia for aid. Despite the dissolution of the Soviet Union, Russia has not gone away, and Ezekiel has not changed his mind! The Russians will embrace their new allies, hoping to regain their position as a global superpower. The Russians will hastily put together a coalition of anti-Semitic nations. This coalition will precipitate the invasion of Israel that Ezekiel foresaw (chaps. 38–39) and that is described in

Revelation 9:12–21. The moment the massive armies of Russia, Islam, and their allies cross into Israel, God will act. The demise of Russia and Islam will remove these two major obstacles from the Antichrist's path. His way will now lead directly to global power. The remaining nations of the earth will hasten to make their peace with him (Rev. 13:4).

With the whole world under his sway, the Antichrist will have no further use for Israel. He will seize the rebuilt temple and install his image in the Holy Place (Matt. 24:15; Rev. 13:15). He will then compel all men to receive his mark. Those who resist will be marked for extermination. Thus, the Great Tribulation will begin (Rev. 13:15–17).

Paul tells us that the Antichrist himself will sit "in the temple of God, showing himself that he is God." The word for "showing himself" is *apodeiknumi.* Having taken his seat in the temple and proclaimed his deity, the Antichrist will "set himself forth" as God. He will "demonstrate" that he is God. The word is in the continuous tense, indicating that this will be his continuing policy once he has seated himself in the *Jewish* temple. Everything will be directed against the true God.

Satan has been worshiped ignorantly down through the centuries. Satan, after all, is "the god of this world" (2 Cor. 4:4). But he craves open worship. The great role of the Antichrist, in Satan's most secret plan for this world, is to be to Satan what Jesus was to His Father, the channel through whom worship can flow (Rev. 13:4).

(b) Sovereignty delayed (2:5–6)

At this point, Paul inserts a personal note to the Thessalonians. He reminds them of *what they had forgotten:* "Remember ye not, that, when I was yet with you, I told you these things?" (2:5). Evidently, Paul covered a great deal of ground with his converts. Nowadays, we are content to give new Christians some rudimentary instruction on the need for a daily quiet time and prayer, the need to get baptized and find a good church, and to take a stand for Christ. It does not occur to many evangelists and soul winners that new converts need much more than that (Acts 2:42). Doubtless, Paul grounded his converts in "the apostles' doctrine." He gave them crash courses in theology, pneumatology, ecclesiology, angelology, and even eschatology. He considered a good grounding in Bible prophecy as good a preparation for godly, victorious living as anything else. He reminds them that he was not telling them anything new.

He reminds them also of *whom they had forgotten:* "And now ye know what withholdeth that he may be revealed in his time" (2:6). The word used here is *katechō* ("to hold fast, actively and deliberately"). It means "to restrain." "You know what is restraining him (the Antichrist)," Paul says. They knew because they had already been told. He adds the reason why the restraint is in force, "that he may not be revealed before his proper time," that is, before the rapture of the church. The neuter is used here—"the restraining thing." In the next verse, Paul makes clear that the One who is holding back the final development of lawlessness on this planet is the Holy Spirit.

b. The mystery of sin (2:7–12)
  (1) The present conflict (2:7)

"For the mystery of iniquity doth already work: only he who now letteth [*katechō,* "holds fast"] will let [hold fast], until he be taken out of the way." A "mystery" in Scripture is a truth that once was hidden but is now revealed. About a dozen such mysteries are mentioned in the New Testament.[2]

The "mystery of iniquity" is the secret working of lawlessness. From the beginning, it has been a goal of Satan and his wicked spirits in the heavenlies (Eph. 6:11–12) to overthrow God's purposes regarding this planet.

The word for "work" here means "to work actively." The word is used to describe the active power of God's Word. Paul thanked God for the Thessalonians because they received the Word of God "as it is in truth, the word of God, which *effectually worketh* also in you that believe" (1 Thess. 2:13).

Satan is tireless in his efforts to bring his plans to fruition, but he is up against a major obstacle. There is One who "hinders and will hinder, until he be taken

2. There are the mysteries of *the kingdom of heaven* that detail the secret progress of God's purposes in this age (Matt. 13:3–50). There is the mystery of *Israel's blindness* to the gospel during this age (Rom. 11:25). There is the mystery of the *Rapture* (1 Cor. 15:51–52; 1 Thess. 4:14–17). There is the mystery of *the church as the body of Christ,* made up of both Jews and Gentiles (Rom. 16:25; Eph. 3:1–11; Col. 4:3). There is the mystery of *the church as the bride of Christ* (Eph. 5:28–32). There is the mystery of *Christ living in the believer* (Gal. 2:20; Col. 1:26–27). There is *the mystery of Christ, the incarnate fullness of God* and in whom all divine wisdom manward subsists (1 Cor. 2:7; Col. 2:2, 9). There is the mystery of *godliness,* the process whereby godlikeness is restored to us. There is the mystery of the *seven stars* (Rev. 1:20). There is the mystery of the religious system called *"Babylon"* (Rev. 17:5–7). Then, too, there is *the mystery of iniquity* (here in 2 Thess. 2:7; Matt. 13:33).

out of the way." The word for "letteth" (hinders) is *katechō,* the same word that is translated "withholdeth" in 2 Thessalonians 2:6. Satan encountered this divine restraint when he sought harm to Job (1:6–2:8).

There is a change from the neuter ("ye know *what* withholdeth," 2:6) to the masculine ("*he* who now letteth," 2:7). This suggests that the Restrainer can be spoken of as a thing or a person. The Holy Spirit can be spoken of in both neuter and masculine genders. Tertullian interpreted the Restrainer as the Roman Empire, the neuter participle referring to the state and the masculine to the emperor. This interpretation, although it illustrates the use of neuter and masculine genders, is wholly inadequate for a context so heavily charged with the supernatural.

The only One who can restrain Satan and his angels is the Holy Spirit. The instrument of that restraint, ever since Pentecost, has been the church, the mystical body of Christ into which believers are baptized by the Holy Spirit (1 Cor. 12:13).

Nothing can happen, prophetically, until a change occurs and the mighty power that is now restraining Satan and his minions is removed: "Only he who now hinders will hinder until he be taken out of the way." As long as the Holy Spirit and the church remain on earth, the day of grace continues. As long as it is a day of grace, God cannot pour out His judgments and His wrath upon this planet. The Flood could not come until Noah was safely in the ark. Fire could not fall from heaven until Lot was safely out of Sodom. Judgment cannot come until the church is removed from this planet.

The removal of the church will mean that God's method of doing things will revert to the Old Testament era. The Holy Spirit will cease baptizing people into the mystical body of Christ. He will no longer hinder the rapid acceleration of wickedness in the world. The way will be clear for Satan and the Antichrist to take over the world. People will be left to learn for themselves what the world will be like once unrestrained wickedness is given full rein. The book of Revelation gives us the dread details.

Although the Holy Spirit will no longer restrain the development of the mystery of iniquity, that does not mean that it will be impossible for people to be saved or that God will no longer have those on earth to bear witness to Him. On the contrary, millions of people will be saved after the Rapture. The two witnesses (Rev. 11:1–7) and the 144,000 witnesses will reap a vast harvest (Rev. 7:1–17). These saved people will not, of course, be in the church, but they will be in the kingdom. Moreover, they will pay a high price for their confession of faith. Countless millions of people will be martyred by the Antichrist.

(2) The prophetic climax (2:8–10)

Now the Holy Spirit moves the story on to the end and answers three questions concerning the coming Man of Sin—when? who? and why? He tells us *when:* "And then shall that Wicked be revealed, whom the Lord shall consume with the spirit of his mouth, and shall destroy with the brightness of his coming" (2:8). The Antichrist will be revealed. That is, he will have his apocalypse (as in 2:3), his unveiling, his revealing to the world. Throughout the history of the church age, it has been the method of the Holy Spirit to allow evil to rise to a certain level and then send a church-born, spiritual revival to hurl it back.

How people underestimate the church! They see it weak, ineffective, torn asunder, riddled by cultic abnormalities, shaken by scandals, espousing wrong causes, and often represented before the world by unsaved or weak and carnal men. What they see is not really the church but *Christendom.* The very gates of hell cannot prevail against the true church (Matt. 16:18–19). Its foes, in the heavenlies, understand that far better than we do. The false, the fanatical, and the faulty in the church do not deceive them. They see the church as it really is—"spread out through all time and space, rooted in eternity, terrible as an army with banners," as C. S. Lewis once described it. They fear it as the body of Christ and for its ability to be in touch with God's throne.

When the Great Revolution burst upon the unhappy land of France, the streets ran red with blood as the suddenly released citizenry flexed its muscles, drank the heady wine of power, and revenged itself on the nobility of France. Men marched to the stirring strains of "The Marseillaise." They stormed the Bastille and freed its political prisoners. They scaled Notre Dame and tore the cross from on high and flung it to the streets below. "We are going to pull down everything that reminds you of God," a revolutionary told a peasant. The people hated the arrogant Roman Catholic Church as much as they did the arrogant aristocracy. The guillotine worked night and day. The great nobles of France were hauled off in farmers' carts to meet their fate amid the jeers and cheers of the people.

In England people watched and waited. Conditions in England were about as bad as those in France. The people of England were ripe for revolution, too. A haughty, privileged aristocracy rode high, wide, and handsome. A careless church offered people stones for bread, and its fox-hunting parsons disgraced the gospel. Moral conditions among the poor were never at lower ebb. Crime, drunkenness, and immorality reigned supreme. All that England needed was a spark from across the channel, and it, too, would be set ablaze. The peers of England knew what to expect.

Then came the Wesleys, and revival broke out. Millions of people turned to Christ. The historian Lecky wrote, "The Methodist revival saved England from bloody revolution." What saved England was not the British navy—given half a chance, the sailors would have sided with the insurgents. It was not the army that saved England, nor was it parliamentary reform, nor the indecision of the common people. It was a Holy Spirit revival.

John Wesley preached 42,000 sermons, traveling 250,000 miles to do so. His brother Charles wrote six thousand hymns, four thousand of which are so popular that they were published and sung from one end of the land to the other. The Wesleys reached the heart and conscience of England. Everywhere they went, they left behind converts by the thousand, a trail of churches fired with the message and hosts of Spirit-filled preachers to conserve the fruit and spread the work. Nor did it end there. Other revivals followed, and from the English-speaking world went out armies of missionaries to carry the news to other lands. Moreover, reformation followed hard on the heels of revival, and social conditions improved.

Rapture! The church gone! The Restrainer no longer operating through the church, the mystical body of Christ, to arrest corruption and decay! The way will be cleared at last for the Man of Sin. Satan will be swift to seize the initiative once the obstacle that he has fought and feared so long is mysteriously and supernaturally removed. As for the revivals that will follow the Rapture, he will know how to deal with those. Individual believers, not baptized into a mystical body, will be easy prey. He will simply stamp them out. He tried that with the church, but it didn't work. The church always came back with fresh revivals.

But, with the church gone, he will be able, at last, to reveal his man. Here he is called "that Wicked (one)." The word means "the lawless one." He will be the last in a long line of rebels. Nimrod, whose name means "the rebel," was one such satanic type of the Antichrist. In the early dawn of time, right after the Flood, Nimrod set out to build a world empire. There was to be a one-world *society* as symbolized by a common language, a one-world *sovereignty* as symbolized by the city, and a one-world *sanctuary* as symbolized by the Tower of Babel. The key phrase is a thrice repeated, humanistic "let us," answered in the end by God's divine "let Us" (Gen. 11:1–9).

The Antichrist, then, will be revealed, but not until after the rapture of the church. The Holy Spirit hastens to record his certain doom: "whom the Lord shall consume with the spirit of his mouth, and shall destroy with the brightness of his coming." The word for "consume" is *analiskō*. It means "to destroy." Thus,

James and John wanted to call down fire from heaven to "consume" certain Samaritan villagers who would not receive Christ because He was evidently going to Jerusalem (Luke 9:54). Destruction of the Antichrist will be the sole prerogative of the Christ, the very One he has vilified so long and whose people he has so terribly persecuted.

Nor will it take much. He will destroy him with "the spirit of his mouth." Some scholars render that phrase "with the breath of his mouth." In the Apocalypse, it simply says that he was "taken." The word used means that he was arrested (Rev. 19:20). His day is over. His doom is upon him. A sword from the Lord's mouth slays the armies mobilized at Meggido (Rev. 19:21). Evidently, all that the Lord has to do is speak!

Not only will the Antichrist be consumed but also he will be destroyed by "the brightness of his coming." The word for "destroy" here means "to render inactive, to spoil," "to make useless or void," "to abolish." The word is used to show how the barren fig tree made useless the space that it occupied (Luke 13:7). It is used to describe the cessation of the special transition gifts in the early church, notably the gifts of "prophecy" and "knowledge" (1 Cor. 13:8). (A different word marks the permanent end to "tongues.") The word is used to show how complete will be the Lord's triumph over death: "The last enemy that shall be *destroyed* is death" (1 Cor. 15:26).

One glimpse of "the brightness of his coming" and all of the boasted schemes of the Antichrist will be brought to nothing. As a bright light shining into some junk-piled attic reveals all of the dust, dirt, cobwebs, and broken, useless odds and ends, and crawling creatures too, so the brightness of the Lord's coming will reveal the tarnish, the tinsel, the grotesqueness, the tawdry shoddiness, the uselessness, the shame, the crime and guilt, and the cheapness of Satan's imitation Christ and the importance of Antichrist's phony kingdom.

The apostle has told us when; now he tells us *who:* "even him, whose coming is after the working of Satan with all power and signs and lying wonders, and with all deceivableness of unrighteousness in them that perish" (2:9–10a). God is going to give Satan unhindered license to *behave* as he wants and will give him enough rope to hang himself; He is going to give the sinner an unhindered opportunity to *believe* as he wants and will give him enough rope to damn himself.

Satan will certainly rise to the bait. His final and consummate masterpiece of deception will be the unveiling of the Man of Sin. First, he is going to have a "coming," a *parousia.* His presence will be revealed to his own, to a godless world that has long since rejected the Lord Jesus Christ.

His coming will be "after the working of Satan." The word is *energeia,* the same word used to describe the energetic working of the mystery of iniquity (2:7). Satan's activity will become feverish after he is thrown out of the heavenlies and his dark machinations are restricted to this planet (Rev. 12:7–17). It will now dawn upon him that his time is short. Like Hitler—who, once he realized that the war was lost, determined to do all of the damage he could before finally committing suicide—Satan will refuse to acknowledge defeat and will work all the harder to harm the human race, which he hates with a malice and a vindictiveness that defy description.

He will bring his man onstage. The seal judgments will reduce the world to such chaos that the people will be eager to find a man able to bring order and sanity back to the world (Rev. 6). Satan will clothe his man with power.

The word for "power" is *dunamis,* untrameled, unequaled power. Satan once exercised this kind of power. Jesus authorized His disciples, however, to confront him: "Behold," He said, "I give unto you power [*exousia*] to tread on serpents and scorpions, and over all the power [*dunamis*] of the enemy" (Luke 10:19). This was a foretaste of things to come.

After the Lord's resurrection and ascension and the coming of the Holy Spirit at Pentecost, this was changed. *Dunamis* was vested in the church, the body of Christ, the body through which Satan is currently held in check: "Ye shall receive power [*dunamis*], after that the Holy Ghost is come upon you" (Acts 1:8); "I am not ashamed of the gospel of Christ," Paul said, "for it is the power [*dunamis*] of God unto salvation to every one that believeth" (Rom. 1:16).

During this age, Satan's power is described by the word *exousia* ("authority, power subject to another power"). Thus, Satan is called "the prince of the power [*exousia*] of the air" (Eph. 2:2). We are delivered from "the power [*exousia*] of darkness" and are "translated . . . into the kingdom of his dear Son" (Col. 1:13). Paul's testimony was that God had commissioned him to preach to the Gentiles "to open their eyes, and to turn them from darkness to light, and from the power [*exousia*] of Satan" (Acts 26:18).

Since Pentecost, Satan has been under restraint. The Antichrist cannot be revealed until the restraining power of the church is removed. It is evident from 2 Thessalonians 2:9 that Satan not only regains his lost *dunamis* but also bestows the same kind of power on his protégé, the Antichrist.

The Antichrist will be invincible. He will bring the whole world under his sway for a limited time. The world will quickly acknowledge the futility of offering him any resistance (Rev. 13:4). The Antichrist's personal charisma and political cunning will be enhanced by his power to work miracles. He will dazzle the world with "signs and lying wonders."

The word for "signs" is the common word that John used to describe the miracles wrought by the Lord Jesus. It occurs forty-eight times in the Gospels. John uses it seventeen times. (In four places—2:18; 4:48; 6:30; 20:30—it is translated "sign" in the King James text. In the other places, it is translated "miracle"). The word points especially to the *significance* of the wonder wrought. It is intended to emphasize the reason, the object, and the purpose of the sign. The signs that the coming Antichrist will give will be lying signs intended to deceive, if possible, the very elect (Matt. 24:23–24). The word for "lying" in the text is *pseudos,* the usual word for falsehood. The signs of the Antichrist are designed to deceive. In this, the Antichrist betrays the family likeness. Jesus said to the Jewish authorities: "Ye are of your father the devil, and the lusts of your father ye will do. He was a murderer from the beginning, and abode not in the truth, because there is no truth in him. When he speaketh a lie [*pseudos*], he speaketh of his own: for he is a liar, and the father of it" (John 8:44). The purpose of these lying signs is to convince the world that the Antichrist's claim to be God is true.

The word for "wonders" is *teras.* It refers to something marvelous, something that produces a marked effect on those who witness the miracle. Signs appeal to the intellect; wonders appeal to the imagination. Satan can, and does, perform miracles. The word, as used of Christ's miracles, underlines the excitement produced. When used, the word is always found in connection with signs. The signs that the Antichrist will perform will be spectacular and will convince the world.

The era will be one of miracles. Miracles in the Bible are comparatively rare. An outburst of miracles occurred in the days of *Moses and Joshua* to get Israel out of Egypt and into Canaan. Then they ceased, and God gave the people His Word (the Pentateuch, the early histories, the Davidic psalms, and the other poetic books). An outbreak of miracles occurred in the days of *Elijah and Elisha,* when Israel and Judah stood at the Great Divide, poised on the brink of total apostasy. Then they ceased, and God gave His people more of His Word. The writing prophets came, and more books were added to the sacred Scriptures—the histories of the kings and the writings of the preexilic prophets. A brief flurry of miracles occurred in the days of *Daniel.* Then they ceased, and God added yet more books to the Bible—the closing historical and prophetic books of the Old Testament. A mighty outpouring of miracles occurred in the days of *Jesus and the apostles.* Then they ceased, and God gave us the New Testament (1 Cor. 13:8–10). The completion of the canon of Scripture and the breakup of the Jewish nation put an end to miracles as such. The principle is given by Peter who, having recorded one amazing experience that he had once had with Jesus (2 Peter 1:16–18), turns away at once from voices and visions and points to that "more sure word of prophecy," or "scripture," as he calls it in the next verse (2 Peter 1:19–21).

Miracles will abound during one more period. *The Lord will have His two men* down here, and they will perform mighty miracles of judgment, as did Moses and Elijah of old (Rev. 11:3–7). *The Devil will have his two men* down here (the Beast and the False Prophet), and they will perform miracles (Rev. 13:2, 11–18). The lying signs and wonders of Satan's men will be much more popular with the people than the judgment miracles of God's two witnesses. Indeed, when the Antichrist succeeds in slaying the two witnesses, there will be universal rejoicing (Rev. 11:9–10).

Paul now tells us *why* God will permit Satan this one brief hour of triumph: "because they received not the love of the truth, that they might be saved" (2:10b). Millions of people will be saved after the rapture of the church, but no one who has received adequate presentation of the gospel in this age and rejected it will be saved in that judgment age. All of those people who have been brought up under the sound of the gospel, all who have heard it and understood it but who have had no love for it, will put themselves beyond the hope of salvation once the Rapture occurs. They will be left behind for judgment. Thus it was in the days of Lot and Noah, and thus it will be again. Paul goes on to elaborate.

(3) The practical conclusion (2:11–12)

For those thus left behind, there will be *delusion:* "And for this cause God shall send them strong delusion, that they should believe a lie" (2:11). What a startling revelation! It is a sobering fact that men are free to choose their own way and God is free to confirm them in their delusions. Just before he put down his pen, the great prophet Isaiah issued this warning from God: "I also will choose their delusions, and will bring their fears upon them; because when I called, none did answer; when I spake they did not hear; but they did evil before mine eyes, and chose that in which I delighted not" (Isa. 66:4).

Before He rained down hell from heaven upon the wicked people of Sodom, God first smote the vile practitioners of perversion with blindness (Gen. 19:4–11).

Before the Flood came to cleanse a world given over to pornography (Gen. 6:5, 12), He confirmed them in their willful ignorance of Himself (Matt. 24:37–39; 2 Peter 2:5).

Paul warns that a time comes in the personal history of an unbeliever when God gives him up (Rom. 1:24–32). God warns, "My spirit shall not always strive with man" (Gen. 6:3). A poem I remember from childhood puts it this way:

> There is a line by us unseen
> That crosses every path;
> The hidden boundary line between
> God's mercy and His wrath.

Belshazzar crossed that forbidden frontier (Dan. 5:17–30). King Saul passed it (1 Sam. 15:22–29). When he found that he could no longer get an answer when he knocked on the door of heaven, he knocked on the door of hell. To his surprise, it was opened, and he was pushed through it to his doom (1 Sam. 28:6–7). Balaam crossed that unseen line (Num. 22:15–22; Josh. 13:22; Jude 11; Rev. 2:14). The epistle to the Hebrews warns against crossing that line (Heb. 6:4–8; 10:26–31).

God will send to those who have heard and rejected the gospel "strong delusion." The word for "delusion" means literally "to wander," "to forsake the right path." It refers to a deviation in both doctrine (2 Peter 3:17; 1 John 4:6) and morals (Rom. 1:27; 2 Peter 2:18).

For those who thus reap the due reward of their deeds, there will be *damnation:* "That they all might be damned who believed not the truth, but had pleasure in unrighteousness" (2:12). It is inevitable, in any sphere of life, that those who refuse truth embrace error. A person may choose to believe that two multiplied by two is ten, but all he has done is embrace a lie. A person may choose to disbelieve a medical truth—that he has cancer, for instance—but all he does is hasten and ensure his death; he has embraced a deception. What is true of a scientific truth is true of a spiritual truth; to turn from it is to embrace some form of error. Here Paul says that, in a coming day, having rejected the truth (whether in this gospel age or the truth proclaimed by the two witnesses or the 144,000 witnesses) will be to embrace a lie—literally "*the* lie"—the lie of the Antichrist, "that he is God" (2 Thess. 2:4).

How terrible! It is not unbelief but *faith* that will be the snare of the last days. "God shall send them strong delusion, that they should *believe* a lie." They will embrace it with zeal and a fanaticism equal to or exceeding that with which people embrace humanism, communism, or Islam.

The amazing receptivity of the soul's soil for this coming lie has two causes, one negative and one positive. The negative reason is that "they received not the love of the truth, that they might be saved." It is not merely that they received not the truth. God is patient with our blindness and unbelief, and His grace can triumph, at last, in a heart that has rejected it for years. However blind and dark people are, God still has His vice-regent in their soul. Conscience remains with its love of the truth. But conscience can be distorted and eventually seared. How great is the peril of that person who refuses to love what he knows to be right. What folly to trifle with the convicting of the Holy Spirit, to play games with the Scriptures, to find excuses for unbelief.

The second reason for man's ready response to the lie is positive: they "had pleasure in unrighteousness." The root cause of all rejection of God, the Bible, and the gospel does not lie in any defect of the intellect or in the reason of the mind. These are excuses for unbelief, not reasons. The ultimate reason people reject the truth is not mental but moral; it lies in man's love of sin and his pleasure in unrighteousness.

"God shall send . . ." Terrible words, indeed! A divine principle is at work here. Goodness practiced develops into greater goodness; even so, wickedness does not stand still. It matures. As someone has said, "One leprous spot makes at last the full-blown leper." God made the laws, which thus operate in the moral world, as He made the laws that govern in the material world.

After the Rapture, God will remove all moral and spiritual restraints, and man's momentum toward evil will be free. I've heard it said, "The greyhound strains after the hare, but slip the leash and he is gone like lightning." A lost eternity awaits all those who turn away from the truth.

Paul now turns from the greatness of the coming Lie to help instruct his beloved Thessalonians in the everyday, workaday world in which they lived.

B. The greatness of the Christian life (2:13–3:15)
   1. The believer is chosen (2:13–14)
      a. The sovereignty of God (2:13a–b)

"God is still on the throne." He is Lord and sovereign, and His purposes are all "yea and amen" in Christ (2 Cor. 1:20). "But we are bound to give thanks alway to God for you, brethren," Paul says (2:13a). We can almost hear the audible sigh of relief as the apostle returns from a contemplation of the dark days of the foretold Antichrist and from a consideration of the consummation of human unbelief in a belief most vile. He thinks once more of his dear converts away there in Thessalonica. Them? In the Great Tribulation? No, indeed! Thank God, indeed! There was something for which to be *thankful.* That dark world of hatred and horror is not for us.

Some years ago, I was in London and while there visited Madam Tussaud's, the famous wax museum. I moved around the main hall and made nodding acquaintance with a dozen English kings. There was William the Conqueror and Henry VIII and his wives. There was the current queen and members of the royal family. There, too, was Churchill, Ghandi, and a few American presidents, along with celebrities from the world of entertainment. It was all bright lights, sparkling jewelry, and rich costumes.

But there was an underworld. I went down to the Chamber of Horrors. There the lights were low, just the faintest glow. The place looked like a dungeon with a guillotine towering over all. The atmosphere was chilling. Horrors were everywhere. In the eerie atmosphere, one could rub shoulders with murderers who have made history. Some of them were depicted in the very act of dismembering a victim. Some looked beastly and ferocious. Others looked astonishingly sane. At one point, I turned a corner and almost ran into Charles Manson, the demoniacal American mass murderer, who was able to hypnotize others into, doing for him, dark deeds of crime. Crippin was there, too, and the Brides of the Bath murderer, and others of the same dreadful ilk.

I wondered what it would be like to be locked in for the night, alone and in the dark. For an imaginative person, it would indeed be a chamber of horrors. Even with the dim lights glowing and people milling around, it seemed, after a while, that this grisly underworld was the whole world, a world gone mad, a world of cruelty and crime, a world of sinister shapes and suggestive shadows, a gloomy suburb of hell. I found myself looking at my watch. I did not want to be accidentally locked in there.

Then I went through a door or two and stepped back into a world of sunshine and stability, a world of traffic lights and double-decker buses and benevolent policemen. After all, that dark, dungeon world was no home of mine. I belonged to another world far away on another shore. That Chamber of Horrors was still there, but it had no claim upon me. One step and I came back from the past to the present. How thankful I was!

"But ye, brethren!" With one step, Paul came back from the nightmare future, from the Antichrist's very real Chamber of Horrors, to the present. He came back to a chosen people, a throne of grace, and a world where salvation and sanctification of the Spirit was still possible and still available to all.

There was also something about which to be *thoughtful:* "because God hath from the beginning chosen you to salvation through sanctification of the Spirit and belief of the truth" (2:13b). They would never believe the lie; they had believed the truth. The "salvation" in focus here is almost certainly salvation (deliverance) from the Antichrist and the coming delusion, just as in the first epistle the salvation (deliverance), in connection with the Rapture, is salvation from the wrath of God to be poured out upon this planet (1 Thess. 5:9).

God's electing process takes place in eternity—"from the beginning" (see John 8:44). God Himself has chosen this for His people that they, those who believe in this age, members of the mystical body of Christ, shall escape the coming storm. Our sanctification by the Holy Spirit ensures it. Our belief in Him who is the Truth guarantees our escape from him who is the Lie.

Some people use such verses as this to bolster belief in mistaken ideas about the sovereignty of God. The sovereignty of God, they maintain, is exercised arbitrarily and independently of human powers of choice.

God is God. He is omnipotent, omniscient, and omnipresent. He is God over all, blessed forevermore. He is sovereign Lord of the universe. He is eternal, uncreated, and self-existent. It is impossible for Him ever to be mistaken, deceived, or thwarted. He has complete knowledge of all of the data in the universe. He knows everything there is to know, including the names of all of those who, in the process of time, accept Christ as Savior, in all dispensations and under all conditions.

God is God. He cannot violate His own character. He is absolutely holy. He is also the very essence and source of all love. When God created other wills in the universe besides His own, He sovereignly limited Himself, within certain parameters known and controlled only by Himself, and determined by the character, calling, and capacity of those created beings. All of the factors implied by the existence of such wills, including the possibility that they might be used in defiance of His will, were foreknown to Him. In other words, God has set up certain rules by and within which these other wills can operate. He has to respect those wills otherwise, in the case of the human race, for instance, he would not have created people but puppets.

C. S. Lewis reminds us that omnipotence does not mean that God can do what is fundamentally impossible. "We can attribute miracles to God," he says, "but not nonsense." God cannot give a creature a will of its own and, at the same time, withhold free will from that creature. God cannot do two mutually exclusive things at the same time.[3] We can't have it both ways. Either God has created

3. C. S. Lewis, *The Problem of Pain* (New York: Macmillan, 1959), 16.

other wills in the universe, or He hasn't. If He has, He can certainly control them without violating them.

For instance, a novice plays a game of chess with a chess master. The pieces are put on the board. Each has a measure of sovereignty over the board. Within the rules of the game, each has the power of choice and the right to decide which moves to make. The game proceeds, but after half a dozen moves, the chess master announces that the game is over. Not once did he violate his opponent's power of choice. However, his mastery of the game and his sovereignty over the board was such that he could overrule the other's moves.

Thus, God allows us to make our choices in life, but He overrules them. All other wills can function properly only when they cooperate with the will of God. When they are set up in opposition to God's will, they create confusion. God is quite able to take all of those factors into account and ensure that, in the end, all ministers to His glory and to His eternal purpose. Nor does He ever violate other wills to do so.

God will not violate the human will. But, by the same token, neither will He allow Satan to violate it. Satan can tempt, but he cannot compel; he can persuade, but he cannot push; and he can entice, but he cannot force. He could persuade Eve to eat of the forbidden fruit, but he could not push it down her throat.

This is equally true of salvation. The human will is active in the decision to accept or reject God's magnanimous offer of salvation. The Holy Spirit never forces us. He convicts but does not compel. He has thousands of ways to speak, enlighten, and "strive," but He never makes the decision for us. He woos but does not ravish. In the end, the decision is ours. We can say, "I will," or "I won't," to the gospel call. He can and does quicken but can be and sometimes is quenched.

In the end, God endorses the decisions we make. He does not send people to hell; they send themselves. A person says, "I will not accept Christ." God finally says, "Your will be done. Live forever without Him."

An example of God's moral judgment of His people is seen in the history of Israel. When the people heard the report of ten of the spies and discovered that giants were in the Promised Land, they cried, "Would God that we had died in . . . Egypt! or . . . in this wilderness!" (Num. 14:2). They had now provoked God ten times (Num. 14:22), and God answered their prayer and endorsed their choice: "Say unto them, As truly as I live, saith the LORD, as ye have spoken in mine ears, so will I do to you: Your carcases shall fall in this wilderness . . ." (Num. 14:28–29).

God, in His omniscience, has anticipated all of this. We dwell in three tenses of time, but God dwells in the eternal present. He describes Himself as I AM. Thus, the moment He chose me was the same moment I chose Christ. Past, present, and future are human phenomena. God transcends time. He knows the end from the beginning. He is able to choose, elect, and predestinate because the future is all foreknown to Him (1 Peter 1:2).

God does not preordain certain people to be saved and certain people to be lost. God's ability to elect is based on His foreknowledge (1 Peter 1:2). There is the moral factor, too. His decisions are in keeping with His omniscience and His righteousness. "Shall not the Judge of all the earth do right?" Abraham asked when pleading for Sodom (Gen. 18:25). Of course, God always does what is right. He is righteous, just, and holy. Moreover, He is a God of love. All He does is in keeping with His infinite compassion and love. His purpose in predestinating people is wholly benevolent. He wants all of His own to be like His well-beloved Son.

b. The salvation of God (2:13c–d)

The believer is chosen by God to be set apart for Himself. Separation and sanctification are two sides of the same coin. Sanctification is accomplished by the Holy Spirit's indwelling the believer. The necessary prerequisite is "belief of the truth." This is not only a matter of the mind and heart. It is ultimately a matter of the will. Jesus said to the unbelievers of His day, "If any man will do his will, he shall know of the doctrine . . ." (John 7:17).

c. The splendor of God (2:14)

"Whereunto he called you by our gospel, to the obtaining of the glory of our Lord Jesus Christ." Far from being destined to the doom and gloom of the Great Tribulation and the dark shadow of the Antichrist, the church is destined for glory. We will come back with Him when He comes in power and great glory to overthrow His foes. We shall be "fair as the morning, bright as the day." As the old hymn "The Crowning Day," by Daniel Whittle (lyrics) and James McGranahan (music), puts it,

> The heav'ns shall glow with splendor,
> But brighter far than they
> The saints shall shine in glory,

As Christ shall them array,
The beauty of the Savior
Shall dazzle every eye,
For the crowning day is coming
By and by.

2. The believer is challenged (2:15–3:5)
   a. To trust (2:15–17)

Now Paul gets down to the practical challenge of the believers. All of his epistles combine doctrine and behavior. "Therefore, brethren, stand fast, and hold the traditions which ye have been taught, whether by word, or our epistle" (2:15). It has been well said that whenever we see that word *therefore* in the Bible, we should pause and see what it's there for! In other words, it draws our attention directly to the preceding context.

What a terrific context it is. We are to escape all of those end-times horrors that are soon to burst upon the world. We have been chosen to share, instead, in the end-times glories of Christ; therefore, we must stand fast and hold fast. The fact that we are going to escape the climactic horrors of the consummation of the age, the fact that God has decided for us that we shall share the splendors of His Son and be shown to the world as partakers of His glory, makes certain demands upon us. We must live, even now, as those who are members of the royal family of heaven. That is our *responsibility.*

"Thou shalt eat bread at my table continually," David said to poor, lost Mephibosheth. He was a man typical of the human race, lame on both his feet, without any standing, not to say without any possibility of walking (2 Sam. 9:3, 7). But David knew all of that when he sent the messengers of his grace to find him in distant Lo-debar. All that he asked of Mephibosheth was that he come and hide his poor, lame feet under the king's own table and that he accept the rank and dignity of one who henceforth was to be counted as one of the king's sons (2 Sam. 9:11). That, however, imposed on Mephibosheth a responsibility as well as a right. He must henceforth conduct himself, not as a fugitive and a vagabond on the earth but as a member of the family of David. It would be most improper for Mephibosheth to have lounged around the royal palace looking like a beggar, or to frequent haunts in Jerusalem where he would bring dishonor on that high table that he now graced.

But Mephibosheth did not have what it took to live this new life. So David bestowed upon him, as a further act of his grace, all that he needed, henceforth, to appear before David and all other men as a member of David's family (2 Sam. 9:7). Which introduces our *resources* (2:16–17): God knows that even when we accept the royal invitation and come in all of our ruin and rags to Jesus, even when, by His sovereign grace, He puts us in His own family (John 1:12) and sits us at His won table (1 Cor. 11:23–28), we do not have, in and of ourselves, the spiritual resources necessary to live the Christian life. So He gives us all that we need.

We note *whence these resources come:* "Now our Lord Jesus Christ himself, and God, even our Father, which hath loved us" (2:16a). We are to "stand fast" because God has now given us a standing before Him (2:15). The word is in the present continuous tense. It is a position that we must always maintain. The Thessalonians had moved away doctrinally from the firm foundation of truth on which Paul had placed their feet.

The "traditions which ye have been taught" was the apostolic truth in which Paul had grounded them. The word *traditions* has been much abused because it has come to mean human teachings and religious practices that often contain a great deal of error interwoven with truth. The word used is *paradosis,* meaning something that has been delivered from one person to another. It is, of course, a fact that New Testament truth was transmitted orally at first. It was handed on thus by the Lord Jesus to His disciples and His chosen apostles (1 Cor. 11:23). It is not to be compared with the traditions handed on by the Jews and that later comprised the Talmud (Matt. 15:1–3), of which the Jews were so zealous and about which the Lord roundly rebuked them. Nor is it to be compared with the traditions of which the Roman Church is the custodian and that she treats as being of equal weight with the Scriptures, even though they frequently contradict the Scriptures.

The Holy Spirit kept the oral traditions (teachings) of the early church pure. He kept their memory alive and supernaturally revealed deeper aspects of the truth as time passed. The Lord foretold the entire process: "But the Comforter, which is the Holy Ghost, whom the Father will send in my name, he shall teach you all things, and bring all things to your remembrance, whatsoever I have said unto you" (John 14:26). That covers the Gospels.

"When the Comforter is come, whom I will send unto you from the Father, even the Spirit of truth, which proceedeth from the Father, he shall testify of me: and ye also shall bear witness, because ye have been with me from the beginning" (John 15:26–27). This covers the book of Acts.

"I have yet many things to say unto you, but ye cannot bear them now. Howbeit when he, the Spirit of truth, is come, he will guide you into all truth: for he shall not speak of himself; but whatsoever he shall hear, that shall he speak" (John 16:12–13). That covers the New Testament epistles.

"And he will show you things to come. He shall glorify me" (John 16:13b–14a). That covers the book of Revelation. The Holy Spirit supernaturally protected *these* oral traditions from any admixture of error. All of them were written down before the last of the apostles died, and they contain all that is needed for faith and practice.

The apostle told the Thessalonians that they were to "hold" these traditions. The word is *krateō,* meaning "to be strong," "powerful," "to be master of." They were to grasp the truth firmly. Because the Thessalonians had been shaken by false teaching, the warning was needed (2:2). Paul reminds them that they had been taught the truth "by word," that is, by his oral teaching before he left town, and "by epistle," that is, by the first epistle that he wrote to them—eventually, of course, by all of the inspired New Testament writings.

The resources are thus available to us to stand fast and firmly, to grasp the truth, and to live the life itself, and they all come from the Lord Jesus Christ and from our Father. Paul adds, "who loves us." The present tense here does not point to one moment of time or to one particular occasion. God lives in the present tense. All moments and occasions are ever before Him. The tense is used, rather, to remind us that God's love is timeless. We have the same thing in Ephesians 2:4.

In concluding this particular challenge, Paul reminds us not only whence these resources come, and they are infinite, but also *what these resources convey:* "and hath given us everlasting consolation and good hope through grace . . ." (2:16b). The comfort that the Lord Jesus and the Father give to us is eternal. It is quite different from the comfort that this world affords. Often, at the funerals of unsaved people, we hear adulation and eulogies and all kinds of flattering things said, supposedly to comfort the bereaved. It is the best that a lost world has to offer. But how shallow and hollow it is to those who know the true comfort of the Lord and His people and who have that "blessed hope" to shine its light into the darkness of the tomb. We have, indeed, what Paul calls here "a good hope." Hope may be defined as "a well-grounded expectation." It is not wishful thinking but a firmly held and solidly based prospect. The "blessed hope" (the Rapture) dominates the entire future skyline of the child of God. Jesus is coming again and before the Antichrist comes. God's grace is our guarantee. Our prospect is grace, not wrath; escape, not tribulation.

The Lord Jesus, the Father Himself, the God of all love and consolation, "comfort your hearts, and stablish you in every good word and work," writes Paul (2:17). The fires of persecution were still burning there at Thessalonica. Meanwhile, let them draw on all of the resources of the Godhead. God Himself would "stablish" them—the word is *stērizō,* "to set fast," or "to fix firmly."

The believer then is challenged and called to trust. God is still on the throne! As the old hymn by Joseph Hart, "How Good Is the God We Adore," says,

> How good is the God we adore,
> Our faithful unchangeable Friend;
> His love is as great as His power,
> And knows neither measure nor end.

b. To travail (3:1–2)

First comes an *exhortation:* "Finally, brethren, pray for us" (3:1a). We never arrive at the place in our Christian life and ministry where we no longer need people to pray for us, just as we never arrive at a degree of holiness where we can no longer be tempted. The greatest of all of the apostles solicited prayer from his converts. "Pray for us," he said. Paul not only felt his need for prayer warriors to help pin down the enemy and soften hearts and open doors but also wanted to give his converts an opportunity to share thus in his ministry.

Prayer can place us in a village in Africa or in a hut on the Amazon. It can put us in a peasant's cottage or a royal palace. It can sit us alongside a suffering saint or raise a roadblock in the path of a scoundrel. It can do its work in the heart of a seeker at the close of a service. It can change the course of empires. It can put to rout spiritual forces of wickedness in high places, and it can bind evil spirits and set their captives free. Prayer links us with the throne of the universe. It connects us with the mind, heart, and will of God. Why this should be is a mystery. Prayer is one of the forces of the universe, as real as the forces of gravity, electricity, and magnetism. God always takes into account the factor of prayer when He is resolving the total equation of the universe. "Pray for us," said Paul. And no wonder!

Then comes *an explanation* (3:1b–2). Paul wanted his friends to pray for the *proclamation of the message:* "that the word of the Lord may have free course, and be glorified, even as it is with you" (3:1b). The apostle wanted all hindrances to the gospel swept aside that it might make rapid progress in the world. The enemy is very clever at hindering, as Paul reminded his Thessalonian friends in his first epistle (2:18). Paul was often hindered. He was hindered by the suspicion with which he was regarded in Jerusalem by even Jewish Christians. He was hindered by the active malice of the Jews of the Diaspora. He was hindered by imprisonment, by shipwrecks, by the opposition of apostates such as Elymas the sorcerer and the demons that possessed the soul of the slave girl at Philippi. He was hindered at times by his own discouragement. He told the Corinthians later that he knew what it was to be handicapped on all sides, to be puzzled and persecuted. Prayer was the only power of which he knew that could clear away all obstacles.

He wanted his friends to pray for *the protection of the messengers:* "And that we may be delivered from unreasonable and wicked men: for all men have not faith" (3:2). The Thessalonians had experienced that. They knew what happened when enemies of the gospel tried to hinder its progress by stirring up attacks against those who proclaimed it (Acts 17:5). People working in lands where Islam, Hinduism, and other false religions and creeds control the government and the courts know what it is like to face the opposition of unreasonable and wicked men, men who are utterly devoid of saving faith. Satan is a skilled player on life's chessboard. He knows how to move his men to check the advance of the gospel. But he is no match for the Holy Spirit. Prayer can annul even his formidable advantages. Who would have thought that, within the compass of a single year, the Iron Curtain would be torn down and that Bibles, evangelists, and Christian workers would be able to move freely into Russia and her former satellite states? Certainly prayer changes things. The Lord Jesus reminds us that *He* has the key. He is the one "that openeth, and no man shutteth; and shutteth, and no man openeth" (Rev. 3:7).

c. To triumph (3:3–5)
   (1) Because of the Lord's reliability (3:3–4)

Yes, indeed! We are on the winning side! Paul mentions *the Lord and His purposes.* They are twofold. He intends to ground His own and to guard His own: "But the Lord is faithful, who shall stablish you, and keep you from evil" (3:3). Paul looks away from the dangers that he himself had so often faced and comes back to consider the dangers that the Thessalonians were facing. The Lord would give them both stability and protection. "The Lord is faithful," he reminds them.

God does not exempt His people from the natural disasters and ills of life. He does not promise immunity from dislike, discrimination, detention, and even death. What He does promise is that He will temper the wind to the shorn lamb.

He will not allow Satan to go beyond a certain line that He Himself draws with an unerring hand (Job 1:12; 1 Cor. 10:13). Moreover, He promises to make a way of escape, and often that escape is a result of His own sufficient grace (2 Cor. 12:7–10).

Paul concentrates next on *the Lord and His people:* "And we have confidence in the Lord touching you, that ye both do and will do the things which we command you" (3:4). Paul's confidence was not misplaced. It was in the Lord. That's where Job's confidence was. Disaster after disaster had rolled over him in a series of tidal waves. They were utterly senseless so far as he could see. His friends—Eliphaz, Bildad, and Zophar—had each come to sit and stare. Each of them had said his first piece, more or less accusing Job of secret sin. Job had answered them argument for argument. Zophar had been particularly brutal. "Wisdom will die with you," Job said sarcastically. Then, reaffirming his faith, he cried, "Though he slay me, yet will I trust in him" (Job 13:15). His confidence was in the Lord.

Moses' confidence was in the Lord. The children of Israel had marched out of Egypt only to find themselves trapped. The waters of the Red Sea rolled before them, barring their way. The Egyptian army was behind them, marching to avenge the devastation of their land and the death of their firstborn sons. The Israelites were in a panic. The forward look was hopeless; the backward look was terrifying. They quite forgot the upward look. Then Moses spoke: "Stand still," he said, "and see the salvation of the LORD" (Exod. 14:13). He had hardly finished speaking when the ominous Shechinah cloud moved from before them to stand between them and the foe.

It is no vain thing to have confidence in the Lord. Paul, as much as he loved the Thessalonian believers, did not place his trust and confidence in them; he had confidence in the Lord. He appealed to God regarding them. He said, "Ye both do and will do the things that we command you." This was not because of his apostolic authority—he never felt the need to threaten that with them, as he sometimes did with others—but because he had confidence in the Lord regarding them. After all, they were the Lord's people, not his.

George Müller of Bristol used the same approach. He would remind the Lord that the homeless boys and girls under his care were the Lord's orphans, not his. He tells us the arguments he used when pleading with God.

1. That I set about the work for the glory of God, i.e., that there might be a visible proof, by God supplying, in answer to prayer only, the necessities of the orphans that He is the living God, and most willing, even in our

day, to answer prayer: and that, therefore, He would be pleased to send supplies.

2. That God is the "Father of the fatherless," and that He therefore, as their Father, would be pleased to provide (Psalm lxviii. 5).
3. That I have received the children in the name of Jesus, and that, therefore, He, in these children, has been received, and is fed, and is clothed; and that, therefore, He would be pleased to consider this (Mark ix. 36,37).
4. That the faith of many of the children of God has been strengthened by this work hitherto, and that, if God were to withhold the means for the future, those who are weak in faith would be staggered; whilst, by a continuance of means, their faith might still further be strengthened.
5. That many enemies would laugh, were the Lord to withhold supplies, and say, did we not foretell that this enthusiasm would come to nothing?
6. That many of the children of God, who are uninstructed, or in a carnal state, would feel themselves justified to continue their alliance with the world in the work of God, and to go on as heretofore, in their unscriptural proceedings respecting similar institutions, so far as the obtaining of means is concerned, if He were not to help me.
7. That the Lord would remember that I am His child, and that He would graciously pity me, and remember that I cannot provide for these children, and that therefore He would not allow this burden to lie upon me long without sending help.
8. That He would remember likewise my fellow labourers in the work, who trust in Him, but who would be tried were He to withhold supplies.
9. That He would remember that I should have to dismiss the children from under our scriptural instruction to their former companions.
10. That He would show that those were mistaken who said that, at the first, supplies might be expected while the thing was new, but not afterwards.
11. That I should not know were He to withhold means, what construction I should put upon all the many most remarkable answers to prayer which He has given me heretofore in connection with this work, and which most fully have shown to me that it is of God.[4]

Paul depended in the same way upon the Lord for his converts, that they might grow and be grounded. His confidence was in the Lord.

4. Arthur T. Pierson, *George Müller of Bristol* (New York: Revell, n.d.), 405–6.

(2) Because of the Lord's return (3:5)

"And the Lord direct your hearts into the love of God, and into the patient waiting for Christ." So the King James text reads. This "chimes in happily," Bruce says, with the theme of the Lord's return so characteristic of these two epistles. W. E. Vine and others offer this rendering: "into the patience of Christ" or "the patient suffering of Christ."

The Lord exercised marvelous patience with fallen men during His earthly ministry. How His disciples must have tried His patience at times—as when James and John, for instance, wanted to call down fire on Samaria, or when, after He had just told them that He was on His way to the cross, they began to argue who was going to be greatest in the kingdom. But think of His continuing grace—waiting, like Isaac, for the time to come when he can go to greet his bride (Gen. 24:62–67). We should learn to exercise His patience.

3. The believer is charged (3:6–15)
   a. The need for discipline (3:6–11)
      (1) Paul's exhortation (3:6)

"Now we command you, brethren, in the name of our Lord Jesus Christ, that ye withdraw yourselves from every brother that walketh disorderly, and not after the tradition [*paradosis*] which he received of us."

Here is a clear call for the exercise of church discipline. The word for "withdraw" is *stellō,* the word used for the furling of a sail. It suggests shrinking back from someone. We are not to associate with a believer whose life is disorderly. The idea is that we keep aloof from him. It is an effective way of letting him know that his conduct is unacceptable. There is little enough such discipline exercised in the church today, which, perhaps, explains its lack of power. The word for "disorderly" is *ataktos,* which means "not keeping in rank." They are like soldiers who are out of step. They are out of place, out of order. The following verses detail what was so undisciplined about these disorderly believers.

(2) Paul's example (3:7–10)

Before actually naming the specifics of the case, Paul leads up to it by reminding the Thessalonians of how he and his colleagues had behaved while in their city.

He reminds them of *his integrity:* "For yourselves know how ye ought to follow us; for we behaved not ourselves disorderly among you" (3:7). The missionary party had been an example of self-discipline. They knew how to keep rank among themselves. There had been no vying for position, no insubordination, and no disorderly conduct. Moreover, they had exercised the greatest propriety in their dealings with their contacts and converts. They could say, "Follow us, and you won't go wrong."

He reminds them of *his industry:* "Neither did we eat any man's bread for nought; but wrought with labour and travail night and day, that we might not be chargeable to any of you" (3:8). This was Paul's settled policy on the mission field. Nobody would ever be able to say of him that he was in it for the money. On the contrary, he made tents to pay not only his own expenses but also those of others of the missionary party who, for one reason or another, were unable to support themselves. We can well imagine that Paul kept his colleagues on the go—witnessing if not working. Idleness was abhorrent to him.

Picture Paul, at Corinth, where he was when he penned these words. His friends, Priscilla and Aquilla, were there. They had set up a tent-weaving business in the Jewish quarter. Paul felt at home with them. They were his kind of people. Aquilla's looms would likely be set up in the marketplace under awnings of camel hair—one way to display his own wares.

The women carded the wool. It was washed and made ready for the looms. We can see Paul attach himself to one of them. His hands would be busy with the threads while his feet worked the treadles below. He was an old hand at this trade. With skill and speed, he shot the mounted spools back and forth, forth and back across the frame. He could weave threads of varying color. He was a fast worker and a neat one. There was a sharp sound each time he brought the wooden beam against the framework of the loom. It called on no small amount of skill to bring the board, with its teeth, exactly against the openings in the frame. To Paul it was automatic. It called for no thought at all. It was merely a mechanical function. The rough fibers and the stiff cloth, which was used for tents and sails, dragged at his fingers and hands. Raw or callused skin made no difference to Paul.

Even as he worked at his tent making, he was busy about his soul winning and Bible teaching. All about him in that marketplace of one of the vilest cities of antiquity were drunken sailors, bold-eyed harlots, reprobate priests of various foul religions, sharp-voiced merchants, and penny-pinching buyers. Paul took it all in his stride. He would talk earnestly to a circle of men and women, boys and girls gathered around his loom. Then, night after night, long hours were devoted to evangelism, teaching, and shepherding. Then, bone weary, he would go to his prayers and, at last, to his bed for as few hours of sleep as he could get by with. Then, up in the morning before cock crowing for his quiet time before a bite of breakfast and back to the loom.

That was how it was at Corinth. That was how it had been at Thessalonica. That is how it was almost everywhere. No wonder Paul could say, "Follow me!"

He reminds them of his *intention:* "Not because we have not power [the right], but to make ourselves an example unto you to follow us" (3:9). Paul was not motivated by pride but by purpose. He could well have accepted gifts from his converts as an appropriate means of supplying his needs. Nothing about that was improper. After all, as Paul later wrote to his colleague Timothy, "The scripture saith, Thou shalt not muzzle the ox that treadeth out the corn. And, the labourer is worthy of his reward" (1 Tim. 5:18). He told the Corinthians the same thing (1 Cor. 9:9). There is nothing intrinsically wrong in receiving money for laboring in the harvest field. Paul, however, bent over backward to put to rest the lie that he made merchandise of his converts and that it paid him to be a preacher. It was his avowed intention to set an example of hard work.

He reminds them, too, of his *intimation:* "For even when we were with you, this we commanded you, that if any would not work, neither should he eat" (3:10). That is the Christian work ethic. There was a social security system under the Mosaic Law, but it, too, was based on work. Farmers, when reaping their harvest, were obliged to leave the corners of their fields unreaped, along with the gleanings, or what the scythe left behind at the first sweep through the fields. This was for the poor. The government did not put its hand into the pocket of a hardworking citizen to put money in the hand of a lazy wastrel who had no taste for work. Work was made available. He could follow the reapers and glean what was left. There was no need for anyone to starve.

Likewise, in the New Testament, provision was made for the genuine widow (1 Tim. 5:4–13), but beyond that, social welfare was up to the family. "If any provide not for his own, and specially for those of his own house, he hath denied the faith, and is worse than an infidel" were Paul's pragmatic words (1 Tim. 5:8). So here he reminds his Thessalonian converts that, when he was with them, he had commanded his newfound friends in Christ to work.

(3) Paul's exclamation (3:11)

"For we hear that there are some which walk among you disorderly, working not at all, but are busybodies." Unbelievable! What a lifestyle for a professing Christian!

Remember that the word *disorderly* was used to describe the furling of a sail. What a graphic picture of the lazy man, folding his arms and settling back to do nothing to contribute to the well-being of the community, content to coast along on the efforts of others. Paul was clearly indignant. Love, compassion, and a helping hand should indeed be extended to the poor, the disabled, the aged, and the infirm but not to the able-bodied person who feels that society owes him a living.

The word for "busybodies" is *periergazomai,* which means literally "to be busy about useless matters." It means "to bustle about." It carries the idea of being a meddler in matters that are somebody else's concern. Evidently, these people were minding everybody's business but their own. In the Greek, "work" is *ergazomai,* and "busybodies" is *periergazomai,* so Paul uses here an evident play on words that is not easy to reproduce in English.

b. The nature of discipline (3:12–15)

(1) Discipline avoided (3:12–13)

First, Paul gives *a word of command:* "Now them that are such we command and exhort by our Lord Jesus Christ, that with quietness they work, and eat their own bread" (3:12). The perfect example is the Lord Jesus Himself. He was not born in a palace but in a barn, surrounded by the implements of toil. His mother, though of royal pedigree, was not a princess but a peasant. Joseph, Mary's husband, though equally of royal blood, was not a lord but a laborer. For many years, Jesus Himself toiled at a carpenter's bench. When He became a traveling preacher, He did not have a fancy vehicle in which to ride; He walked. If the Creator of the universe—who could have come in a chariot of fire and commanded twelve legions of angels to smooth His path, having been born in the lap of luxury, and been carried through life on flowery beds of ease—if He chose rather to work and toil, why should we think that we ought not to work, and work hard? With true genius, Paul points to the perfect example. "Occupy till I come." That is the Lord's own word on the matter (Luke 19:13).

The word for "quietness" means "be silent." It calls for tranquility, the kind of quiet calm that arises from within and that causes no disturbance to others. It calls for the very opposite spirit than that which motivates the man who is forever prying into the private affairs of other people.

"Work and eat your own bread!" The Christian is not to be ever on the lookout for a handout. He does not sponge off others. He rolls up his shirtsleeves and gets to work to "bring home the bacon," as we put it today.

Then comes *a word of caution:* "But ye, brethren, be not weary in well doing" (3:13). We should never get weary of doing good. This word of caution perhaps was necessary to prevent an overreaction on the part of the diligent members of the Christian community. Having been ripped off once or twice, it would be easy to decide to abandon social work entirely. There are needy and deserving cases. There are times, too, when we give help even when we know we are being played for a sucker. There might have been a possible reaction, too, against even necessary Christian activity, such as evangelism, teaching, and pastoring. Many people had become drained and discouraged and abandoned all active involvement in the Lord's work. Paul warns against that.

Often, such defeat and discouragement arises from working for the Lord instead of allowing Him, by His indwelling Spirit, to work in us. The Lord, as man, drew also on the illimitable resources of His Father (John 14:10). That is why He was never weary in well doing. Weary with His journey? Yes (John 4:6), but weary in well doing? Never! So now we draw on the inexhaustible resources of our Lord. So it is to be He who does the work (John 14:12–14; 20:21). And He has what it takes.

(2) Discipline advocated (3:14–15)

Paul puts some teeth into the commandment—*excommunication:* "And if any man obey not our word by this epistle, note that man, and have no company with him, that he may be ashamed" (3:14). To be added to the mystical body of Christ, and then to be excommunicated by the local body of the church, leaves one in a very vulnerable position. Paul acknowledged that fact when he urged the Corinthians to receive back into the fellowship an excommunicated brother. He was afraid "lest Satan should get an advantage of us: for we are not ignorant of his devices" (2 Cor. 2:11).

The immediate reason for excommunication was to disassociate the church from any appearance of condoning and encouraging disorderly behavior. The hope was that the brother, thus isolated from the Christian community, would see his behavior in its proper light and would be ashamed of himself. The goal was to bring him to his senses, to make him realize that his behavior was not acceptable. Nowadays, if a local church scripturally disciplines a person for disorderly or immoral conduct or for doctrinal deviation, the offender simply runs down the street to join another church. Thus, the whole purpose of church discipline is circumvented. This was not so easily done in the early church. No little part of the weakness of the local church today lies in its unwillingness to discipline its members and its willingness to receive those who are under the scriptural discipline of another church.

But there was also to be *expectation:* "Yet count him not as an enemy, but admonish him as a brother" (3:15). The aim, in even so severe a discipline as excommunication, is the restoration of the offender. He is to be admonished as a brother because that is what he is. So often believers treat the excommunicated brother to hard looks and harsh words. They gossip about him and treat him with disdain when they should entreat him with compassion. Even if the man were an enemy, which he is not, the Lord tells us to love and pray for our enemies (Matt. 5:44).

PART 4

Conclusion

2 Thessalonians 3:16–18

Just a few last words, and Paul is finished. We have, first, Paul's *last prayer:* "Now the Lord of peace himself give you peace always by all means. The Lord be with you all" (3:16). Their fellow countrymen and the Jews treated them as enemies. Paul prayed that they might know peace. Within the fellowship were those who were causing problems in both belief and behavior. Paul prayed that, no matter what the situation might be, whether in the church or in the world, the peace of God would reign undisturbed in their hearts.

This peace garrisoned the heart of Peter when he calmly went to sleep on what he expected to be his last night on earth (Acts 12:6). He had come a long way since that other night, some few years before, when he had so feverishly denied his Lord out of fear. This peace reigned in the heart of Paul when he stood on the deck of a stricken ship, in the grip of a howling gale and a tempestuous sea, and calmly announced that all would be well (Acts 27:22).

We have also Paul's *last precaution:* "The salutation of Paul with mine own hand, which is the token in every epistle: so I write" (3:17). He drew attention to his signature. The same formula is used in 1 Corinthians 16:21; Colossians 4:18; and Philemon 19. A similar precaution is found in his letter to the Galatians (6:11). It was particularly important that he draw special attention to his personal signature here in 2 Thessalonians because a fraudulent epistle, supposedly bearing his name, had already deceived the church in Thessalonica (2:2).

We have, too, Paul's *last pronouncement:* "The grace of our Lord Jesus Christ be with you all. Amen" (3:18). He ends where he begins—with grace. Grace saves us. Grace sanctifies us. Grace strengthens us. Grace secures us. It is all grace from beginning to end. Thus ends the second of these two magnificent letters dealing with the second coming of Christ.

One of Britain's most illustrious prime ministers was Benjamin Disraeli, a Jew. His father converted to Christianity and had his children baptized, making a parliamentary career possible for his son. (At that time, those who were Jews by religion were excluded from Parliament.) Disraeli was brilliant, eccentric, and immoral. He was extravagant in both money and dress. He became a member of Parliament. It was traditional in the House of Commons for a new member to be extended every courtesy when he made his maiden speech, but this courtesy was denied to Disraeli. His affected mannerism and his foppish dress struck his fellow members the wrong way. He was shouted down, but he refused to be silent.

Raising his voice above the jeers, he said, prophetically enough, *"I will sit down now, but the time will come when you will hear from me."*

That about sums up these two Thessalonian epistles. The Lord Jesus has been insulted and jeered in this dark world of sin. Now He is in heaven. He has taken His place on His Father's throne, "henceforth expecting till his enemies be made his footstool" (Heb. 10:13). There comes then this voice from "the excellent glory"—"I will sit down now, but the time will come when you will hear from me." That time has almost come.